International Perspectives on English Language Teaching

Series editors: **Sue Garton** and **Keith Richards**

Titles include:

Ema Ushioda (*editor*)
INTERNATIONAL PERSPECTIVES ON MOTIVATION

Sue Garton and Kathleen Graves (*editors*)
INTERNATIONAL PERSPECTIVES ON MATERIALS IN ELT

Sarah Rich (*editor*)
INTERNATIONAL PERSPECTIVES IN TEACHING ENGLISH TO YOUNG LEARNERS

Simon Borg and Hugo Santiago Sanchez (*editors*)
INTERNATIONAL PERSPECTIVES ON TEACHER RESEARCH

Chris Jenks and Paul Seedhouse (*editors*)
INTERNATIONAL PERSPECTIVES ON ELT CLASSROOM INTERACTION

Thomas S.C. Farrell (*editor*)
INTERNATIONAL PERSPECTIVES ON ENGLISH LANGUAGE TEACHING

Hugo Bowles and Alessia Cogo (*editors*)
INTERNATIONAL PERSPECTIVES ON ENGLISH AS A LINGUA FRANCA
Pedagogical Insights

International Perspectives on English Language Teaching
Series Standing Order ISBN 978–0–230–30850–3 hardback
978–0–230–30851–0 paperback
(*outside North America only*)

You can receive future titles in this series as they are published by placing a standing order. Please contact your bookseller or, in case of difficulty, write to us at the address below with your name and address, the title of the series and the ISBN quoted above.

Customer Services Department, Macmillan Distribution Ltd, Houndmills, Basingstoke, Hampshire RG21 6XS, England

Also by Hugo Bowles

CONVERSATION ANALYSIS AND LANGUAGE FOR SPECIFIC PURPOSES (*co-editor*)

Also by Alessia Cogo

ANALYSING ENGLISH AS A LINGUA FRANCA
A corpus-based investigation (*co-author*)

LATEST TRENDS IN ELF RESEARCH (*co-editor*)

International Perspectives on English as a Lingua Franca

Pedagogical Insights

Edited by

Hugo Bowles
University of Rome "Tor Vergata", Italy

and

Alessia Cogo
Goldsmiths, University of London, UK

palgrave
macmillan

First published 2015 by
PALGRAVE MACMILLAN

Palgrave Macmillan in the UK is an imprint of Macmillan Publishers Limited,
registered in England, company number 785998, of Houndmills, Basingstoke,
Hampshire RG21 6XS.

Palgrave Macmillan in the US is a division of St Martin's Press LLC,
175 Fifth Avenue, New York, NY 10010.

Palgrave Macmillan is the global academic imprint of the above companies
and has companies and representatives throughout the world.

Palgrave® and Macmillan® are registered trademarks in the United States,
the United Kingdom, Europe and other countries.

ISBN 978–1–137–39807–9 hardback
ISBN 978–1–137–39808–6 paperback

This book is printed on paper suitable for recycling and made from fully managed
and sustained forest sources. Logging, pulping and manufacturing processes are
expected to conform to the environmental regulations of the country of origin.

A catalogue record for this book is available from the British Library.

Library of Congress Cataloging-in-Publication Data
International perspectives on English as a lingua franca : pedagogical insights / edited
by Hugo Bowles, University of Rome Tor Vergata, Italy ; Alessia Cogo, Goldsmiths,
University of London, UK.
    pages cm
ISBN 978–1–137–39808–6 (paperback)
1. English teachers—Training of—Social aspects.   2. English teachers—Training
of—Research—Methodology.   3. English language—Study and teaching—Foreign
speakers.   4. English language—Foreign countries.   5. English language—Social
aspects.   6. Lingua francas.   7. Education, Bilingual.   8. Sociolinguistics.   I. Bowles,
Hugo.   II. Cogo, Alessia.
PE1066.I65 2015
420.7—dc23   2015012283

Typeset by MPS Limited, Chennai, India.

Contents

List of Figures and Tables

Figure

Tables

Series Editors' Preface

There are points in the history of any profession where a movement develops that brings about fundamental changes in the way practitioners think about their work. The disturbances created by such movements are so powerful that they themselves become pulled in different directions, rarely settling to a still point that allows consolidation and consensus to develop. Such is the case with English as a Lingua Franca (ELF).

As Cogo notes in the overview that begins this collection, ELF is now 'a vibrant area of investigation' with its own journal, major ELF corpora and a thriving international community of scholars. The journey to this point, however, has been at times a rocky one, as ELF engaged with fundamental issues in language teaching and learning in ways that disturbed a number of comfortable assumptions. It emerged at a time when the status of 'English', and the pedagogic edifice that had been built around this, was no longer seen as unproblematic. Local voices – and varieties – were at last making themselves heard, and the debate on Global Englishes was broadening out to embrace multilingualism and translanguaging. There were inevitable misunderstandings, not least that ELF was itself a variety, but these are no longer relevant and the emphasis on ELF-aware teaching (so far practitioners seem to have resisted the dubious allure of 'EAT') as reflected in this collection provides an established point of reference.

Arguably the most fundamental shift associated with ELF-aware teaching has been in its emphasis on communication, a concept that has blown around loosely within the orbit of ELT throughout the latter's history but has never before been treated as fundamental. Associated with this is a constellation of concepts and practices that have enriched the language teaching landscape. No longer, for example, is culture regarded as an entertaining add-on but instead moves centre stage in engaging with the dynamics of global communication, a context in which 'local' and 'community' have genuine purchase. How these will eventually shape themselves will be influenced at least in part by the ways in which the challenges they bring are resolved. The concept of community, for example, has long been a matter of debate and the emphasis in ELF on intelligibility raises similar practical and definitional issues. But the concern with co-construction and on awareness raising which lie at the heart of this enterprise offer a way forward in terms of understanding as well as practice.

Just what this practice might involve is addressed by Bowles in his magisterial concluding chapter, drawing related strands together into a coherent picture of the pedagogic landscape of ELF. This and Cogo's elegant opening summary of key issues are likely to become standard reference points in a field that has now established its presence in the teacher education curriculum. As Dewey shows in his important contribution to this collection, introducing ELF into this still faces a number of important challenges, not least with regard to the relative neglect of the practicalities of building ELF into classroom practices. It is therefore particularly encouraging to see how strongly such practicalities feature in the chapters that follow.

Unsurprisingly, the concept of awareness features strongly and different aspects of awareness-raising are given due consideration. Wang's chapter makes this a central concern, but it also features elsewhere. Lopriore and Vettorel's chapter on materials, for example, provides original and inspiring practical suggestions for how basic awareness can be expanded in order to encourage more profound reflection on sociolinguistic dimensions of language use. This orientation complements very effectively Yu's focus in her chapter on the importance of 'languaculture input' and the need to 'de-centralise' the dominant roles of current materials rather than seeking to replace them.

Where challenges are stiffest, the creative flow is often at its strongest and a striking feature of contributions to this collection is their originality. This takes many forms. Focusing on fanfiction on the Internet, Grazzi, for example, draws on the community of *netizens* as his resource, showing how the classroom can be expanded beyond its physical boundaries and, more provocatively, ELF and ELT can be brought into convergence. The originality in Gonçalves' inspiring chapter lies not only in its choice of students but in its disturbing revelations about the nature of linguistic inhibitions. To date, most work in business contexts has focused on white collar contexts, but the focus here is on the communicative practices of migrant domestic workers and the extent to which their perceptions of their own competence is undermined by their orientation to native speaker ideals. The implications of this for approaches to teaching are profound.

As Bowles notes in his conclusion, while there is a strong local focus to this collection, analysis is framed in terms of particular communities rather than geographical areas and it might also be added that the issues writers address have resonance beyond the ELF, narrowly conceived. Schaller-Schwaner's work on oral presentations, for example, addresses the broader issue of intelligibility, exploring a range of resources and making a number of valuable pedagogic suggestions, while the link that Quinn Novotná and Dunková establish between ELF and CLIL offers fresh and intriguing possibilities. The contribution of teacher education and development to this will be important, and it is encouraging to see how the relationship between broader issues and local context features in Bayyurt and Sifakis's description of a distance-oriented project designed to introduce teachers in Turkey and Greece to ELF-oriented concerns.

Each of these contributions reflects in its own way the transformative potential of ELF-aware teaching in our profession. The fundamental shift away from deficit models of language learning in favour of the resource-oriented approaches characteristic of ELF takes us down a path towards a transformed pedagogic world rich with promise. Working together to develop students' resources as effective communicators implies a fundamental shift away from linear models of linguistic accretion towards a dynamic pedagogy of exploration, exchange and engagement, and the prospects and challenges inherent in this are brought eloquently into focus by the contributors to this collection.

Notes on Contributors

Yasemin Bayyurt is a professor in the Department of Foreign Language Education, Boğaziçi University, Turkey. Adding to a number of international publications, she is doing further work in areas including ELF-aware in-/pre-service teacher education; Mobile Assisted Language Learning; telecollaboration and cross-cultural communication. She has various written articles in refereed/indexed national and international journals and chapters in edited books (peer reviewed). Her current publications include two edited volumes: *Mobile as a Mainstream – Towards Future Challenges in Mobile Learning* (2014) and *Current Perspectives on Pedagogy for ELF* (2015).

Hugo Bowles is Associate Professor of English at the University of Rome "Tor Vergata" and specialises in English for specific purposes, literary stylistics and language education. He is co-editor of *Conversation Analysis and Languages for Specific Purposes* (2007) and author of *Storytelling and Drama* (2010), which won the 2012 ESSE Book Award for English Linguistics.

Alessia Cogo is Lecturer in Applied Linguistics at Goldsmiths, University of London (UK), where she teaches modules in sociolinguistics and Global Englishes. She supervises PhD students in Global Englishes, multilingual aspects of ELF and English language pedagogy. She is Reviews Editor of *English Language Teaching Journal* as well as co-founder and co-convenor of the *AILA Research Network on ELF*. Her current research concerns ELF multilingual practices in professional and academic contexts. Her ELF-related publications include journal articles, edited volumes and a monograph with Martin Dewey, entitled *Analyzing English as a Lingua Franca* (2012).

Martin Dewey is a senior lecturer at King's College London, where he teaches modules in Sociolinguistics, Global Englishes and Teacher Education, and supervises PhDs in areas related to the globalization of English and English language teaching. His primary research focus concerns the relevance of ELF in language pedagogy. His current work seeks to re-examine contemporary conceptions of knowledge and expertise in teacher education, particularly to explore the impact on pedagogic practices of adopting an ELF perspective. He has presented and published extensively on work in this field, and is co-author with Alessia Cogo of *Analyzing English as a Lingua Franca: A Corpus-Driven Investigation* (2012), and author of *The Pedagogy of English as a Lingua Franca* (forthcoming).

Jiřina Dunková has a bachelor's degree in English-American Studies and a master's degree in English linguistics from the Department of English Language and ELT Methodology at Charles University in Prague, Czech Republic. Her latest research interest has been the possibility of introducing ELF teaching approaches and methods into the English teaching practice at private language institutions in the Czech Republic. She also works as a freelance English teacher and translator specializing in written technical, medical and other ESP texts.

Kellie Gonçalves received her PhD in English Linguistics from the University of Bern, Switzerland in 2009. She has taught English Linguistics in Bern since 2008 at both the BA and MA level. Her research interests include sociolinguistics, intercultural communication, semiotic landscapes, English as a lingua franca, stylistics, discourse and tourism, language and the workplace, and narrative studies. She has recently been awarded a Marie Heim-Vögtlin grant (Swiss National Science Foundation) for the period of 2015–2017. In this period, she will be working on her Habilitation and second book which focus on the stylistic shifts of place descriptions among L1 and L2 speakers of English within adventure tourism towns.

Enrico Grazzi is a researcher in English Language and Translation at Roma Tre University, Italy, where he teaches English for Communication Sciences. His current research interests are English as a lingua franca, educational linguistics, and sociocultural theory. In 2013, he participated in the research project Intercultural Telecollaboration, in cooperation with the University of Arizona, Tucson (AZ), which was a recipient of the European Language Label Award for Innovative Projects in Language Teaching and Learning, 2012/2013. In 2013, he published a monograph on *ELF and English Language Teaching: The Sociocultural Dimension of ELF in the English Classroom*. Grazzi is a qualified teacher trainer and a textbook writer. He is a past president of TESOL-Italy (2002–2004).

Lucilla Lopriore is Associate Professor in English Language and Translation at Roma Tre University. She holds an MA TEFL from Reading University, UK and a PhD in Italian as a foreign language, University for Foreigners, Siena, Italy. She has worked extensively as a teacher educator in pre- and in-service courses in ELT, CLIL, Italian as a foreign language, educational linguistics, assessment and evaluation; she has designed blended training courses. A course-book writer, she has written general and ESP English course-books and numerous research papers. She was TESOL Italy President (1996–1998), a TESOL International Board of Directors Member (2001–2004) and ELLiE Project Italian coordinator (2006–2010). She was organiser of the 6th International Conference of English as a Lingua Franca in Rome. Her main research interests are ELF, CLIL, teacher education, assessment, terminology, subtitling and early language learning.

Veronika Quinn Novotná teaches in the Department of English Language and ELT Methodology, Faculty of Philosophy and Arts, Charles University in Prague. She also specializes in teaching English to students with special needs (visual and hearing impairment). Her current research interests include World Englishes, pedagogical implications of ELF, language attitudes, linguistic identity and CLIL. She also works as a freelance teacher, teacher trainer and translator.

Iris Schaller-Schwaner is Lecturer in English as Foreign Language at the Language Centre of the University of Fribourg, Switzerland, and the Department of Languages and Literatures, Multilingualism and Foreign Language Education of the same university. She has been teaching English at universities for more than 20 years and been involved in the development and teaching of specific and general English for Academic Purposes course offers, courses for English specialists, introductory seminars in English phonetics and linguistics in a language teacher education programme and in co-organizing events for language teacher development. Her current research focus is English as a Lingua Franca in multilingual academic contexts, but she has also published on pedagogical grammar and English in Swiss billboard advertising.

Nicos C. Sifakis is an associate professor in the School of Humanities of the Hellenic Open University and director of the M.Ed. in TESOL programme. He holds a PhD in language and linguistics from the University of Essex, UK. He has published extensively in various international refereed journals, edited collections and conference proceedings. His book *The English Language and Globalisation: Facets of Present-Day Reality in Greece, Europe and the Rest of the World* was published, in Greek, in February 2012. He is editor-in-chief of *Research Papers in Language Teaching and Learning* (http://rpltl.eap.gr/). His research interests include intercultural communication and pedagogy, teaching and researching English as an international lingua franca, language teaching methodology, distance education, adult education and teacher education.

Paola Vettorel is an assistant professor in the Department of Foreign Languages and Literatures, University of Verona. Her main research interests include ELF and its implications in ELT practices and materials, and ELF and digital media. Publications include 'EIL/ELF and representation of culture in textbooks: only food, fairs, folklore and facts?', in C. Gagliardi and A. Maley (eds) *EIL, ELF, Global English: Teaching and Learning Issues* (2010); 'ELF in international school exchanges: stepping into the role of ELF users', *Journal of English as a Lingua Franca* (2013); 'Connecting English wor(l)ds and classroom practices', *Textus* (2014); and *ELF in Wider Networking. Blogging Practices* (Berlin, 2014).

Ying Wang is Lecturer in Applied Linguistics at the University of Southampton. She is co-organising the 8th International Conference of English as a Lingua Franca. Her research interests include English as a lingua franca, Global Englishes, language awareness, attitude and identity, and language policy and English education. She has presented her research on all these areas in international conferences. Her article 'Non-conformity to ENL norms: a perspective from Chinese English users' is published in *Journal of English as a Lingua Franca* and reprinted in *Global Englishes*, a university coursebook written by Jennifer Jenkins (2015).

Melissa H. Yu is a member of the Centre for Global Englishes Research at the University of Southampton, UK. Her PhD research exploring different aspects of the international spread and use of English in relation to pedagogy, materials, and language policy and curriculum is close to completion. Her professional experience includes English and foreign language instruction in Taiwan and the UK and teacher and research training for Applied Linguistics programmes in UK postgraduate Higher Education. Besides this she is a member of the Editorial Advisory Board of *Englishes in Practice*. Her recent publications appear in *ELT Journal* and companion website materials for Professor Jennifer Jenkins' latest book, *Global Englishes*.

List of Abbreviations

BBC	British Broadcasting Corporation
CAL	Critical applied linguistics
CEFR	Common European Framework of Reference for Languages
CEIL	Content English Integrated Learning
CELTA	Certificate in English Language Teaching to Adults
CertTESOL	Certificate in Teaching English to Speakers of Other Languages
CLIL	Content Language Integrated Learning
CLT	Communicative Language Teaching
CoP	Community of practice
CTEFLA	Certificate in Teaching English as a Foreign Language to Adults
DELTA	Diploma in English Language Teaching to Adults
DTELFA	Diploma in Teaching English as a Foreign Language to Adults
EFL	English as a Foreign Language
EIL	English as an International Language
ELF	English as a Lingua Franca
ELFA	English as a Lingua Franca in Academic Settings
ELF-TED	English as a Lingua Franca Teacher Education
ELT	English Language Teaching
ENL	English as a Native language
ESL	English as a Second Language
ESOL	English for Speakers of Other Languages
ESP	English for Specific Purposes
FG	Focus Groups
FL	Foreign Language
IB	International Baccalaureate
IB DP	International Baccalaureate Diploma Programme
IC	Inner Circle
ICE	Inner Circle English
IE	International English

L1	First language
L2	Second language
LA	Language awareness
LF	Lingua franca
LP	Language policy
MA	Master of Arts
MLS	Multi-lingual speaker
MT	Mother tongue
N	Number
NBLT	Network-based language teaching
NES(s)	Native English speaker(s)
NNES(s)	Non-native English speaker(s)
NNS	Non-native speaker
NS	Native speaker
PEU	Proficient English user
Q	Question
RP	Received Pronunciation
SCT	Sociocultural theory
SE	Standard English
SLA	Second language acquisition
SMLL	Social media language learning
SOL	Speaker of other language(s)
Sts	Students
SUE	Successful user of English
TESOL	Teaching of English to Speakers of Other Languages
Ts	Teachers
UWC	United World Colleges
VOICE	Vienna Oxford International Corpus of English
WE	World Englishes
ZPD	Zone of Proximal Development

1
English as a Lingua Franca: Descriptions, Domains and Applications

Alessia Cogo

There has been a remarkable growth of interest in the phenomenon of English as a Lingua Franca (ELF) in recent years, and as a result this has become a productive field of research, which has now found its place in applied linguistics and sociolinguistics discussions. Interest in this area started with a couple of seminal publications: Jenkins (2000), an empirical study of phonology and related concepts of intelligibility and accommodation in English international contexts, and Seidlhofer (2001), which called for more empirical descriptions of ELF communication and effectively marked the foundation of VOICE (Vienna Oxford International Corpus of English), a corpus of ELF naturally occurring spoken data. This work signed the beginning of ELF research, which, in the 15 years that followed, has increased exponentially and has developed into a vibrant area of investigation. This field today includes numerous scholars from all over the world, a dedicated Research Network under the auspices of AILA (the ELF ReN, www.english-lingua-franca.org), the foundation of two more large-scale corpora (ELFA, English as a Lingua Franca in Academic settings, and ACE, Asian Corpus of English), an annual international conference (which started in 2008 in Helsinki and subsequently took place in Southampton, Vienna, Hong Kong, Istanbul, Rome, Athens and Beijing), and a journal dedicated to work in this area (*Journal of English as a Lingua Franca*) and book series (Developments in English as a Lingua Franca), both published by De Gruyter Mouton.

Since the early publications, developments have been fast and certainly not free of controversies and even heated debates. In this overview, I explore what ELF is, from different definitions, and I cover the empirical work of linguistic description in lexicogrammar and pragmatics, including the debates concerning the nature of ELF communication. I will keep this part relatively brief, as the main aim of this volume is to explore not the description but the applications of ELF research for ELT. So, in the last part, I review sociolinguistic applications of ELF research in professional and academic domains, and finally address implications and applications for English language teaching and teacher education.

What is ELF? Definitions, conceptualisations and debates

Seidlhofer defines 'ELF as any use of English among speakers of different first languages' (2011: 7) and linguacultural backgrounds, across all three Kachruvian circles. In contrast to some earlier definitions and conceptualisations (e.g., Firth 1996; House 1999), this one includes native speakers of English, who may use ELF as an additional resource for intercultural communication. This position is shared by most scholars today (Jenkins 2007; 2014; Mauranen 2012; Cogo and Dewey 2012), but in the past has created a great deal of controversy and debate (Cogo 2008 in response to Saraceni 2008; Cogo 2012a in response to Sowden 2012; and Dewey 2013 in response to Sewell 2013).

Apart from the inclusion-exclusion of native speakers, conceptualisations of ELF also have revolved around key notions such as variety, community and language. Most scholars today would agree that ELF is not a variety, and not a uniform and fixed mode of communication. Nonetheless, corpus research was initially concerned with identifying recurrent and systematic characteristics of ELF as well as co-construction processes of a pragmatic nature. The 'feature' focus, though, was what primarily drew the attention of scholars challenging ELF research and misconstructing it as another attempt to 'create a variety'. Rather, ELF is a flexible, co-constructed, and therefore variable, means of communication. The variability is locally constructed in different geographical areas and domains, but not necessarily geographically constrained, since remote, virtual communities may also develop ELF communicative practices (Jenkins 2014; Mauranen 2012; 2014).

ELF's intrinsic and contingent fluidity and variability therefore challenges traditional notions of 'variety' and 'community'. The concept of 'community of practice' is generally considered a more appropriate conceptualisation of ELF communities (Seidlhofer 2011; Jenkins et al. 2011), which do not fit within the nation-state boundaries and go beyond fixed notions of competence, in relation to nativeness, and language norms. Work on conceptualisation has also emphasised the differences between ELF and English as a Foreign Language (EFL), especially in respect of the linguacultural norms used as points of reference (native speaker norms in EFL contexts), the objectives of communication (such as membership in a NS community) and the processes involved (imitation and adaptation to NS), as Seidlhofer summarises it (Seidlhofer 2011: 18). Jenkins also includes a fundamental difference in paradigm: while ELF is part of Global Englishes, EFL belongs to the Foreign Languages paradigm, whereby languages are learnt in order to communicate and identify with native speakers' communities (cf. Jenkins 2015). Global Englishes, instead, includes communication in Outer circle contexts (normally defined as World Englishes) as well as across Inner and Expanding circle contexts. It is a more inclusive label, which overall emphasises difference and variability, over the reductive, deficient and fixed perspective of EFL (for more on this, see Jenkins 2014).

The emphasis on fluidity and flexibility is a crucial aspect of ELF research and makes it possible to go beyond static descriptions of the formal linguistic properties and focus, instead, on practices and processes, such as 'languaging' and 'translanguaging' (Cogo 2012b; Hülmbauer 2013), which emphasise the multilingual nature of ELF and the language contact situation of most ELF communication. This places more importance on speakers' creative practices in their use of plurilingual resources to flexibly co-construct their common repertoire in accordance with the needs of their community and the circumstances of the interaction.

Conceptualisations of this nature are challenging both for scholars working in the field and for teachers trying to apply an ELF-oriented perspective. The challenge for researchers is to work with the inherent variability of ELF communication and for ELT practitioners to incorporate a difference and variability perspective in their classroom practices. I will now explore the variability in the descriptive work of sociolinguists working in ELF and then turn to the applications for practitioners.

Empirical work on linguistic description

Speakers in ELF encounters normally come from different linguacultural backgrounds, and are likely to display varying levels of competence in English. They are expected to have had different experiences with the language, having learnt it formally in the education system or informally under different circumstances in different parts of the world. In all this, the influence of the local context and the domain in which they function are likely to manifest themselves in various localisations at the different linguistic levels.

Descriptive research of ELF communication has been particularly productive in the past 15 years, especially since the creation of a number of corpora of spoken data (VOICE, ELFA and ACE, as well as some individual and small-scale corpus projects), and increasingly more work on written data too. In this section, for reasons of space, I will provide only a succinct summary of work on the nature of ELF that is relevant for structuring and situating the contributions in this volume. This will include the main findings of research in pronunciation, pragmatics and intercultural aspects. Research in lexico-grammar is not reviewed here as papers in this collection do not involve this aspect in the teaching practices explored.

Pronunciation was the first area of linguistic description to be empirically researched. Jenkins' seminal work (2000) explored intelligibility in ELF spoken communication and the kind of accommodation processes speakers engage in. Her data showed the speakers' ability to accommodate to more or less 'native-like' speech in order to enhance intelligibility. The findings also cast light on the core aspects of pronunciation that are essential for intelligibility – that is, all the consonants (apart from the dental fricatives), consonant deletion in initial clusters, vowel length distinctions and nuclear stress. As such, teaching implications require that practitioners focus more on the pronunciation items that are core and are found to enhance intelligibility, rather than on the entire pronunciation inventory. This research also has fundamental implications for assessment – the ELF pronunciation influenced by speakers' linguistic reper-toires can be considered as legitimate rather than as pronunciation errors (cf. Deterding 2013; Schaller-Schwaner, this volume; Walker 2010).

Research in pragmatics has been more extensive, but has provided similar results in terms of recurrent uses of ELF rather than random learner errors. Numerous pragmatic studies have focused on understanding/non-understanding in the attempt to identify those aspects or expressions that facilitate the solution of understanding problems (see Cogo and Dewey 2012; Kaur 2009; Mauranen 2006; Pitzl 2005). Research has shown that misunderstanding issues are less frequent than might be expected and that interlocutors tend to pre-empt or signal possible issues in a problematic exchange. The focus, therefore, has been on the strategies used for dealing with pre-empting, addressing or resolving issues in communication, such as the use of repetition, paraphrasing or co-construction of idiomatic expressions (Cogo 2010; Kaur 2012; Pitzl 2009; Seidlhofer 2009).

Another aspect of pragmatic investigation is the repertoire of multilingual practices that is creatively co-constructed and flexibly integrated (Hülmbauer 2011; Kalocsai 2013; Pitzl 2012; Vettorel 2014) in ELF communication. This implies strategies involving both code-switching and trans-languaging (Cogo 2012b) for meaning making, expressing a specific orientation to the talk (play-ful, engaged, irritated etc.) and expressing cultural and identity functions.

ELF in business and academic contexts – pedagogical questions

This section is dedicated to specific contexts of ELF research, and includes the applied work of scholars that have examined how ELF works, is constructed and is practised in the business and academic domains.

In international business contexts, especially multinational corporations, the use of English as a 'corporate language' has become a common practice, if not an official recognition of the company's language policy. Business English as a Lingua Franca (BELF for short) is now a requirement in globalised business and, even more, an essential aspect of business knowledge. Kankaanranta and Planken (2010: 399) compare the use of BELF in professional contexts 'to the ability to use a computer: you could not do your work without it in today's international workplace'. The 'it' in this quote, though, is not the English of native speakers, but is ELF in a business context, a mode of communication used among professionals operating globally. Most studies in this area confirm the overall tendency of focusing on content of the message and understanding of business ideas, rather than foregrounding accuracy in linguistic terms. In the words of one professional in Ehrenreich's study, 'I must say I'm confronted with so many levels of correctness that I don't actually care whether something is correct or incorrect. As long as the meaning is not distorted' (Ehrenreich 2010: 418).

It is not uncommon for professionals to make reference to variation in linguistic proficiency among the people they come in contact with in the workplace, and often comments include easiness or difficulty of accents, and native speakers tend to be singled out as the most difficult interlocutors (cf. Rogerson-Revell 2008; Sweeney and Zhu 2010). This is not so surprising if we think that professionals operate with a range of L1 and L2 speakers of English who potentially display variation in their speech at all levels, lexico-grammar, phonology and pragmatics. What makes their communication work, therefore, is not so much adherence to 'native speaker norms', but a flexibility to accommodate the unexpected and adapt their pragmatic and strategic competence to the various communicative challenges of the international workplace. Various scholars have emphasised the importance of accommodation as well as relational talk and rapport-building as essential aspects of communication in BELF environments.

Studies exploring business discourse, notably through the analysis of naturally-occurring data from BELF contexts, have also demonstrated that BELF communication is intrinsically intercultural, and for that business professionals need to be able to deal with not only multiple backgrounds and identities, but also different ways of operating or acting in multiple business cultures (Kankaanranta and Planken 2010). On that basis, because of the cultural hybridity of these contexts, some scholars also focused their research on the negotiation of meaning, the co-construction of understanding and the strategies used to solve non-understanding (Cogo and Dewey 2012; Pitzl 2005; Zhu 2015). This discourse focus has highlighted the importance of collaborative practices at all levels of professional communication and provided important findings in BELF-based interactions, which could partly feed into pedagogical discussions (of which more later).

The other aspect the research in BELF has emphasised is the multilingual nature of most business contexts. Studies have shown that English is not the only language at work in international businesses and professionals normally bring into play a repertoire of resources in their communicative practices. Some studies emphasise that English is a 'must' while a repertoire of resources is appreciated strategically (Ehrenreich 2009, 2011; Pullin 2015); others show how multilingual resources come into play within English in the professional workplace (Cogo 2012b; Hülmbauer 2013; Zhu 2014). In other words, though there is a general understanding that English facilitates communication, there are also studies that explore the issue of language choice and the importance of other languages for work matters, not only for relationship building (Charles 2007; Chew 2005; Erling and Walton 2007; Evans 2013; Zhu 2014). In these studies, BELF is not always seen as the undisputed and natural choice for team communication, and issues concerning English, in its potentially excluding or gatekeeping role, are examined.

Pedagogically, the field of BELF has seen the publication of various papers on the conceptualisation and teaching of BELF in higher education (especially in business schools) and in general business English courses (see for example, Kankaanranta et al. 2015; Pullin 2015, among others).

ELF research has also spread to cover the academic domain: as higher education becomes increasingly international, facilitated by staff and student mobility, academia creates 'a rare opportunity to investigate the intricacies of language contact of unforeseen complexity' (Mauranen 2012: 1). In the words of Mauranen, Pérez-Llantada and Swales, academia 'is one of the domains that has adopted English as its common language, and is one where international communication characterises the domain across the board' (2010: 640). As in business, in ELFA (i.e., ELF in Academic contexts) too the research has focused both on academic discourse and on the practices and attitudes towards English in these contexts. In the rest of this section we are going to address them in turn. As with business contexts, in the academic domain there seems to be agreement that the spoken medium content-orientation is perceived as more important than linguistic 'correctness'.

Starting from discourse, Mauranen and her team in Helsinki have produced various studies based on the ELFA corpus (Mauranen 2010a; 2012; 2014). A good amount of research in this area concerns what is generally considered an essential aspect of ELF(A) discourse, namely explicitness. In order to achieve clarity and deal with unpredictability, different kinds of explicitness strategies are found to be used: metadiscourse, markers of local organisation and negotiation strategies (Björkman 2011; 2013; Cogo and Dewey 2012; Mauranen 2010b; 2012). Other studies have investigated self-repetition, paraphrasing (Cogo 2009; Kaur 2012; Lichtkoppler 2007; Mauranen 2006; 2012) and mediation (Hynninen 2011), which were found to be frequent strategies of academic discourse. Smit (2010) carried out an ethnographic study of classroom discourse exploring, among other things, strategies of negotiation of meaning and repair. These findings concern the area of pragmatics, but further interesting research has been carried out for lexico-grammar, where Ranta (2006) found the innovative use of the progressive forms, such as in 'the air we are breathing' (rather than 'the air we breath'), as indicative of a new function, that of drawing attention to the point the speaker is making. Metsä-Ketelä (2006) also concludes that the use of 'more or less' in spoken academic discourse assumes a minimising function, which is only present in ELF discourse. Emphasising the relation between syntax and intonation, Björkman (2013) stresses the significance of question formulation in ensuring effective communication in academic setting. Her study of a Swedish university also explores attitudes towards non-standard language: here Björkman notes that non-standardness, led by a move towards explicitness, is perceived as neither irritating nor incomprehensible by her participants. Finally, while a lot of research has been carried out to explore ELFA spoken communication, this trend has more recently changed, with an increasing number of studies addressing the written mode, especially research in WrELFA (the corpus of Written ELF in Academic settings, University of Helsinki).

In terms of attitudes and ideologies, ELF scholars have engaged with English language policy in so-called 'international' universities, especially those universities and other educational settings that use English as a medium of instruction (see also Quinn Novotná and Dunková, this volume). Jenkins' recent work in this area (2014) has engaged in compelling criticism of the international universities, whose 'international' students are required to conform to 'national' (i.e., inner circle varieties, and most often UK or US) norms in their use of English, while local students are seldom asked to learn how to accommodate to them. The inequality between English NS and international students is also evident in the orientations towards NS-norm-based exams for university admission, and in the voices of the students themselves, who, in Jenkins' interviews, show the extent to which their academic performance is measured again NS norms, and how they often the extra difficulty they encounter in their English-medium programmes is not being understood. Outside the university settings, the debate around ELFA concerns more specifically writing for research publication and the publishing practices of scholars working outside the English-speaking world. This is a widely-debated topic which intersects the ideologies of standard English, monolingualism and the native speaker (Ingvarsdóttir and Arnbjörnsdóttir 2013; Jenkins 2011; Kuteeva and Mauranen 2014; Lillis and Curry 2010), with a strong tendency towards English at the expense of other local languages and to the detriment of scholars writing and publishing in these languages (Canagarajah 2002; Flowerdew 2008).

To conclude the overview of two of the domains of ELF research, it is important to draw attention to an overarching question that often arises in relation to the role of the learner or user in these settings. The social environments of the classroom and the workplace have their implications for the user/learner dichotomy, and while generally ELF research emphasises the need to see speakers as 'users' in their own right, the situational contexts often require a complex re-consideration of these two roles. In a classroom context, for instance, the learner role may dominate over any other, but outside the classroom, other social parameters may become more relevant. Similarly, in the workplace people can alternate their roles as learners and users. These roles are 'not simple and constant, but assumed situationally' (Mauranen 2012: 5) and they often interplay with considerations of attitudes and identities.

ELF implications for ELT: concluding comments

As research on ELF communication and practices intensifies, questions on the applications of its findings for English language teaching also start to be addressed, and this volume is a contribution in this direction. The pedagogical areas that are strongly influenced by ELF research and implications are teaching approaches and methods, the syllabus, the materials and testing. As a consequence, changes in these areas would, of course, need to be accompanied by appropriate teacher training, which is a topic addressed by many contributions to this volume.

Discussions about the global role of English have constantly accompanied the language teaching profession. However, mainstream ELT activities, in terms of conferences, training and publications, have traditionally been kept rather separate from ELF research. In those cases, when discussions of an ELF-oriented pedagogy have taken place, there have been rather heated debates concerning pedagogical norms and practices. Nonetheless, it is encouraging to see that the ELT industry has recently shown more interest in Global Englishes aspects and also addressed the implications of research in this area. For instance, most IATEFL conferences in the past ten years or so have included papers in ELF and also whole SIG days on ELF-related issues, such as pronunciation. Publications directed at teacher trainers or teacher trainees have been a little more reluctant in including an ELF perspective, though some encouraging developments have appeared, such as Walker's ELF-oriented pronunciation teaching manual (Walker 2010), and various papers have recently appeared in the *English Language Teaching Journal* (Baker 2012; Galloway and Rose 2014; Hall 2014; Suzuki 2011, among others) that more directly address ELF in relation to syllabus, materials and testing. In fact, it is precisely the *ELT Journal*, one of the main publications that brings together research and practitioners in the field of ELT, which has recently included ELF in its Aims. They read as follows:

> ELT Journal is a quarterly publication for all those involved in English Language Teaching (ELT), whether as a second, additional, or foreign language, or as *an international Lingua Franca*. (on page 4 of each issue of *ELT Journal*)

These positive developments in the ELT world have not, however, reached all aspects of pedagogical relevance for teachers and practitioners, and have been especially scarce and non-reactive in relation to materials. Global text-books are still rather conservative in their representations of other varieties of English or of ELF communication. The situation is similar for local textbooks. For instance, Matsuda's study of locally produced textbooks in Japan showed a prevalence of 'US standard sanitized textbook English' (Matsuda 2014; cf. also Matsuda 2012). Although some textbooks showed a few comments or cultural observations on varieties of English and ELF, those would most probably be left unexplored by the teachers, and consequently students, unless teachers are trained to notice, expand and build on them. This further emphasises the importance of teacher education in material development and also of more studies investigating how teachers make use of textbooks and create their own material (see also Lopriore and Vettorel, this volume, for materials in the Italian context; Yu, this volume, for the critical evaluation of materials in the Taiwanese context; Grazzi, this volume, on computer-mediated material, and Goncalves, this volume, for migrant situations).

In terms of testing, ELF research continues to question the viability of exter-nal, normally native-speaker-oriented, norms as a reference for most inter-national and local testing practices. Testing and the issue of how to evaluate proficiency need to be rethought, taking the ELF research findings into account and considering a shift from the notion of native speaker to those of 'educated speaker of English' and 'competent user' (Jenkins and Leung 2013). These concepts need to be specified and operationalised in order to go beyond ENL evaluations as the sole criteria of correctness and appropriateness.

Finally, an ELF approach to language teaching ultimately entails a shift in perspective, a 'change in mindset' (Jenkins 2007) and a 'transformative perspective' (Bayyurt and Sifakis, this volume) on the side of teachers and teacher educators. This also involves an understanding that English is not a monolithic entity and its plurilithic aspects can be integrated and localised in and for the language classroom (see also Wang, this volume, on language awareness; Dewey 2012, and this volume, on a post-normative approach). An ELF-oriented approach to ELT is not about deciding what needs to be taught in the classroom, and not about creating a specific methodology, but enabling teachers to consider ELF research findings and to reflect on their beliefs about the subject English today and how their practices can be adapted to include a more multilingually-sensitive English language pedagogy.

References

Baker, W. (2012). From cultural awareness to intercultural awareness: Culture in ELT. *ELT Journal* 66(1): 62–70.
Björkman, B. (2011). Pragmatic strategies in English as an academic Lingua Franca: Ways of achieving communicative effectiveness? *Journal of Pragmatics* 43(4): 950–964.

Björkman, B. (2013). *English as an academic Lingua Franca. An Investigation of form and Communicative Effectiveness*. Berlin: De Gruyter Mouton.

Canagarajah, S. (2002). *A Geopolitics of Academic Writing*. Pittsburgh, PA: University of Pittsburgh Press.

Charles, M. L. (2007). Language matters in global communication. *Journal of Business Communication* 44(3): 260–282.

Chew, S. K. (2005). An investigation of the English language skills used by new entrants in banks in Hong Kong. *English for Specific Purposes* 24: 423–435.

Cogo, A. (2008). English as a Lingua Franca: Form follows function. *English Today* 24(3): 58–61.

Cogo, A. (2009). Accommodating difference in ELF conversations: A study of pragmatic strategies. In Mauranen, A. and Ranta, E. (eds) *English as a Lingua Franca. Studies and Findings*. Newcastle upon Tyne: Cambridge Scholars Publishing, pp. 254–273.

Cogo, A. (2010). Strategic use and perceptions of English as a Lingua Franca. *Poznań Studies in Contemporary Linguistics* 46(3): 295–312.

Cogo, A. (2012a). English as a Lingua Franca: Concepts, use and implications. *English Language Teaching Journal* 66(1):, 97–105.

Cogo, A. (2012b). ELF and super-diversity: A case study of ELF multilingual practices from a business context. *Journal of English as a Lingua Franca* 1(2): 287–313.

Cogo, A. and Dewey, M. (2012). *Analyzing English as a Lingua Franca: A Corpus-driven Investigation*. London: Continuum.

Deterding, D. (2013). *Misunderstandings in English as a Lingua Franca. An Analysis of ELF Interactions in South-East Asia*. Berlin: De Gruyter Mouton.

Dewey, M. (2012). Towards a post-normative approach: Learning the pedagogy of ELF. *Journal of English as a Lingua Franca* 1(1): 141–170.

Dewey, M. (2013). The distinctiveness of English as a Lingua Franca. *English Language Teaching Journal* 67(3): 346–349.

Ehrenreich, S. (2009). English as a Lingua Franca in multinational corporations – exploring business communities of practice. In Mauranen, A. and Ranta, E. (eds) *English as a Lingua Franca. Studies and Findings*. Newcastle upon Tyne: Cambridge Scholars Publishing, pp. 126–151.

Ehrenreich, S. (2010). English as a business Lingua Franca in a German MNC. Meeting the challenge. *Journal of Business Communication*, Special issue on 'Language Matters' 47(4): 408–431.

Ehrenreich, S. (2011). The dynamics of English as a Lingua Franca in international business: A language contact perspective. In Archibald, A., Cogo, A. and Jenkins, J. (eds) *Latest Trends in ELF Research*. Newcastle on Tyne: Cambridge Scholars Publishing, pp. 11–34.

Erling, E. A. and Walton, A. (2007). English at work in Berlin. *English Today* 23(1): 32–40.

Evans, S. (2013). Perspectives on the use of English as a business Lingua Franca in Hong Kong. *International Journal of Business Communication* 50(3): 227–252.

Firth, A. (1996). The discursive accomplishment of normality: On 'Lingua Franca' English and conversation analysis. *Journal of Pragmatics* 26(2): 237–259.

Flowerdew, J. (2008). Scholarly writers who use English as an additional language. What can Goffmann's 'stigma' tell us? *Journal of English for Academic Purposes* 7: 77–86.

Galloway, N. and Rose, H. (2014). Using listening journals to raise awareness of Global Englishes in ELT. *ELT Journal* 68(4): 386–396.

Hall, C. (2014). Moving beyond accuracy: From tests of English to tests of 'Englishing'. *English Language Teaching Journal* 68(4): 376–385.

House, J. (1999). Misunderstanding in intercultural communication: Interactions in English as Lingua Franca and the myth of mutual intelligibility. In Gnutzmann, C. (ed.) *Teaching and Learning English as a Global Language*. Tübingen: Stauffenburg, pp. 73–89.

Hülmbauer, C. (2011). Old friends? – Cognates in ELF communication. In Archibald, A., Cogo, A. and Jenkins, J. (eds) *Latest Trends in ELF Research*. Newcastle on Tyne: Cambridge Scholars Publishing, pp. 139–161.

Hülmbauer, C. (2013). From within and without: The virtual and the plurilingual in ELF. *Journal of English as a Lingua Franca* 2(1): 47–73.

Hynninen, N. (2011). The practice of 'mediation' in English as a Lingua Franca interaction. *Journal of Pragmatics* 43(4): 965–977.

Ingvarsdóttir, H. and Arnbjörnsdóttir, B. 2013. ELF and academic writing: A perspective from the Expanding Circle. *Journal of English as a Lingua Franca* 2(1): 123–145.

Jenkins, J. (2000). *The Phonology of English as an International Language*. Oxford: Oxford University Press.

Jenkins, J. (2007). *English as a Lingua Franca: Attitude and Identity*. Oxford: Oxford: University Press.

Jenkins, J. (2011). Accommodating (to) ELF in the international university. *Journal of Pragmatics* 43(4): 926–936.

Jenkins, J., Cogo, A. and Dewey, M. (2011). Review of developments in research into English as a lingua franca. *Language Teaching* 44(3): 281–315.

Jenkins, J. (2014). *English as a Lingua Franca in the International University. The Politics of Academic English Language Policy*. London: Routledge.

Jenkins, J. (2015). *Global Englishes*. (3rd ed.) London: Routledge.

Jenkins, J. and Leung, C. (2013). English as a Lingua Franca. In Kunnan, A. (ed.) *The Companion to Language Assessment*, Vol. 4. Hoboken, NJ: Wiley-Blackwell, 1607–1616.

Kalocsai, K. (2013). *Communities of Practice and English as a Lingua Franca: A Study of Erasmus Students*. Berlin: De Gruyter Mouton.

Kankaanranta, A. and Planken, B. (2010). BELF competence as business knowledge of internationally operating business professionals. *Journal of Business Communication* 47(4): 380–407.

Kankaanranta, A., Louhiala-Salminen, L. and Karhunen, P. (2015) English in multinational companies: Implications for teaching 'English' at an international business school. *Journal of English as a Lingua Franca* 4(1).

Kaur, J. (2009). Pre-empting problems of understanding in English as a Lingua Franca. In Mauranen, A. and Ranta, E. (eds) *English as a Lingua Franca: Studies and Findings*. Newcastle upon Tyne: Cambridge Scholars Publishing, pp. 107–123.

Kaur, J. (2012). Saying it again: Enhancing clarity in English as a Lingua Franca (ELF) talk through self-repetition. *Text &Talk* 32(5): 593–613.

Kuteeva, M. and Mauranen, A. (2014). *Journal of English for Academic Purposes*, Special issue on 'Writing for Publication in Multilingual Contexts' 13.

Lichtkoppler, J. (2007). 'Male. Male.' – 'Male?' – 'The sex is male.' – The role of repetition in English as a Lingua Franca conversations. *Vienna English Working Papers* 16(1). Available at: http://anglistik.univie.ac.at/views/archive/ (accessed 1 October 2014).

Lillis, T. and Curry, M. (2010). *Academic Writing in a Global Context. The Politics and Practices of Publishing in English*. London: Routledge.

Matsuda, A. (2012). Teaching materials in EIL. In Alsagoff, L., McKay, S. L., Hu, G. and Renandya, W. A. (eds) *Principles and Practices for Teaching English as an International Language*. New York: Routledge, pp. 168–185.

Matsuda, A. (2014). EIL representation in Japanese EFL textbooks. Presentation given at the ELF7 conference, Athens, Greece, 5 September 2014.

Mauranen, A. (2006). Signaling and preventing misunderstanding in English as Lingua Franca communication. *International Journal of the Sociology of Language* 177: 123–150.

Mauranen, A. (2010a). Features of English as a Lingua Franca in academia. *Helsinki English Studies*, Special issue on 'English as a Lingua Franca' 6: 6–28.

Mauranen, A. (2010b). Discourse reflexivity – A discourse universal? The case of ELF. *Nordic Journal of English Studies*, Special issue on metadiscourse 9(2): 13–40.

Mauranen, A. (2012). *Exploring ELF: Academic English Shaped by Non-native Speakers*. Cambridge: Cambridge University Press.

Mauranen, A. (2014). Lingua Franca discourse in academic contexts: Shaped by complexity. In Flowerdew, J. (ed.) *Discourse in Context: Contemporary Applied Linguistics*. Vol. 3. London: Bloomsbury, pp. 225–245.

Mauranen, A., Pérez-Llantada, C. and Swales, J. M. (2010). Academic Englishes. A standardized knowledge? In Kirkpatrick, A. (ed.) *The Routledge Handbook of World Englishes*. London: Routledge, pp. 634–652.

Metsä-Ketelä, M. (2006). Words are more or less superfluous. *Nordic Journal of English Studies* 5(2): 117–143.

Pitzl, M-L. (2005). Non-understanding in English as a Lingua Franca: Examples from a business context. *Vienna English Working Papers* 14(2): 50–71.

Pitzl, M-L. (2009). 'We should not wake up any dogs': Idiom and metaphor in ELF. In Mauranen, A. and Ranta, E. (eds) *English as a Lingua Franca. Studies and Findings*. Newcastle upon Tyne: Cambridge Scholars Publishing, pp. 298–322.

Pitzl, M-L. (2012). Creativity meets convention: Idiom variation and remetaphorization in ELF. *Journal of English as a Lingua Franca* 1(1): 27–55.

Pullin, P. (2015) Culture, curriculum design, syllabus and course development in the light of BELF. *Journal of English as a Lingua Franca* 4(1).

Ranta, E. (2006). The 'attractive' progressive – why use the -ingform in English as a Lingua Franca? *Nordic Journal of English Studies* 5(2): 95–116.

Rogerson-Revell, P. (2008). Participation and performance in international business meetings. *English for Specific Purposes*, 26: 103–120.

Saraceni, M. (2008). English as a Lingua Franca: Between form and function. *English Today* 24(2): 20–26.

Seidlhofer, B. (2001). Closing a conceptual gap: The case for a description of English as a Lingua Franca. *International Journal of Applied Linguistics* 11(2): 133–158.

Seidlhofer, B. (2009). Accommodation and the idiom principle in English as a Lingua Franca. *Intercultural Pragmatics* 6(2): 195–215.

Seidlhofer, B. (2011). *Understanding English as a Lingua Franca*. Oxford: Oxford University Press.

Sewell, A. 2013. English as a Lingua Franca: Ontology and ideology. *ELT Journal* 67(1): 3–10.

Smit, U. (2010). *English as a Lingua Franca in Higher Education*. Berlin: De Gruyter Mouton.

Sowden, C. (2012). ELF on a mushroom: The overnight growth in English as a lingua franca. *ELT Journal* 66(1): 89–96.

Suzuki, A. (2011). Introducing diversity of English into ELT: Student teachers' responses. *ELT Journal* 65(2): 145–153.

Sweeney, E. and Zhu, H. (2010). Accommodating toward your audience. Do native speakers of English know how to accommodate their communication strategies toward nonnative speakers of English? *Journal of Business Communication*. Special issue on 'Language Matters' 47(4): 477–504.

Vettorel, P. (2014). *ELF in Wider Networking. Blogging Practices*. Berlin: De Gruyter Mouton.

Walker, R. (2010). *Teaching the Pronunciation of English as a Lingua Franca*. Oxford: Oxford University Press.

Zhu, H. (2014). Piecing together the 'workplace multilingualism' jigsaw puzzle. *Multilingua* 33(1–2): 233–242.

Zhu, H. (2015). Negotiation as the way of engagement in intercultural and lingua franca communication: Frames of reference and interculturality. *Journal of English as a Lingua Franca* 4(1).

2
Promoting Awareness of Englishes and ELF in the English Language Classroom

Lucilla Lopriore and Paola Vettorel

Introduction

Research on ELT textbooks has repeatedly shown that materials have traditionally tended to focus on 'established' and standard representations of language, most often presenting British – and to a certain extent American – Standard varieties as the sole valid exemplifications of the English language, failing 'to acknowledge the increased use of English among non-native speakers of English' (Matsuda 2012a: 171). This approach has contributed to the promotion of a simplified monolithic view of the English language; furthermore, given the diversification brought about by the spread of English at a global level, it has been argued (e.g. McKay 2002, 2003; Matsuda 2003, 2012b; Seidlhofer 2004, 2011; Dewey and Leung 2010) that such an approach does not adequately prepare learners for the dynamic variety and plurality they will meet as English users.

An investigation related to some recently published textbooks and materials in the Italian upper secondary school context has focused on whether, how and to what extent a perspective on Englishes and ELF has been taken into consideration in pedagogical terms (Vettorel and Lopriore 2013). Findings have shown that, apart from a more inclusive view in relation to intercultural awareness, materials in the corpus do not consistently account for the diversity of English, nor do they aim at fostering awareness of its current plurality in terms of teaching activities.

Yet the manifold contexts in which English is used, its widespread and plurilithic presence in the media and in the environment at large, and the fact that bilingual speakers of English outnumber by far its native speakers (e.g. Crystal 2003; Graddol 2006), ideally require didactic materials and classroom practices that provide a more balanced and up-to-date representation of this reality. In other words, as Matsuda notices, 'one of the most important goals is to develop awareness of and sensitivity toward differences – in forms, uses and users – and learn to respect (or at least tolerate) those differences. EIL teaching materials must support this' (Matsuda 2012a: 170).

Stemming from our analysis of recent ELT materials in the Italian context, and taking into consideration recent developments in literature in relation to classroom practices informed by World Englishes, English as an International language (EIL) and ELF, the present chapter aims to: (a) identify core aspects of possible WE and ELF-orientation in course-book organisation and syllabi in taking into account the diffusion of Englishes and ELF both in terms of contents and teaching approaches; (b) set out some suggestions and recommendations for publishers, teacher educators and teachers aimed at fostering awareness of Englishes and ELF in teaching materials and classroom practices; and (c) provide examples of activities and materials that can be used in the classroom to raise awareness of the extended contexts of English use in today's world and to familiarise learners with WE and ELF.

English(es), ELF and textbooks

From several recent research studies on ELT textbooks analysis, it appears that the tendency to introduce aspects of global Englishes is usually visible in those sections aimed at developing (inter)cultural awareness or CLIL (Gray 2002; Vettorel 2010a, 2010b; Lopriore and Ceruti 2012; Vettorel and Corrizzato 2012; Naji Meidani and Pishghadam 2013; Vettorel and Lopriore 2013). It less frequently occurs in recorded materials or in the interactions among the characters in the book (Kivistö 2005; Eggert 2007; Kopperoinen 2011; Caleffi 2014).

The Vettorel-Lopriore investigation (2013) of recently published ELT materials in the Italian context has focused on the degree of inclusiveness for WE and ELF, examining tasks provided in course-books (reading, listening and speaking activities), in their audio, video and web-based materials, as well as in the teacher's guidelines.[1] Taking account of developments in WE and ELF studies, as well as of most recent research in textbook analysis (e.g. Gray 2010; Tomlinson and Masuhara 2013[2]) and materials development (e.g. Matsuda 2012a; McKay 2012a), the core criteria for the analysis were as follows:

1. Presence or absence of references to WE and ELF
2. Awareness-raising activities of WE and/or ELF
3. Promotion of the use of English outside the school environment and flexibility for effective localisation
4. Promotion of the use of effective communication and intercultural strategies.

All criteria were set against the WE and ELF-oriented backdrop that guided our analysis. In line with previous literature, our findings show that, on the whole, there do not seem to be significant changes in relation to the current spread, role(s) and pluralisation of the English language, ELF included.

As regards references to WE and ELF, apart from British and American English differences, and in some cases other Inner Circle varieties (such as Irish, Welsh, Scottish), Standard British English continues to represent the default model, particularly, though not exclusively, for listening materials and vocabulary-development sections.

As to the second criterion – raising awareness of WE and/or ELF – despite the increased presence of several Inner Circle English varieties, few references are made to WE and ELF and, when present, awareness-raising activities are not adequately developed nor clearly defined. Furthermore, despite a growing tendency to include non-native speakers (NNSs) as characters, they are not overtly presented as 'legitimate users of English', and thus viable models and settings for the interactions are mainly native-speaker (NS)/Inner Circle ones. In only two textbooks is explicit reference made to WE and ELF, and in one case the changes English has gone through are mentioned in the teachers' guide. Yet little opportunity for reflection is generally provided in relation to issues and characteristics of WE and ELF communicative settings. It should also be noticed that, in the overwhelming majority of cases, the characters in the recorded materials sound like native speakers, or as if their NNS pronunciation was being imitated by NSs.

Similarly, connections to potential opportunities to use English in the outside-school environment are very rarely considered,[3] despite a few course-books fostering awareness of pragmatic differences between the learners' L1 (Italian) and English, and in one textbook drawing attention to other languages, too.

The area where more encouraging findings emerge is that of intercultural awareness and culture-devoted sections – '*civiltà*', as they are conventionally called in Italian; these sections are increasingly inclusive of elements referring not only to British (or American) cultural aspects, but to different countries and languacultures, too. Reflective activities, also related to the learners' own culture, are well represented, thus providing opportunities for language use which are at the same time broader (that is, not solely related to the Anglophone world) and more localised, for example in relation to topics such as food or sports. This appears to be an important point, not least given that participants in ELF contexts belong by default to different languacultures, and this diversity plays a relevant role in interactions and meaning negotiation (Cogo 2010; Seidlhofer 2011; Leung 2013). It should be noticed, however, that communication strategies are often included only with reference to self-study and exam skills, rather than involving students in tasks that take into account the relevance of these strategies in the diversity of (ELF) settings where English is currently used.

Recent developments in pluralistic approaches to English in classroom practices

A debate over the implications of findings in the research areas of WE and ELF for ELT and pedagogic practices has recently seen important developments, and several proposals can be found in literature, mostly oriented at an inclusive and more pluralistic approach in connection to the developments and changes English has gone through. Some proposals are related to more general goals in EIL (McKay 2002; Matsuda 2003) and EIL curricula (Brown 2012) or to ENL, ESL/WE and ELF/EIL (Kirkpatrick 2007; Matsuda and Friedrich 2011; Wen 2012); others provide exemplifying activities (Farrel and Martin 2009; McKay 2012a; Matsuda and Duran 2012). In some cases more structured activities are set out, either within courses – mostly in higher education – or in modules that can be integrated into a syllabus (Takagaki 2005; Vettorel 2010b; Bayyurt and Altinmakas 2012; D'Angelo 2012; Lee 2012; Sharifian and Marlina 2012). Other proposals have focused on more specific aspects, such as a communicatively oriented curriculum (Sifakis 2006), pragmatics (McKay 2002, 2009; House 2012), or are aimed at the development of language awareness (Seidlhofer 2004) and communication strategies (Canagarajah 2006, 2011; Mariani 2010; Friedrich 2012).

The proposals emerging from the literature can therefore be considered in line with the promotion of plurilithic (vs. monolithic) ELT practices, which are oriented by an Englishes- and an EIL/ELF-informed approach that is set within a broader perspective aiming to make learners aware of the plurality of English today and to provide them with the tools needed to become competent as well as more effective English users.

As the approaches briefly summarised above show, operating within a pluralistic perspective to WE and EIL is not about selecting which 'features' and language elements are to be taught. It has been pointed out very clearly by ELF researchers that to embrace an ELF-informed perspective in ELT would not in any way imply applying a prescriptive pedagogic model, namely 'teaching ELF features' (cf. Seidlhofer 2004; Seidlhofer et al. 2006; Jenkins 2007; Dewey and Jenkins 2008; Cogo and Dewey 2012). Jenkins et al. (2011: 17) state very adamantly that ELF

> is not about determining what should or should not be taught in the language classroom. Rather, ELF researchers feel their responsibility is to make current research findings accessible in a way that enables teachers to reconsider their beliefs and practices and make informed decisions about the significance of ELF for their own individual contexts.

What a pluralistic WE and ELF-oriented pedagogic approach entails is, in the first place, an acknowledgement that English no longer represents a single, monolithic language and culture, and that this diversification is not a distant, far-away and merely theoretical reality, but one that can be frequently encountered in everyday communication.

Adopting a pluralistic perspective on Englishes and ELF is hence neither a matter of 'selecting linguistic features' that ought to be given priority in syllabi and materials, nor of choosing between 'international varieties' such as 'an/the international variety of English' (p. 334), '[s]peakers' own variety of English' (p. 335), or 'an established variety of English' (p. 336), as summarised in Matsuda and Friedrich (2011: 334–337). Instead, it entails a broader shift in perspective, one that 'would enable each learner's and speaker's English to reflect on his or her own sociolinguistic reality, rather than that of a usually distant native speaker' (Jenkins 2006a: 173) and to each local context of learning and use.

As we will see in the next sections, the areas outlined above could be taken into account in order to:

- encourage language use in authentic contexts, similar to the ones learners are already engaged in as L2 users, whether face-to-face, or digitally-mediated;
- foster awareness, and provide a realistic representation, of the pluralities of English today, both in terms of varieties (WE) and of ELF users;
- provide attainable and realistic language models for learners as L2 users;
- connect with the learners' context, environment and L1 as a site of language contact, that can be meaningfully exploited for reflection and critical awareness; and
- provide an overt focus on active and WE/ELF-oriented Communication Strategies (CS) and Intercultural Communication Strategies (ICS).

As regards CS and ICS, if on the one hand it can certainly be said that CS have been part of CLT-oriented curricula, on the other they have traditionally been set against a NS backdrop (e.g., Widdowson 2003; Leung 2005; Berns 2006; Canagarajah 2006, 2011; Jenkins 2006b; Seidlhofer 2011). Given that both CS and ICS are an inalienable element in achieving successful communication, they ought to constitute an important area in ELT, with a focus on real-world communication contexts, particularly in WE and ELF settings (e.g., Leung 2005, 2013).

Awareness-raising in an ELF-oriented pedagogy

As we have seen, the fast changing scenario of global English usage, the complexity of polylingual contexts and the emerging roles and functions of English when used as a lingua franca pose new challenges to commonly held assumptions about language, language teaching and language education (Matsuda 2003; Seidlhofer 2004; Canagarajah 2005; Jenkins 2006a; Matsuda and Friedrich 2011; Cogo and Dewey 2012). As Seidlhofer (1999: 234) anticipated:

'In short, there is a sense of breaking the professional mould, with a broader conception of what it means to teach languages going hand in hand with a more comprehensive view of the languages to be taught'.

This shift in perspective demands for new orientations in language policies and in curriculum design, but it is particularly in ELT courses that careful reconsideration in balancing traditional and new course components and the way language is presented should occur. 'What is needed is a complete revision of the entire program, using an understanding of the use of English in international contexts as a foundation that influences every single aspect of the curriculum' (Matsuda and Friedrich 2011: 13).

Even though they are referring to the curriculum for English as an International Language, what the authors suggest is an approach that may apply to ELF as well. What is needed is an understanding of English as currently used by speakers in naturally occurring interactions within social interaction and multilingual environments as a way to inform the curriculum.

The next sections will deal with the way in which this ELF-informed perspective can be developed in relation to four main areas:

- ELF-awareness in ELT education;
- course book and syllabus organisation;
- inclusive approaches; and
- activities and materials.

ELF-awareness and ELT education

Changes towards an awareness-based approach to a WE and ELF curriculum would inevitably involve different types of ELT practitioners: teachers, teacher educators, material and course-book writers, and test developers. Each of these practitioners, however, may understand, use and implement this pedagogical approach, in which learners gradually gain insights into language and into how language works, differently. It is thus important to identify, implement and share successful activities, tasks and materials that promote and sustain learner awareness of different instantiations of English.

The following two sections are specifically addressed to two main types of ELT practitioner – teacher educators and materials writers.

Teacher educators – raising teacher awareness

This section introduces three areas in which teacher education can raise teacher awareness of ELF:

- the importance of exposure and observation;
- the need to redefine communicative competence; and
- teacher reflection on suitable activities.

Re-consideration of language and language learning in terms of the role and function of English varieties and of ELF should be included as the underlying component of teacher education courses since it is in initial education and teaching communities that awareness of language, language varieties and multi-language competence may best be developed (Cook 2002; Alptekin 2010).

A useful starting point would be to expose teachers-to-be during training to a variety of social contexts in which ELF is actually used, either through audio materials, films or documentaries or by tasks on extracts from corpora of English, of WE varieties and of ELF, and to invite them to observe what people actually do with language when they communicate and to discuss different notions of English, varieties of English and ELF in terms of effectiveness of communication (Dewey 2012; Cogo and Dewey 2012).

One of the issues emerging from ELF studies is, for example, the redefinition of communicative competence, which is too often only acknowledged as 'adherence to established norms', or perceived as 'native speaker idealization', rather than being considered as the ability to effectively move in and across communities that use English (Leung 2005; Alptekin 2010; Cogo and Dewey 2012). These types of issue could usefully be included in teacher education workshops, since they provide a unique opportunity to challenge teachers' commonly shared beliefs about language, language competence and English. Tasks could include discussion and joint redefinition of the notions of communicative competence (Leung 2005), multilingual competence, language proficiency and, as a consequence, assessment (McNamara 2011).

Trainee teachers need to reflect upon the most effective activities for language learners who are aiming to become proficient users of English in multilingual contexts. Trainers should therefore provide opportunities for teachers to devise formats and tasks for which the model for their language learners is not the native speaker, but rather an effective and intelligible communicator. In this respect, asking trainees to plan activities in which their learners would be using language to carry out successful communicative tasks, e.g. through online projects between international schools, may represent a springboard for pooling ideas and evaluating learner strategies within NNS interaction rather than just aiming at the correct use of traditional language norms.

As Gray (2010: 191) points out, rather than passive consumers (of materials), '[t]eachers need to begin to see themselves as powerful and begin to make demands on publishers'. This resonates with Seidlhofer's call for teachers to be 'agents of change' in using materials as 'resources for adaptation' (1999: 236) and thus play an active and major role in promoting awareness of Englishes and ELF not only in selecting the most appropriate materials, but also in using them in a context-appropriate way (cf. also Seidlhofer 2011: 199, 201; McKay 2012a, 2012b) – hence the importance of teacher education (Lopriore 2010).

Materials writers

Course-book syllabi traditionally rely on basic organisational language-related components such as grammar, vocabulary, pronunciation, language skills and language functions, but they also provide sections on subject specific topics, for example CLIL, and on cultural and intercultural issues. As we have already seen, in recent research studies of course-books, the evidence of a shift towards a more WE and ELF-oriented position is so far mainly in terms of the type of intercultural issues presented in the materials. It would be important on the other hand to provide information through a more comprehensive approach to language work, where teachers may be able to resort to a variety of multi-modal resources and learners would thus be exposed to multilingual contexts with real non-native proficient speakers who use English in authentic exchange contexts. For example, extracts from news about international meetings where non-native public figures (politicians, artists etc.) talk in press conferences or use English to communicate and interact with other ELF users.

Audio and/or video materials drawn from 'real' contexts of use may provide both textbook authors and teachers who develop their own teaching materials an opportunity to devise activities where learners are engaged in 'noticing' (Schmidt 2001), i.e. paying conscious attention to language use, and 'languaging' activities (Swain 2006: 96), that is, activities involving 'the use of strategies for making sense, negotiate meaning, co-constructing understanding, and so on, in short the strategic exploitation of the linguistic resources of the virtual language that characterises the use of ELF' (Seidlhofer 2011: 198).

One of the drawbacks in materials and course-book production is that materials writers are restricted in their use of source material by issues such as privacy and copyright. It is cheaper and easier for publishers to record their own non-authentic material using writers' scripts and actors. To counter this problem, training courses should therefore offer teachers the opportunity to devise and produce their own materials, encouraging them to use and exploit for teaching purposes what is available on the web, particularly on YouTube, where different authentic uses of English in real contexts are accessible. Being engaged in producing their own materials and/or activities would lead teachers to reflect on the kind of English their students are being presented with. This can be and is already being done in several training courses, but unfortunately writing materials is time-consuming for teachers and many of them, once their course is finished, prefer to resort to the course book only.

Course-book and syllabus organisation

Course-book organisation is largely dependent upon market demand, but text-books are initially conceived and developed in relation to the way authors view and conceptualise language and the process of language learning and teaching.

In the case of ELF, '[...] without a radical shift in the way language is under-stood as a concept, and then positioned in the curriculum, there seems little prospect of there being any uptake of an ELF perspective' (Cogo and Dewey 2012: 172).

There are two closely related assumptions that would sustain a shift towards WE and ELF orientation in course-books:

1. A view of the learner who:
   - is capable of personal and social decisions in normal conversational inter-action and uses (Lantolf and Thorne 2006; Larsen-Freeman 2012: 299);
   - has the capacity to draw on his/her multilingual repertoire (Canagarajah 2007a: 229; Kramsch 2009: 43);
   - can become an agent of change (Norton and Toohey 2011: 419), as teach-ers can (Seidlhofer 1999).
2. A view of the language as a complex and adaptive system (Ellis and Larsen-Freeman 2009: 4), a polylithic variety (Seidlhofer et al. 2006; Seidlhofer 2011), in which language change is a natural phenomenon, and learners' language competence includes their ability to display their identity as members of a community (Canagarajah 2007b). In short, a view of English as a discursive construct (Widdowson 2003). It is within this view that ELF defies all previous traditional representations of language varieties since it 'operates across conventional sociolinguistic boundaries rather than within them' (Cogo and Dewey 2012: 165).

These assumptions relate to both the contents and the approach that should be adopted in course-books and materials development. Rather than a mere provi-sion of examples of, or exposure to, the plurality of Englishes, it is how these pluralities are presented to the learners, how learners are being engaged and challenged through tasks and activities within and beyond the school context that makes a shift in perspective for both teachers and learners possible.

Inclusive approaches in the WE and ELF-oriented classroom

Given the dynamic and hybrid nature of ELF settings, where constellations of speakers – together with their linguistic and cultural backgrounds – are also very changeable, the complexity of the communicative strategies characteris-ing these encounters ought to constitute a point for reflection in class. Matsuda identifies three main reasons for an inclusive approach to Englishes. According to her (Matsuda 2012a: 175),

1. it is important that the materials used in class represent both native and non-native speakers, particularly those similar to learners themselves. Such an inclusive representation represents the profile of English users more

accurately and helps learners develop a more realistic expectation about their future interlocutors;
2. this could foster 'the sense of ownership of English', which can be done in several ways, 'from having the opportunity to use English for authentic purposes to meeting someone with a similar background using English effectively to having explicit discussions in it';
3. the inclusion of people who are similar to the learner is important because they serve as the role model. Specifically, it allows learners to see themselves as someone who can become a legitimate user of the language.

One of the major areas where one's view of the language is represented is grammar, both in terms of its conceptualisation and of learning sequences. In spite of widely known theories and approaches to grammar, such as systemic-functional linguistics with its integration of grammar into discourse, or of 'grammaring', the dynamic process of relating form and structure to meaningful units, very little of these approaches is represented in course-books or even grammar books. Grammar is still presented as a set of clearly outlined verb paradigms, rules about linguistic forms and rules to be practised and implemented in de-contextualised activities. On the other hand, FL teaching and learning approaches based on how second languages are acquired and developed (Larsen-Freeman 2003, 2006; Ellis 2008) share a focus on the users, in particular on their experience of processing language while simultaneously constructing it, and identify the notions of 'attention', 'awareness' and 'noticing' as crucial for fostering acquisition. Such an approach would certainly fit a WE and ELF orientation where the learner should be encouraged to observe and to notice language in use in naturally occurring interactions.

Activities and materials for raising student awareness

What is most needed in the plurality of contexts where English is being used and taught is an approach based upon awareness-raising activities implemented through a WE- and ELF-oriented curriculum. Learners need to pay attention to and become aware of the language they are being exposed to in order to be able to understand its use. The notion of attention in language acquisition, often taken as a synonym of consciousness (Ellis 2008), plays a crucial role in the learning process, insofar as it helps raise awareness of the language in use. But learners should also be gradually encouraged to use their multilingual repertoire by code-switching and effectively exploit the available language resources.

In the next section we propose some examples of WE- and ELF-oriented activities. These have been subdivided into four main areas according to their main purpose, namely: WE and ELF awareness, out-of-school exposure, intercultural communication strategies and intercultural sensitivity.

Awareness of the plurality of English: related activities

Developing learners' awareness of the natural phenomenon of language change, the varieties of English and the global emergence of ELF should constitute the backbone of teacher education courses and of teaching materials. This would require, on the part of both teacher educators and of course-book writers, some preliminary reflection on teachers' and learners' notions about what language is and what language change involves, as well as on their beliefs about English and about what the core syllabus of an English course should be composed of.

In order to activate learners' awareness, it is also necessary to expose them to samples of L2 diachronic and synchronic changes, both written and oral, that have occurred or are still occurring in the English language. Group projects aimed at enhancing learners' ability to notice ways changes occur in time and in different languacultural contexts would be particularly appropriate. These might include the use of multimedia with both visual and spoken input, and stimulate their learning strategies in parallel with their spoken and written production and interaction. Sources of input for this kind of activity might include suitable materials such as David Crystal's video seminars[4] on how English has changed and is continuously changing in everyday texts, and written material such as language corpora and dictionaries of contemporary English, or the Internet, with learners using webquests to find samples of specialised language usage or English language changes, for example, in songs and music.

As well as observing language change, learners also need to be made aware of diversity. They should therefore be increasingly engaged in observing how English is differently realised in different contexts and of how they themselves may have been personally exposed to different Englishes or engaged as L2 users in ELF exchanges. Given the widespread presence of English, and its increasing role as a lingua franca in the world, it is most likely that learners have come into contact not only with several varieties of English in the media, but that they have also directly experienced an active role as ELF users. Contacts with people of other languacultures most frequently take place via the increased opportunities for mobility, which may be virtual or physical, and for a variety of purposes – holidays, study, such as school or Erasmus exchanges, or work. These contacts may involve encounters with speakers of different varieties of English, both native and non-native, as well as of different L1s; in most cases, it is English that works as the shared lingua franca allowing communication to take place, while learners would be actively 'languaging' the English they are learning.

Materials suitable for this approach to diversity might include: excerpts of TV series from different parts of the English-speaking world, videos on different varieties of English, interviews with famous native and non-native politicians, actors, singers and sports champions who use English as an international means of communication. These materials can be used to elicit learners' reflection, allowing them to draw inferences and make comparisons – also with their mother tongue – in terms of degrees of formality and informality, pragmatic features and uses of local varieties and/or slang. A reflective approach can be enhanced through noticing activities, mainly through listening and reading, requiring learners to spot differences and similarities with what they are presented with in their course-books and grammar books. Listening and reading activities are pivotal in this context since learners are likely to encounter WE varieties mostly through aural comprehension. Listening is a complex and active process of interpretation, in which listeners match what they hear with what they already know and develop specific metacognitive and cognitive strategies. The listening activities should thus provide space for development of strategic comprehension skills and for focussed attention on intelligibility. This process can for instance be easily enhanced when learners are exposed to non-dubbed films or films with intralingual subtitles.

A number of activities could be devised, either as part of course-books or by teachers themselves, not only to familiarise learners with, and foster reflection on, the plurality of ways and settings in which English and ELF are used, but also to enhance their independence in searching for examples of what the previous activities have triggered in terms of awareness. For instance, students could:

- be asked to work upon, and possibly retrieve from the Internet, examples of songs, videos, video clips and films related to different varieties and samples of WE or ELF. Working in groups, characteristic linguistic features occurring in interactions could be identified, and then shared with the class in group presentations;
- work in groups, designing a questionnaire to interview students (and members of their families or communities) of a different language background that are largely present in most European schools, in order to find out what variety of English is spoken in the contexts they come from, as well as the role English retains in those areas.

Out-of-school exposure: related activities

The role of out-of-school exposure to English is one of the most important variables for successful language learning and for establishing the learners' own identity as language users. There is a close relation between the extensive availability of WE and of ELF exchanges outside the school walls and the importance of fostering learners' awareness through guided observation of the different representations and use of English in their environment. This is why a specific component of an ELT course-book should be devoted to activities where the link between classroom reflective study and what takes place in real life is established and where learners are invited to carry out projects that foster opportunities for connections with language use. Young people are generally familiar with digital spaces that provide networking opportunities, particularly social networking sites (SNS); in these internationally-oriented arenas, English as a lingua franca is the main language of communication.

Opportunities for exposure to English outside the classroom might include inviting speakers of English to visit a school or setting up a partnership with an international school (Vettorel 2013). Particularly valuable in this sense are the networking and social interaction opportunities provided through computer-mediated communication (CMC), such as the eTwinning European portal,[5] through which exchanges can be organised by means of digital virtual tools provided in the platform dedicated spaces (Vettorel, forthcoming) or in the *European Tandem Portal*, which through the *International e-tandem Network*[6] has opened up a space to educational institutions all over the world where people from different language and cultural backgrounds can meet and use English to interact.

As Alsagoff points out, '[s]uch global discourse communities are useful resources for EIL teaching because they offer possibilities of imagined communities and hybrid identities that allow EIL learners to explore and engage with English in truly authentic EIL contexts outside the classroom' (2012: 112). Indeed, personal websites, blogs and SNS are 'authentic international and multilingual communicative situations' (Matsuda 2012a: 181) that learners are very likely to be familiar with.

As regards particular out-of-school activities involving English, students could be required to

- investigate the presence of English (and other languages) in the linguistic landscape, in the digital media and in advertising of the context they live in and carry out tasks to understand the purpose and features of the English used;
- record in a diary all the English they hear, see and meet (cf. McKay 2012b: 43) in the environments they live in, either for a day or for longer. Findings could then be discussed in groups, followed by a reflection on the roles and functions English plays in their local context (for the linguistic landscape cf. Sayer 2010; Vettorel 2010a, 2014);
- identify and monitor, through specific guidelines and follow-up activities, the communicative strategies they have used in interacting with their partners on the web, whether in educational (e.g., eTwinning or Tandem) or in their private exchanges. Their comments may then become the object of group activities where learners report and compare the strategies used, through their functions as well as their effectiveness. The inclusion of examples of effective communication would also provide students with language

they are likely to meet in their out-of-school experiences. These, as pointed out by Matsuda, would also 'allow learners to see themselves as someone who can become a legitimate user of the language' (2012a: 175).

Communication strategies for effective and cooperative intercultural interaction

Since the 1980s mainstream ELT has been largely constructed around communicative methodologies, in which 'communicative strategies' have played a significant part. Although they have been classified in different ways within that time (see, e.g., Rubin 1987; Oxford 1990; Cohen and Macaro 2007), what they have in common is that they are all based on NS–NS communication strategies rather than on intercultural communicative ones. The ELF perspective on communicative strategies is rather different. Within an ELF-oriented perspective, Seidlhofer (2011: 199) writes that 'the criterion for selecting language to be taught is not whether it is proper English as measured against standard norms or the convention of NS usage but whether it is appropriate English – locally appropriate to the purpose of developing a capability in the language'. In order to develop learners' ability to initiate, establish and maintain meaningful and effective communication when interacting with speakers of WE or with other non-native speakers, learners can be involved in noticing activities, for example of the communication strategies as used by characters in video extracts, as well as of those the learners normally use in their L1. Learners may then be engaged in interactive tasks where they are required to actively use these strategies for effective communication. Given the likelihood that our students' opportunities of language use in the 'real world' will see a plurality of Englishes, not least in ELF settings, it would seem appropriate and useful to expose them to how L2 speakers effectively communicate in different contexts. This would provide them with a perspective on how they 'can be(come) effective users of English' (Seidlhofer 2011: 197; cf. also Hino 2012). Rather than mimicking NS speech, within contexts which are mostly – or only – related to NSs, it would seem more sensible for learners to be exposed and encouraged to experiment with effective uses of English involving both native and non-native, bilingual users of English; 'in this view, learners are not learning *a language* but learning *to language*' (Seidlhofer 2011: 197, emphasis in original).

Possible activities for raising learners' awareness of communicative strategies would expose learners to samples of social exchanges from video extracts of contemporary TV programs and focus their attention upon the use of effective communication strategies.

Intercultural communication and cross-cultural sensitivity: related activities

Intercultural communication in face-to-face as well as virtual activities within a WE and ELF-informed curriculum would further expand learners' sensitivity to other cultures and languages through the use of English as a means of communication. Today English is *de facto* entwined with a variety of cultures (Alptekin 2010; Matsuda 2012a) and the study of global topics and cultures can favour learners' awareness even of their own culture (Cortazzi and Jin 1999; McKay 2002; Matsuda 2012a: 176). An important tool for enhancing learners' intercultural communication skills and sensitivity to other cultures would thus be the use of forms of telecollaboration (Kohn and Warth 2011; Guth and Helm 2012; Grazzi 2013). Specially created dedicated blogs, Facebook pages or the aforementioned eTwinning and Tandem spaces can offer valuable opportunities for learners to interact in realistic situations and to experiment with the language in ELF intercultural contexts. As Ware, Liaw and Warschauer point out, the 'power of digital media in the classroom stems in part from its potential to bridge in-class activities with out-of-class use, to blur the lines between formal instruction and informal learning, and to validate the wide range of registers and uses of English on the global scene' (2012: 77). The authors add that 'learners in the EIL classroom grapple with real interaction, in which the messages they send and receive – the literal, linguistic meanings as well as the symbolic and cultural import underneath the words – position them as representatives of their communities and cultural groups' (2012: 78).

The core syllabus should include activities for developing awareness of and sensitivity to different languacultures and traditions, as well as to diverse realisations of identities, forms of communication and expression of feelings and politeness. The activities should be developed in a perspective that, as Seidlhofer notes below, uses materials and tasks to enable learners to face situations by extending, as well as appropriately adapting, their linguistic resources to the contexts they are going to be working in:

> How much language learners acquire is ultimately irrelevant. What matters is the extent to which whatever parts they have learnt can serve to activate their capability for using, and therefore for further extending, their linguistic resource. This capability will then also serve them well subsequently, for instance when they do find they need (or wish) to conform to standard norms where such conformity is contextually appropriate. (Seidlhofer 2011: 198)

Conclusions

The increasing plurality which the English language has developed over the last decades involves its demographics, in terms of both WE and ELF since bilingual speakers of English outnumber by far its native speakers, as well as the diversity of its speakers and contexts of use. This plurality of forms and functions cannot any longer be ignored in teacher education as in materials and classroom practices.

The representation of native varieties of English only in ELT materials is problematic as it is 'incomplete and may result in a limited and skewed understanding of who speaks English and for what purposes' (Matsuda 2012a: 171). In the ELT world ELF is still a debated issue (e.g. Maley 2010), and 'traditional' teachers' expectations and beliefs in terms of 'language models' certainly do play a relevant role (e.g., Kivistö 2005; Dewey 2012), as do the gate-keeping (and levelling) role of assessment methods (e.g., McNamara 2011; Takahashi 2011).

The development of sociolinguistic awareness (e.g. Bayyurt 2013) and of receptive skills in relation to the diversity of speakers and contexts – of WE as of ELF – should thus be prioritized in teacher education, ELT materials and pedagogic practices. As we have sought to outline in our contribution, the possibilities to include a reflective didactic approach on these changes are manifold, and can be developed along a continuum, taking into account several aspects aimed not only at fostering awareness of the sociolinguistic plurality of English, including its widespread presence in the environment and its active contexts of use, but – and most importantly – at acquainting learners with how English is effectively used in its plurality of forms and functions.

The suggestions offered so far are in terms of:

- ELF-orientation in coursebooks, materials, teacher education and classroom activities;
- Awareness-raising approaches through languaging in both teacher education courses and language classroom;
- Use of currently available audio, video and web resources in material development and classroom activities take into consideration the fact that changes are by nature slow to be implemented, and demand for a shared understanding on the part of both teachers, course-book authors and publishers.

Many current ELT course-books may already offer some opportunities for teachers to widen the materials and activities by including samples of Englishes in a WE and ELF-related perspective. As we have sought to exemplify, tasks can go beyond awareness-raising initial steps, and can be devised to foster deeper reflection on sociolinguistic aspects of language use, as well as to empower learners to explore and analyse language, while becoming independent users. In parallel, the current plurality of English and of the contexts where it is used ought to be taken into account more consistently by material writers and developers too, while teacher education should take on a plurilithic approach, with specific components of contact and reflection on the diversity of forms and functions English retains today. Acknowledging this diversity would provide both teachers and learners with a more realistic perspective on their pedagogic (as well as 'real-language') aims as multicompetent L2 users.

Engagement priorities

1. An overt focus on WE/ELF-oriented communication implies the development of effective intercultural communication strategies (ICS) within ELT teacher education programs, materials and course-books and classroom activities. Discuss its possible implementation in your own context and implications for trainers, teachers and materials writers.
2. ELT materials and activities in a WE/ELF-oriented approach ought to connect with the learners' context and environment as a site of language contact, that can be meaningfully exploited for reflection and critical awareness. Several activities are suggested in this chapter, such as investigating and reflecting upon the presence of English and other languages in the learners' context or reflecting upon pragmatic features of the learners' L1. What practical implications do you see in your own context? What education level do you think this type of activities is most appropriate/feasible for? What other types of activities would enhance learners' awareness of WE/ELF?
3. Among the different reasons for an inclusive approach to Englishes, Matsuda (2012a: 175) identifies the importance of fostering 'the sense of ownership of English', which can be done in several ways, 'from having the opportunity to use English for authentic purposes to meeting someone with a similar background using English effectively to having explicit discussions in it'.

   Thinking of your own context, would you agree on the importance of fostering 'the sense of ownership of English' and on the ways suggested by Matsuda to enhance an inclusive approach to Englishes? What would the implications in terms of learner identity be?
4. The chapter suggests that the use of 'audio and/or video materials drawn from "real" contexts of use may provide both textbook authors and teachers who develop their own teaching materials, with an opportunity to devise activities'.

   Discuss the implications of this suggestion for teachers, teacher trainers and publishers in your own context.
5. The chapter often suggests that learners should be engaged in 'noticing' (Schmidt 2001), that is, in paying conscious attention to language use, and in 'languaging' (Swain 2006: 96) activities whereby language is being used to make meaning. Languaging 'involves the use of strategies for making sense, negotiating meaning, co-constructing understanding [...], in short the strategic exploitation of the linguistic resources of the virtual language that characterises the use of ELF'. (Seidlhofer 2011: 198)

   Discuss your understanding of 'noticing' and 'languaging' in an ELF-oriented approach and hypothesise possible training and teaching activities.

Notes

1. The corpus comprised ten textbooks published between 2008 and 2013 by Italian and British publishers, widely used in Italy in upper secondary school; all units were analysed according to the four criteria described above.
2. To our knowledge, Tomlinson and Masuhara's article is the first to have included ELF-related criteria in an otherwise general overview of recent ELT course-books.
3. However, it should be acknowledged that additional materials downloadable from publishers' dedicated websites, when available, frequently focus on 'noticing' the presence of English in different, and often localised, contexts.
4. Many of these are retrievable on YouTube.
5. http://www.etwinning.net/en/pub/index.htm [Accessed 10/09/2014]
6. www.slf.ruhr-uni-bochum.de, http://www.cisi.unito.it/tandem/email/idxeng00.html [Accessed 10/09/2014]

References

Alptekin, C. (2010). Redefining multicompetence for bilingualism and ELF. *International Journal of Applied Linguistics* 20(1): 95–110.

Alsagoff, L. (2012). Identity and the EIL learner. In L. Alsagoff, S. L. McKay, G. Hu and W. A. Renadya (eds), *Principles and Practices for Teaching English as an International Language*. London: Routledge, pp. 104–122.

Bayyurt, Y. (2013). Current perspectives on sociolinguistics and English language education. *The Journal of Language Teaching and Learning* 3(1): 69–78.

Bayyurt, Y. and Altinmakas, D. (2012). A WE-based English Communication Skills course at a Turkish University. In A. Matsuda (ed.), *Principles and Practices of Teaching English as an International Language*. Bristol: Multilingual Matters, pp. 169–182.

Berns, M. (2006). World Englishes and communicative competence. In B. B. Kachru, Y. Kachru and C. L. Nelson (eds), *The Handbook of World Englishes*, Oxford: Blackwell, pp. 718–730.

Brown, J. D. (2012). EIL curriculum development. In L. Alsagoff, S. L. McKay, G. Hu and W. A. Renadya (eds), *Principles and Practices for Teaching English as an International Language*. London: Routledge, pp. 147–167.

Caleffi, F. (2014). *World Englishes, English as a Lingua Franca and English Language Teaching: Analysis of English Accents in a Corpus of Upper Secondary School ELT Textbooks in Italy*. Unpublished MA thesis, University of Verona.

Canagarajah, A. S. (ed.) (2005). *Reclaiming the Local in Language Policy and Practice*. Mahwah, NJ: Lawrence Erlbaum Associates.

Canagarajah, A. S. (2006). Negotiating the local in English as a Lingua Franca. *Annual Review of Applied Linguistics* 26: 197–218.

Canagarajah, A. S. (2007a). *A Geopolitics of Academic Writing*. New Delhi: Orient Longman.

Canagarajah, A. S. (2007b). Lingua Franca English, multilingual communities, and language acquisition. *Modern Language Journal* 91(5): 921–937.

Canagarajah, A. S. (2011). Codemeshing in academic writing: Identifying teachable strategies in translanguaging. *Modern language Journal* 95(3): 401–417.

Cogo, A. (2010). Strategic use and perceptions of English as a Lingua Franca. *Poznań Studies in Contemporary Linguistics* 46(3): 295–312.

Cogo, A. and Dewey, M. (2012). *Analysing English as a Lingua Franca*. London/New York: Continuum.

Cohen, A. D. and Macaro, E. (2007). *Language Learner Strategies*. Oxford: Oxford University Press.

Cook, V. (ed.) (2002). *Portraits of the L2 User*. Clevedon: Multilingual Matters.

Cortazzi, M. and Jin, L. (1999). Cultural mirrors: Materials and methods in the EFL classroom. In E. Hinkel (ed.), *Culture in Second Language Teaching*. Cambridge: Cambridge University Press, pp. 196–219.

Crystal, David. (2003 [1997]). *English as a Global Language*. Cambridge: Cambridge University Press.

D'Angelo, J. (2012). WE-informed EIL curriculum at Chuko: Towards a functional, educated, multilingual outcome. In A. Matsuda (ed.), *Principles and Practices of Teaching English as an International Language*. Bristol: Multilingual Matters, pp. 121–136.

Dewey, M. (2012). Towards a *post-normative* approach: Learning the pedagogy of ELF. *Journal of English as a Lingua Franca* 1(1): 141–170.

Dewey, M. and Jenkins, J. (2008). English as a Lingua Franca in the global context: Interconnectedness, variation and change. In M. Saxena and T. Omoniyi (eds), *Contending with Globalization in World Englishes*. Bristol: Multilingual Matters, pp. 72–92.

Dewey, M. and Leung, C. (2010). English in English language teaching: Shifting values and assumptions in changing circumstances. *Working Papers in Educational Linguistics* 25(1): 1–15.

Eggert, B. (2007). *Global English and Listening Materials. A Textbook Analysis*. EngelskaCupsatts: Karlstads Universitet Essay.

Ellis, R. (2008). *The Study of Second Language Acquisition*. Oxford: Oxford University Press.

Ellis, R. and Larsen-Freeman, D. (eds) (2009). Language as a complex adaptive system. Special Issue *Language Learning*, 59 Supplement 1.

Farrel, T. S. C and Martin, S. (2009). To teach standard English or World Englishes? A balanced approach to Instruction. *Forum* 47(2): 2–7.

Friedrich, P. (2012). EIL, intercultural communication and the strategic aspect of communicative competence. In A. Matsuda (ed.), *Principles and Practices of Teaching English as an International Language*. Bristol: Multilingual Matters, pp. 44–54.

Graddol, D. (2006). *English Next*. London, England: British Council. Available at http://www.britishcouncil.org/learning-research-english-next.pdf (accessed 10 September 2014).

Gray, J. (2002). The global coursebook in English language teaching. In D. Block and D. Cameron (eds), *Globalization and Language Teaching*. London: Routledge, pp. 151–167.

Gray, J. (2010). *The Construction of English. Culture, Consumerism and the Promotion in the ELT Global Course-book*. Basingstoke: Palgrave Macmillan.

Grazzi, E. (2013). *The Sociocultural Dimension of ELF in the English Classroom*. Roma: ANICIA.

Guth, S. and Helm, F. (2012). Developing multiliteracies in ELT through telecollaboration. *English Language Teaching Journal* 66(1): 42–51.

Hino, N. (2012). Endonormative models of EIL for the Expanding Circle. In A. Matsuda (ed.), *Principles and Practices of Teaching English as an International Language*. Bristol: Multilingual Matters, pp. 28–43.

House, J. (2012). Teaching oral skills in English as a Lingua Franca. In L. Alsagoff, S. L. McKay, G. Hu and W. A. Renadya (eds), *Principles and Practices for Teaching English as an International Language*. London: Routledge, pp. 186–205.

Jenkins, J. (2006a). Current perspectives on teaching World Englishes and English as a Lingua Franca. *TESOL Quarterly* 40(1): 157–181.

Jenkins, J. (2006b) Points of view and blind spots: ELF and SLA. *International Journal of Applied Linguistics* 16(2): 137–162.

Jenkins, J. (2007). *English as a Lingua Franca: Attitude and Identity.* Oxford: Oxford University Press.

Jenkins, J., Cogo, A. and Dewey, M. (2011). Review of developments in research into English as a Lingua Franca. *Language Teaching* 44: 281–315.

Kirkpatrick, A. (2007). *World Englishes. Implications for International Communication and English Language Teaching.* Cambridge: Cambridge University Pres.

Kivistö, A. (2005). *Accents of English as a Lingua Franca: A Study of Finnish Textbooks.* University of Tampere ProGradu Thesis. Available at: http://www.helsinki.fi/englanti/elfa/ProGradu_Anne_Kivisto.pdf (accessed 10 September 2014).

Kohn, K. and Warth, C. (eds) (2011). *Web Collaboration for Intercultural Language Learning.* Verlagshaus Monsenstein und Vannerdat OHG Münster, www.mv-wissenschaft.com, available at http://gepeskonyv.btk.elte.hu/adatok/Anglisztika/Kohn_Warth_Webcollab/Kohn_Warth_Webcollab_EN_FINAL_v3.pdf (accessed 6 June 2015).

Kopperoinen, A. (2011). Accents of English as a Lingua Franca. *International Journal of Applied Linguistics* 21(1): 71–93.

Kramsch, C. (2009). *The Multilingual Subject.* Oxford: Oxford University Press.

Lantolf, J. P. and Thorne, S. L. (2006). *Sociocultural Theory and the Genesis of L2 Development.* Oxford: Oxford University Press.

Larsen-Freeman, D. (2003). *Teaching Language: From Grammar to Grammaring.* Newbury House: Heinle & Heinle.

Larsen-Freeman, D. (2006). The emergence of complexity, fluency, and accuracy in the oral and written production of five Chinese learners of English. *Applied Linguistics* 27: 590–619.

Larsen-Freeman, D. (2012). Chaos/complexity theory for second language acquisition. *The Encyclopedia of Applied Linguistics.* Published online 5.11.2012. Available at: http://onlinelibrary.wiley.com/doi/10.1002/9781405198431.wbeal0125/ (accessed 10 September 2014).

Lee, H. (2012). World Englishes in a high school English class: A case from Japan. In A. Matsuda (ed.), *Principles and Practices of Teaching English as an International Language.* Bristol: Multilingual Matters, pp. 154–168.

Leung, C. (2005). Convivial communication: Recontextualizing communicative competence. *International Journal of Applied Linguistics* 15(2): 119–144.

Leung, C. (2013). The 'social' in English language teaching. *Journal of English as a Lingua Franca* 2(2): 283–313.

Lopriore, L. (2010). World Englishes and language teacher education in a world in migration: A shift in perspective. In C. Gagliardi and A. Maley (eds), *EIL, ELF, Global English: Teaching and Learning Issues.* Bern: Peter Lang, pp. 69–91.

Lopriore, L. and Ceruti, M. A. (2012). Lexicon and intercultural competence in EFL manuals. In R. Facchinetti (ed.), *A Cultural Journey Through the English Lexicon.* Newcastle-upon-Tyne: Cambridge Scholars Publishing, pp. 235–264.

Maley, A. (2010). The reality of EIL and the myth of ELF. In C. Gagliardi and A. Maley (eds), *EIL, ELF, Global English: Teaching and Learning Issues.* Bern: Peter Lang, pp. 25–44.

Mariani, L. (2010). *Communication Strategies.* Milan: Learning Paths/Tante Vie Per Imparare.

Matsuda, A. (2003). Incorporating World Englishes in teaching English as an International Language. *TESOL Quarterly* 37(4): 719–729.

Matsuda, A. (2012a). Teaching materials in EIL. In L. Alsagoff, S. L. McKay, G. Hu and W. A. Renadya (eds), *Principles and Practices for Teaching English as an International Language.* London: Routledge, pp. 168–185.

Matsuda, A. (2012b). Introduction. In A. Matsuda (ed.), *Principles and Practices of Teaching English as an International Language.* Bristol: Multilingual Matters, pp. 1–14.

Matsuda, A. and Duran, C. S. (2012). EIL activities and tasks for traditional English class-rooms. In A. Matsuda (ed.), *Principles and Practices of Teaching English as an International Language*. Bristol: Multilingual Matters, pp. 201–237.

Matsuda, A. and Friedrich, P. (2011). English as an international language: A curriculum blueprint. *World Englishes* 30(3): 332–344.

McKay, S. L. (2002). *Teaching English as an International Language*. Oxford: Oxford University Press.

McKay, S. L. (2003). EIL curriculum development. *RELC Journal* 34(1): 31–47.

McKay, S. L. (2009). Pragmatics and EIL pedagogy. In F. Sharifian (ed.), *English as an International Language*. Bristol: Multilingual Matters, pp. 227–341.

McKay, S. L. (2012a). Teaching materials for English as an International Language. In A. Matsuda (ed.), *Principles and Practices of Teaching English as an International Language*. Bristol: Multilingual Matters, pp. 70–83.

McKay, S. L. (2012b). Principles of teaching English as an International Language. In L. Alsagoff, S. L. McKay, G. Hu and W. A. Renadya (eds), *Principles and Practices for Teaching English as an International Language*. London: Routledge, pp. 28–46.

McNamara, T. (2011). Multilingualism in education: A poststructuralist critique. *Modern Language Journal* 95(3): 430–441.

Naji Meidani, E. and Pishghadam, R. (2013). Analysis of English language textbooks in the light of English as an International Language (EIL): A comparative study. *International Journal of Research Studies in Language Learning* 2(2): 83–96. Available at: http://profdoc.um.ac.ir/articles/a/1029016.pdf (accessed 27 October 2013).

Norton, B. and Toohey, K. (2011). Identity, language learning, and social change. *Language Teaching* 44(4): 412–446.

Oxford, R. (1990). *Language Learning Strategies. What Every Teacher Should Know*. New York: Newbury House.

Rubin, J. (1987). Learner strategies: Theoretical assumptions, research history and typology. In A. L. Wenden and J. Rubin (eds), *Learner Strategies in Language Learning*. Englewood Hills: Prentice Hall, pp. 15–19.

Sayer, P. (2010). Using the linguistic landscape as a pedagogical resource. *ELT Journal* 64(2): 143–154.

Schmidt, R. (2001). Attention. In P. Robinson (ed.), *Cognition and second language instruction*. Cambridge: Cambridge University Press, pp. 3–32.

Seidlhofer, B. (1999). Double standards: Teacher education in the Expanding Circle. *World Englishes* 18(2): 233–245.

Seidlhofer, B. (2004). Research perspectives on teaching English as a Lingua Franca. *Annual Review of Applied Linguistics* 24: 209–239.

Seidlhofer, B. (2011). *Understanding English as a Lingua Franca*. Oxford: Oxford University Press.

Seidlhofer, B., Breiteneder, A. and Pitzl, M. L. (2006). English as a Lingua Franca in Europe: challenges for applied linguistics. *Annual Review of Applied Linguistics*, 26: 3–34.

Sharifian, F. and Marlina, R. (2012). English as an international language (EIL): An innovative academic program. In A. Matsuda (ed.), *Principles and Practices of Teaching English as an International Language*. Bristol: Multilingual Matters, pp. 140–153.

Sifakis, N. C. (2006). Teaching EIL – teaching international or intercultural English? In R. Rubdy and M. Saraceni (eds), *English in the World. Global Rules. Global Roles*. London: Continuum, pp. 151–168.

Swain, M. (2006). Languaging, agency and collaboration in advanced language proficiency. In H. Byrnes (ed.), *Advanced Language Learning: the Contribution of Halliday and Vygotsky*. London: Continuum, pp. 95–108.

Takagaki, T. (2005). Raising students' awareness of the varieties of English. *English Teaching Forum* 43(2): 4–7, 16–17.

Takahashi, R. (2011). *English as a Lingua Franca in a Japanese Context: An Analysis of ELF-oriented Features in Teaching Materials and the Attitudes of Japanese Teachers and Learners of English to ELF-oriented Materials.* Unpublished dissertation. University of Edinburgh. Available at: http://hdl.handle.net/1842/5269 (accessed 10 September 2014).

Tomlinson, B. and Masuhara, H. (2013). Adult course-books. *ELT Journal* 67(2): 233–249.

Vettorel, P. (2010a). EIL/ELF and representation of culture in textbooks: Only food, fairs, folklore and facts? In C. Gagliardi and A. Maley (eds), *EIL, ELF, Global English: Teaching and Learning Issues.* Bern: Peter Lang, pp. 153–185.

Vettorel, P. (2010b). English(es), ELF, Xmas and trees: Intercultural Communicative Competence and English as a Lingua Franca in the primary classroom. *Perspectives – A Journal of TESOL Italy* 37(1): 25–52.

Vettorel, P. (2013). ELF in international school exchanges: Stepping into the role of ELF users. *Journal of English as a Lingua Franca* 2(1): 147–173.

Vettorel, P. (2014). Connecting English wor(l)ds and classroom practices. *Textus* 27(1): 137–154.

Vettorel, P. (forthcoming). English, Englishes, ELF: A project with primary school pupils. In Y. Bayyurt and N. C. Sifakis (eds), *English Language Education Policies and Practices: A Mediterranean Perspective.* London: Pearson.

Vettorel, P. and Corrizzato, S. (2012). World Englishes and ELF in ELT textbooks: How is plurality represented? In R. Facchinetti (ed.), *A Cultural Journey through the English Lexicon,* Newcastle-upon-Tyne: Cambridge Scholars, pp. 201–234.

Vettorel, P. and Lopriore, L. (2013). Is there ELF in ELT course-books? *Studies in Second Language Learning and Teaching* 3(4): 483–504.

Ware, P., Liaw, M.-L. and Warschauer, M. (2012). The use of digital media in teaching English as an International Language. In L. Alsagoff, S. L. McKay, G. Hu and W. A. Renadya (eds), *Principles and Practices for Teaching English as an International Language.* London: Routledge, pp. 67–84.

Wen, Q. (2012). English as a Lingua Franca: A pedagogical perspective. *Journal of English as a Lingua Franca* 1(2): 371–376.

Widdowson, H. G. (2003). *Defining Issues in English Language Teaching.* Oxford: Oxford University Press.

3
Developing Critical Classroom Practice for ELF Communication: A Taiwanese Case Study of ELT Materials Evaluation

Melissa H. Yu

Introduction

In the past two decades the use of English language for intercultural communication has gained wide recognition via empirical research into English as Lingua Franca (ELF). One key aim of ELF studies is to capture the linguistic and cultural dynamics as well as the complexity of intercultural exchanges occurring in a range of contexts and for various purposes (Jenkins et al., 2011). The new understanding of linguistic, cultural phenomenon has challenged established concepts/theories that underpin English language teaching (ELT) and raised pedagogical concerns (Seidlhofer, 2011). English language education continues to underplay the pedagogical concerns of these studies to various degrees in both ELT classrooms and published materials. In order to understand how and why the ELF perspective is not well integrated into classroom practice, one needs to scrutinise ELT materials as well as teachers' and learners' use of these materials.

From an SLA (second language acquisition) perspective, materials, teachers and learners are recognised as three major input sources for language learning (Ellis, 2012). This chapter will focus on how these sources interact and their impact on classroom practice. I will therefore examine the interplay among these three input elements and the impact of each element on teaching and learning. In particular, this chapter presents the so-called linguacultural input provided by curricular materials and analyses how this input informs classroom practices at the tertiary level in Taiwan. Furthermore, I will suggest that through interaction between teachers and students new opportunities emerge for pedagogical transformation that move beyond the mere reproduction of material-focused linguacultural input toward the creation of an ELF-informed practice of teaching and learning.

Due to its small sampling size, this chapter makes no attempt to generalise how teachers and students perceive ELT materials in relation to ELF or to draw conclusions concerning the pedagogical implications of the classroom practices illustrated below.[1] Instead of urging teachers to completely adopt the ELF approach[2] or to abandon current practices, my aim is to offer strategies to integrate the ELF approach into existing classroom practice as well as teacher education, and to encourage further classroom-based ELF research. This chapter begins with a literature review of ELT materials and of ELF-informed research for ELT material and classroom practice. Next, the methodological frame underpinning data collection and analysis is outlined, followed by a discussion of findings related to the teaching practices of ELT professionals, and the benefits of the ELF approach in evaluating and using materials in similar contexts. The chapter concludes with practical suggestions on how ELT professionals can apply a critical and flexible approach to their teaching practices and how teacher educators can prepare trainees for ELF-relevant teaching.

Teachers, learners and materials – the problem areas

Materials and linguacultural representations

For learners of English, teaching materials used in the classroom often represent its culture and language use, and it is around teaching materials that classroom lessons are usually organised by teachers. Yet teaching materials found in textbooks are neither neutral nor unbiased. In this regard, Gray (2010a: 715) argues that global textbooks tend to take a 'dominant-hegemonic' approach to make 'English mean in particular ways'. Examples of Gray's point are that NES (Native English Speaking) writers who tend to take an Anglo-American approach (Shin et al., 2011) to develop materials and to ascertain the linguistic accuracy of ELT materials (Dat, 2008). Linguistic variation of English and/ or its cultural representation beyond the Anglo-Saxon/European world proves to be either inadequately represented or occasionally inaccurate (e.g. Baker, 2015; Dat, 2008; Matsuda, 2012). Hence, textbooks fail to represent the real world language use and context, showing a mismatch between not only prescribed NES(-like) texts and unpredictable real-world communication but also contexts of language learning and language use (Crawford, 2002). These observations suggest that the NES approach is the dominant one. If so, the input offered to students through teaching materials depicts English in ways that correspond more to NES-oriented linguacultural norms for communication, and less to a dynamic perspective of negotiating linguacultural variations and co-formulating communication norms *in situ*. Therefore, students' learning of English is likely to be shaped by the dominant linguacultural representation of English as it is presented in the textbooks that they are exposed to.

Teachers' awareness, evaluation, and use of materials

The question one can raise then is how do teachers become aware of and deal with the dominant linguacultural representation of English in textbooks during their teaching? Furthermore, how can one foster this awareness through teacher education? To address the latter, Dewey (2012) proposes that teacher education should cultivate teachers' awareness of dominant linguistic classroom discourse. On one hand, current teacher training courses tend to offer more theoretical than practical support (Korthagen, 2001). On the other hand, raising TLA (Teacher Language Awareness) seems to be more concerned with teaching knowledge, and less concerned with teaching practice. This creates a mismatch between teacher education courses and classroom reality. Therefore, I argue that raising TLA about ELF offers a good starting point for re-theorising teaching practices, and I suggest that ELF-informed pedagogy should be ensured on a practical level. Rendering TLA productive for pedagogical practice becomes possible only when TLA combined with teaching practice shows a linkage to ELF communication that in turn informs ELF teacher training programs and pedagogy. Hence, the emergent questions concern practices of not only teaching but also teacher education.

Many teachers tend to take a static, impression/experience-based approach to materials evaluation. A case in point is teachers' 'predictive' and 'retrospective' approach to ascertaining which material suits their teaching purposes before use, or whether the selected material serves their purposes well after use (Ellis, 1997). It seems common that teachers rate materials before and/or sometimes after teaching. This points to the absence of a practice whereby teachers are capable to evaluate the teaching material during the actual teaching. Indeed, the processes and the shifts in evaluating materials pre-, during- and post-teaching are not well-documented, nor are the teachers' decisions to improve or adapt materials (Reinders and Lewis, 2006). It therefore appears that empirical evaluation of materials during teaching and in real time situations is far less common than impression-based or retrospective evaluation. The discussion above highlights the absence as well as the importance of a dynamic, practice- and process-based approach to assess materials.

Repositioning learners

Gray (2010b) views students as the main consumers of textbooks, but often they remain uninvolved in the process of rating or selecting materials. Students' limited involvement in choosing and evaluating materials leads to heavy reliance on teachers' knowledge, evaluation and use of materials. This offers little space for students' critical evaluation of linguacultural input via textbooks. Canagarajah (1999: 91) has criticised the absence of students' feedback in regard to teachers' pedagogical decisions, indicating thus that students' critical engagement in reviewing and reinterpreting linguistic, cultural dominance represented in textbooks is a part of the process of learning. In a similar vein, Pennycook (2001: 159–160) and Kumaravadivelu (2012: 82) propose critical engagement activities whereby students can problematise and reinterpret the taken-for-granted learning as a form of language acquisition.

This chapter will discuss students' views on and ways to deal with the linguacultural input via teaching materials. It will further illustrate students' knowledge of English language and its use by evaluating the described input resources with the researcher. By presenting students' evaluation of teaching materials, I will exemplify the possible way to negotiate ELF-relevant classroom practice from the students' perspectives and in their own terms. Also, the examples, I will offer, of student critical engagements and evaluation of input sources from teaching materials, can also provide teacher trainers and trainees with new ideas for creating their own context-friendly engagement activities and can more generally inform approaches to teacher education and teaching practices.

Materials evaluation in the classroom: a case study

Interest in materials from the ELF perspective has recently flourished in expanding circle contexts, such as China (Xiong and Qian, 2012), Finland (Kopperoinen, 2011), Japan (Matsuda, 2002), Korea (Song, 2013), Spain (Garcia, 2005), Taiwan (Ke, 2012) and Asia (Dat, 2008; Shin et al., 2011). Some researchers look at local textbooks, others at global ones; still others examine both, often taking a critical and/or multicultural approach to secondary and tertiary levels. These studies utilise content or critical discourse analysis to reconsider Anglo-centric ideology and American/NES cultural dominance (Song, 2013), explore idealised American social and/or cultural norms as well as global ones (Ke, 2012), and examine content from an intercultural, local and international standpoint (Feng and Byram, 2002; Shin et al., 2011). Still, research findings point to the prevalence of a monolingual, monocultural approach to ELT materials, in particular the NES approach to linguacultural norms against which local, global ELT material is developed. Nevertheless, most research has only focused on identifying the dominant linguacultural discourses represented in materials. Rather little research has looked into how teachers/students evaluate and use materials to support or challenge the dominant linguacultural representation in materials during teaching/learning. This emergent implication for research is addressed below.

The case study: questions and context

This chapter examines how the textbooks *Reading Explorer 3* (Douglas, 2010) and *Communicating Effectively in English* (Porter and Grant, 1992), as well as *Friends* supplementary material, develop undergraduates' listening and speaking in Taiwan, and considers the relevance of each to ELF communication. First, content analysis is used to illustrate linguacultural representation as well as to identify dominant linguacultural input of these materials before exploring how such dominance was reproduced and resisted via teaching/learning and how reproduced linguacultural input hinders ELF-informed alternatives' realisation in classrooms. To this end, the following research questions were formulated:

1. What ELT materials serve as major input sources to develop students' listening and speaking?
2. How do teachers select ELT materials, and what reasons do they cite?
3. How are language and culture represented in selected materials?
4. How do teachers and students use these materials for listening and speaking training?

The study[3] was conducted at one state (University A, henceforth UA) and one private university (University B, henceforth UB) in Taiwan, a context of teaching/learning English as a Foreign Language. English language education in Taiwan universities is described as NES/AmEng-oriented (Chang, 2014).[4]

Data was collected from classes whose teachers Victor and Grace used widely-recognised global ELT textbooks and supplementary material to teach different courses to students from a wide range of disciplines. Convenient sampling was mainly used to recruit the teachers and 48 of their students, who participated in a short-answer questionnaire survey, classroom observation and on-site interviews. For confidentiality, pseudonyms were used for teachers and codes for their students: e.g., VS1 for Victor's Student 1 and GS2 for Grace's Student 2. For the purposes of this chapter, quantitative content analysis is used to account for the frequency of cultural, linguistic representation in materials.[5]

Teachers' use of materials in the classroom

Based on the questionnaire survey into selection and use of materials, Victor reported that he considers 'whether topics are interesting and whether the language is colloquial' when rating and selecting textbooks. He nevertheless indicated that his choice of *Reading Explorer 3* resonates with the objective of university curriculum to develop students' reading. Grace indicated that the course coordinator chose *Communicating Effectively in English* to facilitate oral proficiency; she knew little about 'selection criteria'. Curriculum and syllabus clearly influence a teacher's choice of materials to various degrees, such that Grace had no chance to evaluate and pre-select her textbook, which will be further discussed in the next section.

Besides text, Victor often used the TV sitcom *Friends* to develop listening, while Grace did not use supplementary materials. Most of Victor's students (about 91%) viewed *Friends* as primary and textbooks as secondary material for training listening. Over half of Grace's students (62.5%) saw textbooks as the key material for speaking training. The answers to the questionnaire survey showed that textbooks were a primary teaching material. The results indicate that a textbook/material-free approach encounters resistance or textbook/

material-based teaching persists, indicating that ELT materials are major linguacultural input sources in classroom practice.

Materials analysis – identifying the dominant linguacultural input

Given their considerable dependence on textbooks, Victor's and Grace' frequently-used materials for Freshman English and Oral Training were analysed and considered in terms of how the culture and language representation of these two books reflects the multilingual, cultural nature of ELF-related intercultural communication. To this end, quantitative content analysis was adopted to count the people, places, languages, and events presented and related to particular cultural groups in both textbooks. Tables 3.1 and 3.2 exhibit quantitative content analysis of cultural representation in two textbooks, categorised as US-, Taiwan-, or World (neither Taiwan nor US)-related.

Table 3.1   Content analysis of *Reading Explorer 3 (National Geographic)*

Unit	Taiwan	US	Other localities	Major perspective
1	0	15	95	Multicultural
2	0	8	49	Multicultural
3	0	8	52	Multicultural
Review	0	2	40	Multicultural
4	0	27	83	Multicultural
5	3	2	101	Multicultural
6	0	0	114	Multicultural
Review	0	2	25	Multicultural
7	0	19	26	Multicultural
8	0	1	273	Multicultural
9	0	31	75	Multicultural
Review	0	13	65	Multicultural
10	0	2	11	Multicultural
11	0	8	113	Multicultural
12	0	9	41	Multicultural
Review	0	10	102	Multicultural
Sum	3 (0.2%)	157 (11.0%)	1,265 (88.8%)	1,425

Table 3.2   Content analysis of *Communicating Effectively in English*

Unit	Taiwan	US	Other localities	Major perspective
1	0	4	32	Multicultural
2	2	31	2	US
3	14	10	14	Multicultural
4	1	49	1	US
5	0	3	0	US
6	0	73	0	US
Sum	17 (7.2%)	170 (72.0%)	49 (20.1%)	236

Table 3.1 shows *Reading Explorer 3* incorporating World and US-related subjects into almost every unit, while Taiwan-related (local) content is more limited at less than 1%. Table 3.2 shows four of the six units in *Communicating Effectively in English* featuring US-related content; world and local perspectives constitute a mere 37%, with the American perspective prominent in terms of frequency in each unit and overall percentage of content in the book. *Communicate Effectively in English* takes the American approach to content to enhance NNES learners' English. The content of *Reading Explorer 3* reflects various parts of the world, affording students more exposure to subjects from diverse cultural groups. By contrast, *Communicate Effectively in English* provides mainly US-based content, giving rather inadequate exposure to non-US NES/NNES input sources. As for teaching supplements to enhance listening, Victor uses *Friends*, in which NES actors and actresses in America portray six characters' lives in New York City, suggesting that linguacultural input from the show is greatly US-based. In sum, a US-related influence on the content of the analysed materials is persistent and sometimes dominant, as the reviewed literature indicates.

As Kirkpatrick (2007) has highlighted, an ELF approach to textbooks is still neither well-developed nor widely available to teachers. Even if ELF-tailored textbooks were available, not all teachers get full freedom to choose; some may select textbooks according to other approaches and/or curricula. Responses to the questionnaires show that Taiwanese teachers tend to rely on textbooks for listening and speaking training; it seems unrealistic to propose a material-free approach for teaching or advocate immediate shifts in selecting and using ELF-tailored materials unless these concerns are adequately addressed and ELF-materials are well-developed and available to teachers and students to choose and use. For this reason, the next section focuses on teachers' and students' roles in evaluating materials, their criticality on available materials and their ways of dealing with limitations of linguacultural representation in textbooks.

Key incidents in the classroom

The two audio-recorded classes discussed in this chapter consist of approximately six hours of classroom teaching from Victor's Freshman English and ten hours of teaching from Grace's Oral Training course. I selected classroom practices that are either regarded as typical teaching or as uncommon or specific teaching practice of two Taiwanese teachers. For the purposes of this chapter, one typical event from Victor's teaching and one specific event from Grace's were selected for analysis based on the relevance of the chosen events to ELF. Analysis of these two incidents discusses teacher's orchestration of student involvement, plus how all the participants collectively construct the meaning of classroom discourse, as Walsh (2011) suggests. Classroom discourse analysis at the micro-level explores the Initiation-Response-Feedback (IRF)[6] sequence of each teacher's practice and students' response to teaching, showing how classroom discourse is controlled in terms of the forms of reproducing or resisting US-related linguacultural input via the use of materials. Post-teaching interviews with teachers and students are also analysed to support the interpretation of classroom discourse analysis. Below is the analysis of teachers' most frequent and one particular use of materials for listening and speaking.

Key incident 1: Maintaining the status quo and reproduction

Victor's classroom practice focuses on the content of *Friends*, his main listening material; students were observed listening to each scene/episode the first time without English subtitles and then answering questions about its content. Each scene was replayed for students to check answers. Extracts 1 and 2, taken from post-teaching interviews, demonstrate Victor's views on *Friends* for teaching and the ways he uses it over two semesters. Extract 3 presents a shortened transcript from a 4'30" recording of Victor's routinised listening training, showing that sequence, choice of topics, and linguistic items to be taught are pre-determined and based on *Friends*.

Extract 1
Victor: Why I chose this (*Friends*)?
Researcher: Yeah...
Victor: I think first I consider its topics. I feel it (the language that characters of Friends used to elaborate the topics) is similar to daily language use. So (.) I think, speaking (.) Ummm, many students would like to learn **English which reflects spoken language use in daily life** ... I chose *Friends* because of students' preference. Subjects of *Friends* are less controversial and disputable for most people and **are related to daily lives** ... Of course, some students may prefer science fiction films or others, of that kind, investigation-related, like *CSI* ... but I think issues addressed in these films are subject-specific. In addition, ***Friends* that (.) the English use in *Friends* is colloquial. It should be quite suitable for them** (students).

Extract 2
Researcher: That is ... hmmm ... another focus of your teaching is your use of *Friends* to develop students' listening. You have used *Friends* for two semesters?
Victor: Yes, **two semesters.**

Extract 3
I: Ok, Scene 1 starts here, all ready? Then, here we go. ((playing *Friends*[19] and pause))

R: ((Students write answers.)){12}
I: Continue ((continue playing *Friends*[10] and pause))
R: ((Students write the answers and then listen)){17}
    ... ((Continue playing and pausing the player)) /40/
I: And then Joey said 'I will be done by then.' ((continue playing *Friends*[5] and pause))
R: ((Students write the answers and continue listening)) {19}
I: All right then, Joey goes ((continue playing *Friends*[30] to the end of this scene))=

Victor cites topics, students' preference and language as reasons for adopting *Friends* (Extract 1). He also assumes that language presented in *Friends* reflects language use in daily life (Extract 1). Given the aforementioned limitation of choosing inclusive material, how Victor evaluates and uses chosen materials and his students' response to the use of *Friends* for listening training become pedagogically indicative. Extract 2 shows consistent use of *Friends*, suggesting considerable dependence on one kind of material, with little space for others. Extract 3 illustrates how students receive substantial input from *Friends* every class and Victor's failure to re-evaluate *Friends* with regard to the longitudinal reproduction of similar linguistic input while teaching. Implications arise from the analysis for teachers from similar teaching contexts regarding exploring how the learning and perception of English usage for intercultural communication is influenced by the length and amount of delivery of similar input based on the same material and teachers' lack of re-evaluation during and after teaching. To consider these implications, Victor's perception of cultural and linguistic input through *Friends* will be examined (Extracts 4 and 5).

Extract 4
Researcher: ... And I also would like to know more about how you feel about their (actors' and actresses' English) language?
Victor: Culture, yeah, yeah, yeah, we mentioned culture.
Researcher: Yeah.
Victor: ... in fact, I did not really consider this issue. Ummm ... of course, it is fairly ... ummm ... **American** ... as I said, it is not easy to choose inclusive materials. If TV sitcom is chosen and used as teaching materials, then these TV series are specific to certain culture in the first place. For example, ***Friends* is American culture-oriented**. If I want to select material with multicultural input sources, I think it is fairly difficult ... now tracing back to the past...(.) **English language education in Taiwan seems American English (AmEng)-based**. Right (.). From primary to tertiary level, most Taiwanese may have been

> taught by British teachers ... **most English language input is AmEng-based.** Therefore, I think **this (AmEng) is more likely for them (students) to accept it (*Friends*)**, yeah.

Researcher: Is it because they (students) have background (of American English-based education)?

Victor: Yes.

Extract 5

Researcher: So (.) you feel this is easier for students to accept? In other words, they have gained basic familiarity with it (AmEng)?

Victor: Yeah, and ... I remember that the course evaluation of a semester (.) it ... I remember students wrote, **one to two of them, said that they wanted to know about the US.** He specified 'American culture' and hoped I could introduce him more American-related culture and language use. Or (.) then another student knows that I was an exchange student to the US and wants to know about the US. He said I should talk about that (his exchange experience in the US). Then, I feel (.) that the US or, the US culture or American English in Taiwanese (.) Errm, in fact, **the dominance of AmEng has been recognised and I should not reinforce its dominance but somehow I still chose *Friends* ...**

In Extract 4, Victor refers to culture-specific material as inevitable and shows his cultural awareness that input from *Friends* is US-oriented, while highlighting the unavailability of inclusive material for multicultural input. He also points out that the students' acceptance of AmEng input from *Friends* is based on his assumption about their extensive learning experience under the AmEng-based English language education system in Taiwan. He decides to maintain the status quo of the AmEng approach to ELT, showing little resistance to AmEng dominance. According to Victor, his students are interested in American culture (hereafter, AmC), which he uses to support his resistance to the introduction of a non-American approach to oral English and culture (Extract 5).

Victor indicates the dominance of AmEng and AmC input that lingers within Taiwan's educational system; he also claims that it should be discouraged. Victor's choice and use of *Friends* are in contrast to his critical awareness of AmC, AmEng input, representing his maintenance and reproduction of US-related linguacultural input and resistance to pedagogical alternatives (Extracts1, 3). It seems that his listening training aims to augment AmEng/AmC by getting 'correct' answers in conformity with linguistic norms represented by *Friends*. His longitudinal use of *Friends* demonstrates a form of resistance to other materials as well as to alternative ways to use *Friends*. In Extracts 6 and 7 Victor's students critique *Friends* for listening training.

Extract 6

Researcher: Do you find *Friends* helpful?

VS1:   Yeah.

VS2:   It helps ... at least **the accents** (presented in *Friends*) **become clearer to** me

VS3:   I feel I made progress (in understanding *Friends*).

Extract 7

Researcher: So do you feel you are used to, say, Monica's (one character in *Friends*) English?

VS4:   We have listened to *Friends* **for a long time.**

Researcher: Are you suggesting your teacher should change materials?

VS4:   **There are different kinds of movies.**

Extract 6 illustrates how Victor's students took it for granted that his longitudinal use of *Friends* benefits their learning; they support Victor's choice and use of this teaching supplement. Nevertheless, Extract 7 exemplifies one student's critical awareness of dominant AmEng/AmC-based input as well as his resistance to long-term use of material. Two questions pertaining to linguacultural awareness arose from the critical exchanges between researcher and students: the first is whether similar interaction is undertaken for teachers to gauge students' language and intercultural awareness for their teaching preparation, and the second is how a monolithic approach to representation of one specific kind of English and culture in textbooks affects learning. The aspect for teacher educators to ponder is how teacher training programmes develop pre-, in-service teacher's criticality when dealing with NES approach to materials and teaching practice. These questions are addressed at the end of this chapter.

Key incident 2: de-dominance, negotiation and resistance

Extract 8 is a shortened classroom discourse transcript of Grace's teaching, describing her critical inquiry into culture represented by a textbook while teaching. Extract 9 shows her opposition to a monolithic approach and preference for an open approach when using textbooks to develop students' oral proficiency.

Extract 8

Grace: ... of course, like this kind of statement, ok, basically it doesn't really (.) hmm ... we don't go to America to live. We are not immigrants. We won't feel sympathy with the statement ... That's immigrants' business, **none of our business ...**

Extract 9

Researcher: ... I actually heard you saying that ... **you let students choose and/or use the topic to discuss,** and you said to them that some topics are US-relevant and ...?

Grace:	In Oral 2, **the textbook clearly suggests that students explore and speak on topics of their own** based on their interests, knowledge. I thus suggest students they should not explore topics that they do not really know about or classmates may not be interested in. **Maybe they should not consider topics provided by textbooks, which may be challenging for them to talk about or prepare for.**
Researcher:	So your teaching avoids topics that are country-specific?
Grace:	I never consider country-specific teaching. No.
Researcher:	Despite dominance of AmC input via textbook, it seems you feel that students should address topics to their audience (classmates) and make audience understand their points.
Grace:	I **do not consider geographic perspective** because I want my students to focus on the content of matters for discussion.
Researcher:	Sounds like you are blurring cultural or geographic boundary in terms of choosing subjects?
Grace:	Exactly. **Why should topics (*in textbooks*) be country-bounded or culture-specific? I don't like that.**

Based on the authors' guide for using their textbook, Grace first advises that students should use their own topics for speaking training. Then, taking a critical approach, she challenges the US-oriented text, highlighting the irrelevance of the topics to students during (Extract 8) and after teaching (Extract 9). She also indicates that her focus on oral training via textbook has less to do with country-specific topics and more with how students elaborate on a subject, posing resistance to country-specific content (Extract 9). Extracts 8 and 9 exemplify Grace's open approach to de-centralising US-based input and urging students to discuss their own topics. Extract 10 describes the process of Grace's teaching beyond an NES approach and her move towards a critical approach to de-centring the American-based input of textbooks and an open approach to introducing examples from her and her students as NNES resources for classroom practices.

Extract 10

Researcher:	Did Grace teach you one page after another (*based on the textbook*)?
GS1:	No (.), she **selected key points** to teach and gave clear lectures … **not bad.**
Researcher:	What do you mean by clarity and key points? Does that relate to the content of her teaching, say, **an overview of main points**?
GS1:	((**Nodding**)) After that, she gave examples.
Researcher:	She used the examples in textbook?

GS2:   No, **she explains in her own term.**

Researcher: For example? Could you recall any example?

GS1:   She asked us to give and write examples. (.) **She first provided her example** and then asked us to practice. After that, **she wrote what we said on blackboard, no matter we gave good or bad answers; she let us make comments on each other's answers afterwards.**

Grace's teaching is not completely structured according to textbook content (Extract 10). Through an open approach, Grace selects and uses parts of the textbook rather than the entire thing to teach, and she refers to her own and her students' examples as learning resources. This avoids exclusive reliance on the textbook for input and simultaneously formulates modes of de-centring or resisting NES input in the textbook. In contrast, Victor's adherence to NS input through his longitudinal use of *Friends* gives him and his students limited chances to critically evaluate the NES input through *Friends* in relation to the learning outcome. Grace's open approach to non-AmEng/AmC-oriented resources, in theory, supports her critical approach, which resists pre-packaged AmEng/AmC dominance represented in textbooks, and in practice allows for the introduction of NNES-based input sources (her own and her students' examples) in dialectical interplay with her teaching and students' learning.

Applying an ELF approach to the selection and use of materials

Scholars and other contributors to this volume advise that teachers raise students' awareness of NES approaches to the linguacultural representation of materials. The evidence of my research confirms this view; simultaneously, the research recognises the importance of raising teachers'/teacher trainers' awareness of the dominant linguacultural input as well as understanding an ELF approach for teacher and teacher educators to reconceptualise the input embedded in classroom discourses. Richards (1998: 65) discusses how researching findings inform teaching and proposes that good teaching entails the 'application of research findings' and that teaching practices that are studied serve as 'primary data for a theory of teaching'. The above results can be useful for the development of teachers, teacher educators and training programmes in relation to an ELF approach through a re-conceptualisation of teacher education courses as well as classroom practices for transformative changes in pedagogy. For this kind of pedagogical transformation to occur, practical suggestions are required to help ELT practitioners and teacher trainers put the notion of raising linguacultural awareness into practice. These suggestions should address how teachers, educators and students transcend ideological/theoretical critiques of dominant NES approaches so as to enhance thinking, teaching and learning 'the other way around' in class. As Pennycook (2012: 139) advises:

> critical pedagogical enterprise is not foremost about ideology critiques of schooling or the curriculum, nor about teaching subject matters we believe may empower students, nor merely opening a space for our students to speak. Rather, it is about ethical and political demands to think otherwise, to develop a form of critical resistance, to see other possibilities.

In line with Pennycook's advice, this chapter has exemplified teachers'/ students' use of materials for/against ELF and analysed the possibility of negotiating alternative uses of materials for teaching. These results are of direct practical relevance to an ELF approach to classroom practice and teacher education. To apply the findings of this chapter to teacher education and teaching, three different types of recommendation are proposed below for teacher training, teacher strategies and classroom activities.

Teacher training

The findings suggest that an ELF approach could be incorporated into teacher education programmes to lend trainees theoretical as well as practical support to critically evaluate, use materials and then teach beyond NES approaches to linguacultural input. In theory, student teachers' insights into ELF-related concepts that they develop from teacher education could help trainees apply an ELF perspective to re-theorise ELT, SLA and other theories of teaching. For instance, teacher educators should encourage student teachers to constantly evaluate their materials through a comparative perspective involving an ELF approach and other teaching theories through training courses. Moving from theory to practice, quantitative content analysis, as outlined in the above textbook analysis, can offer examples of an ELF approach to analysing linguacultural representation in materials, which can be used by trainee teachers to practise identifying dominant linguistic, cultural input through analysing the textbooks themselves. Going beyond the product-/process-based approach to materials analysis, teacher training should consider letting trainees observe, evaluate and discuss the use of materials embedded in the recorded classroom discourses from ELF in opposition to other pedagogical perspectives: e.g., trainees compare Victor's and Grace's approach to using materials or other aspects of teaching from an ELF and a non-ELF perspective. This activity echoes Richards' (1998: 124) discussion about using the observation of classroom practices to train student teachers not only to identify teaching strategies but also to develop profound understanding of various approaches to teaching. Through visualising other teacher's use of materials to student teachers, trainees can familiarise themselves with ELF-(ir)relevant approaches to evaluating materials during teaching in order to integrate content and utilise it for teaching in class. Alongside this theoretical and practical support, teacher education should then consider merging critical evaluation and the use of global or local US/NES-based materials into training courses, letting trainers and trainees practise evaluating various materials as well as exploring possible ways to adapt materials from ELF-relevant perspectives. Teacher education should adapt and apply these processes and practices to prepare teacher trainers, as well as trainees, for ELF approaches to the evaluation and use of materials.

Teaching strategies

Thornbury (2013: 215) suggests that 'the role of pre-packaged materials' should be 'arguably less central' and teachers should manage learning to make materials 'potentially even counterproductive'. In alignment with Thornbury's critical approach to the evaluation and use of materials, the following are teaching strategies that were developed from Victor's and Grace's teaching and their students' learning. One implication of Victor's and Grace's teaching for formulating teaching strategies towards ELF-oriented classroom practice is to consider how theories of teaching and learning support longitudinal or persistent adherence to or critical resistance to NES input through materials and its influence on student's perception of language and language use. Another implication of their teaching is to develop strategies for critical teaching practice that refers to alternative thinking and teaching which challenges and de-centres established, taken-for-granted NES approaches to materials, as Thornbury (2013: 215) and Pennycook (2012) suggest. To realise these implications, a critical approach is first suggested to evaluate and use the chosen materials for teacher trainers and trainees and to problematise dominant linguacultural representation in textbooks. An open approach to content and use of material is then recommended, thus permitting sufficient flexibility for teacher educators and student teachers to draw on other teaching/learning resources to challenge pre-packaged NES approaches to content materials and then seek alternatives. For example, teachers should avoid inclusive adoption of specific materials and limited evaluation of materials during teaching to de-centralise US/NES-related materials in contrast with Victor's consistent use and limited evaluation of a kind of material. Alternatively, de-centralising the dominant roles of US/NES-based material can be achieved by introducing non-NES/US-based input sources, as Grace did when she drew on her own and her students' examples as learning resources.

Critical engagement activities

Pennycook (2001: 159–160) and Kumaravadivelu (2012: 82) propose that 'critical engagement' activities should be undertaken to enable students to be open to 'personal transformation', i.e. the ability to critically problematise and re-interpret the taken-for-granted learning/teaching. Extracts 6 and 7 exemplify a type of critical engagement activity that can be organised for teachers and their students to co-challenge the NES/US approach to materials or any dominant linguacultural representation in materials. Students' engagement in critical discussion allows them to recognise dominant input sources as well as ferret out possible ways to deal with discussed dominance from their own viewpoint, in their own terms. The result of the proposed discussion lays the foundation from which teachers can modify an ELF approach to materials that is suitable for students' level of language and intercultural awareness. For instance, teachers could organise a critical engagement activity for students to discuss Victor's students' different views on the dominant US-related input and reflect on the received input in relation to their learning. This activity aims to help students understand and practise how they approach materials from ELF perspectives and reconsider longitudinal reception of US-related input as well as its impact on their learning.

Conclusions

This chapter aims to avoid presenting a static approach to materials or imposing suggested pedagogical ideas on classroom practice. To achieve this aim, adapting and integrating the proposed ideas of teaching with other theories of teaching/learning is recommended to support ELF-informed teaching, which is contingent upon each teaching/learning context. As indicated in the introduction to this chapter, the suggestions for teacher education above are not made in order to encourage trainees to transmit the whole set of knowledge of the ELF approach to materials or to persuade trainees to abandon NES/US-based materials entirely or thoroughly change their use. These notions are being offered in order to add to teachers' and teacher educators' repertoire of teaching examples, which they can then draw on during teaching and teacher training, (re)formulating principles and (re)-navigating their teaching and teacher training beyond a US/NES approach to textbooks and towards ELF-relevant input.

Engagement priorities

Johnson (2009: 98) argues that research into second language classrooms tends to reproduce theory/practice dichotomy, or attends to what theory says should happen in practice rather than to how theory and practice should inform one another. Recently, the implications of ELF research for pedagogy have been reconsidered in terms of practicality. Below, I present topics in three aspects of ELT for further discussion in relation to the practicality of an ELF-informed approach to ELT and how classroom practice in turn informs future ELF research.

1. ELF approach to research: To what extent does classroom-based research support re-theorisation of an ELF approach in order to develop context-friendly ELF-oriented classroom practice? What aspects of teaching/learning should be explored in order to establish a two-way relationship between ELF and classroom practice?
2. ELF approach to teacher education: How could teacher educators help trainees develop their own ELF-informed teaching strategies to expand their repertoire of teaching examples, rather than transmit the proposed strategies and suggestions as a set of teaching knowledge?
3. ELF approach to teaching and learning: How are the proposed strategies and activities at the end of this chapter feasible in your teaching contexts and are there any other alternatives to the proposed ones?

Appendix 3.1   Transcription convention

Grace:	teacher
Victor:	teacher
I:	Initiating teaching
R:	student's or students' response
VS1:	Victor's student 1
VS2:	Victor's student 2
GS1:	Grace's student 1
GS2:	Grace's student 2
(Word):	Single parentheses contain author's descriptions rather than transcription
((Word)):	Double parentheses contain researcher's description of classroom practice/participant's behaviours
(.):	a short pause between utterances
Bold Letters:	Bold letters indicate author highlighting of participants' accounts
[4]:	duration of the audio material played; length given in seconds
{4}:	duration for students to write their answer; length given in seconds
...:	cycle of similar classroom practice
/4/:	the duration of similar classroom practice; length given in seconds
=:	turn continues, or one turn follows another without any pause

Notes

1. Nor does the chapter imply criticism of any in-service teacher or student for not taking an ELF approach to teaching and learning; in-service teachers and their students have myriad pedagogical concerns. Likewise, there is no attempt here to evaluate particular textbooks/material as ELF or not-ELF, or to persuade textbook writers/publishers to produce ELF materials.

2. In this chapter, the ELF approach to ELT refers to classroom practice that is informed by or connected to linguacultural phenomena of communication through English as a Lingua Franca.
3. 'The study' refers to the author's PhD research (Yu, 2015). Due to limited space, this chapter only details part of the research.
4. This chapter accounts for the compulsory Freshman English course, which supports non-English majors' general English competence, and the Oral Training course, which supports English majors' speaking. Most student participants had already had about ten years of English learning experience. Teachers see Freshman English in UA as reading-oriented and UB syllabus oral-proficiency-based. Few Taiwanese students have opportunities to select textbooks or supplementary materials; UA and UB materials are not locally published.
5. Pennycook (2003) points out that geographic scope offers a restricted account of the linguacultural dynamics and complexity of English and its use in a global context. Accordingly, the nation-based content analysis of cultural representation for this chapter does not aim to fully address the cultural diversity/complexity within one region/country but to give a preliminary sketch of dominant cultural discourses represented in materials. To capture the actual provision and reception of this kind of dominance through teaching, political discourse analysis, 'a form of argumentation for or against particular ways of acting' (Fairclough and Fairclough, 2012: 1), was applied to scrutinise teachers' and students' justification and practice for/against using their materials.
6. Walsh (2011: 17) identifies IRF as one of the typical and predictable classroom discourses. It consists of three parts: 'a teacher Initiation, a student Response, and a teacher Feedback'. Some scholars prefer to use the acronym IRE (Initiation, Response and Evaluation).

References

Baker, W. (2015). Culture and complexity through English as a lingua franca: rethinking competences and pedagogy in ELT. *Journal of English as a Lingua Franca* 4(1): 9–30.
Canagarajah, A. S. (1999). *Resisting Linguistic Imperialism in English Teaching*. Oxford: Oxford University Press.
Chang, Y. (2014). Learning English today: what can World Englishes teach college students in Taiwan? *English Today* 30(1): 21–27.
Crawford, J. (2002). The role of materials in the language classroom: Finding the palace. In Richards, J. C. and Renandya, W. A. (eds), *Methodology in Language Teaching: An Anthology of Current Practice*. Cambridge: Cambridge University Press, pp. 80–92.
Dat, B. (2008). ELT materials used in Southeast Asia. In Tomlinson, B. (ed.), *English Language Learning Materials: A Critical Review*. London and New York: Continuum, pp. 263–280.
Dewey, M. (2012). Toward a post-normative approach: Learning the pedagogy of ELF. *Journal of English as a Lingua Franca* 1(1): 141–170.
Douglas, N. (2010). *Reading Explorer 3: National Geographic*. Boston: Heinle, Cengage Learning.
Ellis, R. (2012). *Language Teaching Research and Language Pedagogy*. Chichester: John Wiley & Sons.
Ellis, R. (1997). The empirical evaluation of language teaching materials. *ELT Journal* 51(1): 36–42.

Fairclough, I. and Fairclough, N. (2012). *Political Discourse Analysis: A Method for Advanced Students*. London and New York: Routledge.

Feng, A. and Byram, M. (2002). Authenticity in college textbooks-an intercultural perspective. *RELC Journal* 33: 58–83.

Garcia Mendez, Maria del Carmen. (2005). International and intercultural issues in English teaching textbooks: The case of Spain. *Intercultural Education* 16(1): 58–68.

Gray, J. (2010a). The Branding of English and the Culture of the New Capitalism: representations of the world of work in English language textbooks. *Applied Linguistics* 31(5): 714–733.

Gray, J. (2010b). *The Construction of English: Culture, Consummerism and Promotion in the ELT Global Coursebook*. Basingstoke: Palgrave Macmillan.

Jenkins, J., Cogo, A. and Dewey, M. (2011). Review of developments in research into English as a Lingua Franca. *Language Teaching* 44(3): 281–315.

Johnson, K. E. (2009). *Second Language Teacher Education: A Sociocultural Perspective*. New York and London: Routledge

Ke, C. I. (2012). From EFL to English as an international and scientific Language: Analyzing Taiwan's high school English textbooks in the period 1952–2009. *Language, Culture, and Curriculum* 25(2): 173–187.

Kirkpatrick, A. (2007). *World Englishes: Implications for International Communication and English Language Teaching*. Cambridge: Cambridge University Press.

Kopperoinen, A. (2011). Accents of English as a Lingua Franca: A study of Finnish textbooks. *International Journal of Applied Linguistics* 21(1): 71–93.

Korthagen, F. A. J. (2001). *Linking Practice and Theory: The Pedagogy of Realistic Teacher Education*. Mahwah: Lawrence Erlbaum Associates.

Kumaravadivelu, B. (2012). *Language Teacher Education for a Global Society: A Modular Model for Knowing, Analysing, Recognizing, Doing, and Seeing*. London and New York: Routledge.

Matsuda, A. (2012). Teaching materials in EIL. In Alsagoff, L., McKay, S. L., Hu, G. and Renandya, W. A. (eds), *Principles and Practices for Teaching English as International Language*. New York and London: Routledge, pp. 168–185.

Matsuda, A. (2002). Representation of users and uses of English in beginning Japanese EFL textbooks. *JALT Journal* 24(2): 80–98.

Pennycook, A. (2012). *Language and Mobility: Unexpected Places*. Bristol, Buffalo, and Toronto: Multilingual Matters.

Pennycook, A. (2003). Global Englishes, Rip Slyme, and performativity. *Journal of Sociolinguistics* 7(4): 513–533.

Pennycook, A. (2001). *Critical Applied Linguistics: A Critical Introduction*. London and New York: Routledge.

Porter, P. A. and Grant, M. (1992). *Communicating Effectively in English: Oral Communication for Non-native Speakers*. Boston: Heinle, Cengage Learning.

Reinders, H. and Lewis, M. (2006). An evaluative checklist for self-access materials. *ELT Journal* 66(3): 272–278.

Richards, J. C. (1998). *Beyond Training: Perspectives on Language Teacher Education*. Cambridge: Cambridge University Press.

Seidlhofer, B. (2011). *Understanding English as a Lingua Franca*. Oxford: Oxford University Press.

Shin, J., Eslami, Z. R. and Chen, W. C. (2011). Presentation of local and international culture in current international English language teaching textbooks. *Language, Culture, and Curriculum* 24(3): 253–268.

Song, H. (2013). Deconstruction of cultural dominance in Korean EFL textbooks. *Intercultural Education* 24(4): 382–390.

Thornbury, S. (2013). Resisting coursebooks. In Gray, J. (ed.), *Critical Perspectives on Language Teaching Materials*. Basingstoke: Palgrave Macmillan, pp. 204–223.

Walsh, S. (2011). *Exploring Classroom Discourse: Language in Action*. New York and London: Routledge.

Xiong, T. and Qian, Y. (2012). Ideologies of English in a Chinese high school EFL textbook: A critical discourse analysis. *Asian Pacific Journal of Education* 32(1): 75–92.

Yu, M. H. (2015). Connecting classroom English to real world English: Taiwanese teachers' and students' perspectives on ELF-aware pedagogy. Unpublished doctoral thesis, University of Southampton.

4
Linking ELF and ELT in Secondary School through Web-Mediation: The Case of Fanfiction

Enrico Grazzi

Introduction

This chapter addresses the pedagogical implications of a research project carried out between 2010 and 2012 (Grazzi 2013). The project involved the design and implementation of networked-based activities for the English classroom, whereby two small communities of practice (CoPs) (Wenger 1998), composed of volunteer Italian students of English from five distally-located schools, were required to simulate an ELF-mediated setting and carry out several cooperative assignments. The overall aim was to provide English teachers and ELT practitioners with a model that could be developed and implemented to carry out international educational projects online, via the use of ELF.

The aim of this chapter is to describe and analyse from a pedagogical perspective examples of fanfiction[1] and creative writing tasks. These tasks were aimed at the production of original extracts that were supposed to integrate or change parts of famous English novels and short stories; examples of these activities may include a) adding a description, a dialogue, or a new episode, b) changing the narrator of the story or the narrator's stance, c) writing an alternative denoument, and so on.

The significance of this research project from a teaching perspective is that it takes a blended approach that draws on the results of research in parallel areas of applied linguistics in the fields of ELF (Jenkins, Cogo and Dewey 2011; see also the State-of-the-art Introduction to this volume), educational linguistics (Spolsky 1978; van Lier 2004), sociocultural theory (SCT) (Vygotsky 1978; Lantolf and Thorne 2006), cultural learning (Tomasello 2003), network-based language teaching (NBLT) (O'Dowd and Ware 2009; Guth and Helm 2010) and critical applied linguistics (CAL) (Pennycook 2001). These have lent a fresh perspective to ELT, paving the way for a reconceptualisation of foreign language education that has contributed to the development of an empirical research area within ELF studies that is particularly concerned with ESOL and teacher training (Gagliardi and Maley 2010; Sifakis and Fay 2011; Vettorel and Lopriore 2013; Sifakis 2014; Bayyurt and Akcan 2014). Its main purposes are a) to raise the English teacher's awareness of the nature of ELF and the fundamental role it plays as the main lingua franca in Web-mediated communication (Graddol 2006; Crystal 2011; Campagna et al. 2012), and b) to design new teaching materials and learning activities focused on ELF that are supposed to enrich the ELT syllabus without conflicting with the traditional English as a foreign language (EFL) curriculum.

This project follows on from previous research in the areas of networked learning (Goodyear et al. 2004) and social media language learning (SMLL) (Thorne and Black 2007, Thorne et al. 2009). Moreover, it is consistent with studies that have examined the use of ELF in Internet-based social networking and blogging (Grazzi 2011; Vettorel 2014). The distinctiveness of this project lies in how fanfiction and ELF have been integrated into online collaborative creative writing to design fresh language practice. As this chapter intends to demonstrate, the multicultural and multilingual setting provided by the Web can be used as an affordance to let ELF speakers interact with fellow social networkers. With ELF, the focus on the learner's competence shifts to the pragmatic dimension of communication and the L2-user's performance is considered to be part of a social event that is not subordinate to the standard English (SE) paradigm.

In spite of the fact that EFL and ELF are usually considered independent areas, they tend to converge when the educational context of the classroom is connected to the Internet. In this case the roles of the language learner and that of the L2-user co-occur through their performance. Therefore, the formation of the L2-user's linguacultural identity in Web-mediated discourse is a unifying element, which leads to a dynamic conception of the relationship between the process of EFL teaching/learning – that is largely based on the exonormative native-speaker (NS) model – and the emergence of ELF as social practice. The position taken in this chapter is that the evolution of ELF is part of a natural process enacted by its speakers/learners, who make this language their own through cooperative 'participatory appropriation'[2] in authentic, albeit mostly Web-mediated communicative contexts, and use it as an affordance to carry out communicative tasks in a real intersubjective and intercultural dimension, where the interlocutors' identities concur in their attempt to construct and share meanings.

Kramsch's (2009: 4) critical point of view about traditional schooling and her broad understanding into the nature of the L2-user's identity can be illuminating with regards to the role of ELF in ELT:

> We are fooling ourselves if we believe that students learn only what they are taught. While teachers are busy teaching them to communicate accurately,

fluently, and appropriately, students are inventing for themselves other ways of being in their bodies and their imaginations. [...] Language for them is not just an unmotivated formal construct but a lived embodied reality. It is not simply an agglomeration of encoded meanings, that are grasped intellectually, cognitively internalized, and then applied in social contexts; rather, it is the potential medium for the expression of their innermost aspirations, awarenesses, and conflicts.

The essential pedagogic principle that applies to ELF is that learners should be educated about the value of language varieties as long as these reflect the sociocultural diversity of the communities that use English globally. Hence, at the heart of language education there should be an open-minded attitude toward language change so that students are "in a position to make an *informed* choice by means of having their awareness raised of the sociolinguistic, sociopsychological, and sociopolitical issues involved" (Jenkins 2007: 21–22).

The following sections describe the implementation and results of the creative writing tasks involving fanfiction. It is hoped that they will provide insight into how possible it is to introduce innovative activities in second language education through the use of ELF and Web-mediated communication.

Fanfiction and ELF

The advent of the new digital technology called Web 2.0 has turned the Internet into an interactive environment where social media allow virtual communities of *netizens* to cooperate and share user-generated content (Lantolf and Thorne 2006). This suggests that a different conception of language education is needed in order for language teachers and students to be able to cope with the changes that are taking place in the area of global communication and social networking, where the use of ELF is very common.

Fanfiction and creative writing were chosen as the core activities of the research project, because Italian high-school syllabuses often include the history of English literature, and fanfiction was felt to be an appropriate link between a conventional study of literature and the new approach to reading and writing which takes place on the Internet. The purpose of the study was to interconnect two groups of volunteer high-school students from different Italian cities. They were asked to use English to produce their own creative texts cooperatively. Therefore, their mutual engagement in online activities turned them into two CoPs, which extended beyond the physical space of their classrooms.

Unlike more conventional creative writing tasks, which are part of the EFL curriculum that aims to support the learner's writing skills, the advantages of introducing Web-based collaborative creative writing and fanfiction as teaching/learning activities are many: a) students can work with fellow students from different social backgrounds and benefit from an experience that enhances their intercultural competence, b) they are more autonomous in carrying out their assignments and can also work from home, as they would normally do as social networkers, and c) with fanfiction, a CoP has the option to be visible to the community of fans (*fandom*) who share their same interest and taste in literature. In so doing, CoP members can interact with people from outside the school environment. This stimulates their motivation and bridges the gap between schooling and the thriving digital world.

In fanfiction and collaborative creative writing, negotiation springs from a combination of imagination and language play. Cook (2000: 204) believes that language play is crucial in language learning 'not only because it involves adaptation to a new linguistic and cultural environment, but because play and language are so closely intertwined', while Wenger (1998: 203–204) has emphasised the importance of 'negotiability through imagination':

> Imagination, too, can be a way to appropriate meanings. Stories, for instance, can be appropriated easily because they allow us to enter the events, the characters, and their plights by calling upon our imagination. [...] As a result they can be integrated into our identities and remembered as personal experience, rather than as mere reification. It is this ability to enable negotiability through imagination that makes stories, parables and fables powerful communication devices.

Today, creative writing on the Internet has given rise to a fresh genre, fanfiction, that is being culturally shaped through collaboration and mutual support (Jenkins 2006). Hence, the pedagogical goal of the activities presented in the following sections is to integrate ELF and fanfiction into the framework of the English syllabus.

Phase 1

During the first phase of field research, which took place in the school year 2010/2011, two fifth grade classes from two high schools located in Rome were interconnected online. During organisational meetings, the students and their English teachers were given an outline of the project, their tasks were explained to them and they were trained in how to use the wiki.[3] Work began as soon as the students and teachers joined the wiki.

First of all, the two classes were given a reading list that contained a wide choice of novels and short stories, ranging from 19th- and 20th-century classics of English literature to books that were not usually included in school anthologies. Students were asked to choose two books they would like to read and work on. They selected a novel and a short story that were part of the syllabus for the school-leaving examination that year: Wilde's *The Picture of Dorian Gray* and Joyce's short story *Eveline*, from *Dubliners*.

The teachers and the researcher agreed on what their roles should be in the project. First of all, they were to schedule their lessons in the multimedia laboratories of their schools (at least one hour per week) and make sure that the students carried out their tasks on a regular basis. Because it was impossible to interconnect the two classes at the same time, we decided that the students would work in an online asynchronous connection. The main role of the teachers was to act as facilitators, who would guide the students and give advice when asked. However, they should neither correct the students' work, nor evaluate it. Instead, they were expected to assess it, together with their students, as a work in progress and improve it cooperatively. When the project was over, students were granted extra credits in English.

The wiki contained five thematic pages that corresponded to five different assignments. The first four were about Wilde's *The Picture of Dorian Gray*:

1. *If the picture could speak* ... Students had to change the original narrator of the story and write brand new passages from the point of view of Dorian's picture.
2. *A new preface* ... Students had to create an alternative preface to Wilde's novel.
3. *A new ending* ... Students had to write a different conclusion to the story.
4. *The pact with the devil* ... Students had to rewrite the episode of Dorian putting a spell on his own portrait.

The fifth assignment was about *Eveline*, Joyce's famous short story from *Dubliners*:

5. *Eveline. A different ending* ... Students had to create an alternative denoument.

Working as a CoP, the students could write and share their texts cooperatively, and improve them through their reciprocal advice and corrective feedback. This had rippling effects that turned creative writing into a social event, which in turn fostered language improvement. Interestingly, the use of a facility provided by the wiki called *History* favoured the creation of a Vygotskian *zone of proximal development* (ZPD) (Vygotsky 1978; van Lier 2004; Lantolf and Thorne 2006). Through this facility, learners had the chance to compare at any time the different drafts of each text they had produced and provide reciprocal corrective feedback to improve the intelligibility and the overall quality of their creative work. A peer review process was activated, which not only helped to disambiguate opaque or inappropriate lexicogrammar expressions, but most of all promoted a reflexive attitude. Moreover, it should be observed that this kind of social networking reinforced the students' media literacy and their commitment as members of a CoP.

Occasionally, students used online monolingual and bilingual dictionaries, but they hardly ever used any grammar books.

Here is an example of ELF usage from a passage produced by the students:

> Only Dorian could open the door of the attic. I could hear his footsteps coming to me. [...] His eyes were full of disgust, a disgust that was painted also in mine.

What is interesting to notice is the creative use of language (Seidlhofer 2011: 97) that results in the use of an unconventional loaded expression: *a disgust that was painted also in mine.* This seems to be a case of appropriation and adaptation of the English metaphorical expression *painted on someone's face,* (e.g. *a smile painted on my face*[4]) through the semantic substitution of *face*, the canonical core word of this metaphor, with *eyes*, referred to anaphorically by the deictic *mine*. Hence, instead of the hypernym *face* the students used the hyponym *eyes* (*occhi*, in Italian). This reformulation of the metaphor may be considered an example of semantic transfer of the equivalent Italian metaphorical expression *dipinto negli occhi*, which usually collocates with *terrore* (terror) and therefore has a negative semantic prosody (e.g. *Si svegliava all'improvviso, impaurita, con il terrore dipinto negli occhi*[5] / *He used to awake suddenly, frightened, with terror painted on his face*). In other words, the non-standard metaphor used by the students could be considered a calque, which is a lexical phenomenon that is common in situations of language contact. In this particular case, the learners acted as ELF "languagers [who] exploit the potential of the language, [the] focus [of which] is on establishing the indexical link between the code and the context. [This is a] creative process in that the code is treated as malleable and adjustable to the requirements of the moment" (Seidlhofer 2011: 98).

Hence, the English classroom and the Internet provided the multilingual and multicultural context where the friction of Italian and English led to the emergence of ELF as a natural affordance to accomplish the learners' communicative performance.

Let us focus on another interesting case of "creative idiomaticity" (Prodromou 2008: 52) contained in the following example of ELF usage from a passage produced by the students:

> The perpetual repetition of the identical and the sense of duty had paralyzed her, had made her unable to take the reins of her life. [...]

This sentence shows that students translated an Italian equestrian idiom that is also used in English, only with a slightly different wording. Both expressions, though, are based on the same dead metaphor: *prendere le redini di qualcosa /*

keep a tight rein on somebody/something.[6] Again, we may assume that language transfer was used strategically, and that the students probably translated the Italian idiom word for word into English, not knowing that a similar idiom is also used in this language. In any case, the result of this process was the creation of an alternative ELF metaphorical expression that ensured the transparency of its meaning, at least within our Italian CoP.

The topic of idiomaticity is central in ELF research (e.g. Prodromou 2008: 39–78; Seidlhofer 2011: 132–142). These studies have essentially tackled the problem of idiomatic usage as regards the role of ENL in the acquisition of English. Prodromou's and Seidlhofer's opposite views can be summed up as follows: a) the "pedagogic deficit" (Prodromou 2008: 45) that has traditionally reduced the learner's exposure to ENL idioms and phraseology – especially to formulaic "semi-pre-constructed phrases that constitute single choices" (2008: 50) – affect the student's fluency and communicative competence, and b) the learner's tendency to incorporate ENL idioms as a marker of authenticity in international communicative contexts often leads to "unilateral idiomaticity" (Seidlhofer 2011: 134), i.e. to lack of intelligibility and opacity of meaning. Therefore, the author (2011: 136) claims, "conformity to a native-speaker norm of usage [can be] communicatively dysfunctional in an ELF interaction".

However, the above examples taken from the fanfiction texts produced by the members of our CoP show that the "idiomatizing and metaphorizing" (Seidlhofer 2011: 143) processes activated by ELF speakers do not necessarily take the ENL idioms and metaphors as a model. In fact, it seems that the students' L1 play a fundamental role in the activation of creative idiomaticity through the strategic use of language transfer. This, we may argue, should not only be intended as an expedient used by learners to cope with their inadequate repertoire of native-speaker idioms and language chunks, as Prodromou seems to suggest, but also as a natural predisposition of ELF users to appropriate English and adapt it to their languacultural identity.

Phase 2

During the second phase of fieldwork, which took place in the school year 2011/2012, three fifth grade and one fourth grade classes from three high schools located in Rome, Palermo and Messina were networked. The students interacted through a new wiki[7] and worked on two contemporary short stories: Roald Dahl's *Parson's Pleasure* (1959) and Ron Butlin's *The German Boy* (1987).

In each class the students were divided into two subgroups: one was supposed to work on Dahl's short story and the other on Butlin's. Students could work in pairs and once they had finished writing their texts they would upload them onto the appropriate wiki pages. At this point each of the students who had worked on Dahl's short story could choose one of the texts produced by his/her companions from a different city and rearrange it as he/she pleased. The same could be done by those who had worked on Butlin's short story.

Once this phase of the project was over, the two subgroups swapped roles and worked on each other's texts via the wiki. In this way everyone was able to carry out both assignments and cooperate with the whole CoP.

Similarly to the first phase of my field research, the students were asked to exchange peer feedback in a ZPD, using the wiki facility called *History*. Quite unexpectedly, though, the students tended to focus more on content rather than form in reviewing their cooperative work. This indicates that the use of ELF could well serve the pragmatic needs of the students' CoP. However, since the students shared the same L1, they tended to accept a few expressions which were presumably adaptations of Italian idioms into English, such as the word for word translation of the Italian idiomatic expression: *Dio benedica l'ignoranza / god bless the ignorance*, which is used twice. This could be considered a reverse case of "unilateral idiomaticity" (Seidlhofer 2004: 220), as long as the students tended to borrow this idiom from their L1 rather than use an equivalent ENL idiomatic expression, or paraphrase its meaning. It should be noted that this process of L1 borrowing into ELF by a monolingual class would be likely to cause problems of mutual understanding in a multilingual ELF class.

As regards teaching and learning dynamics, Figure 4.1 shows a diagram of the processes activated throughout this project. The diagram is based on

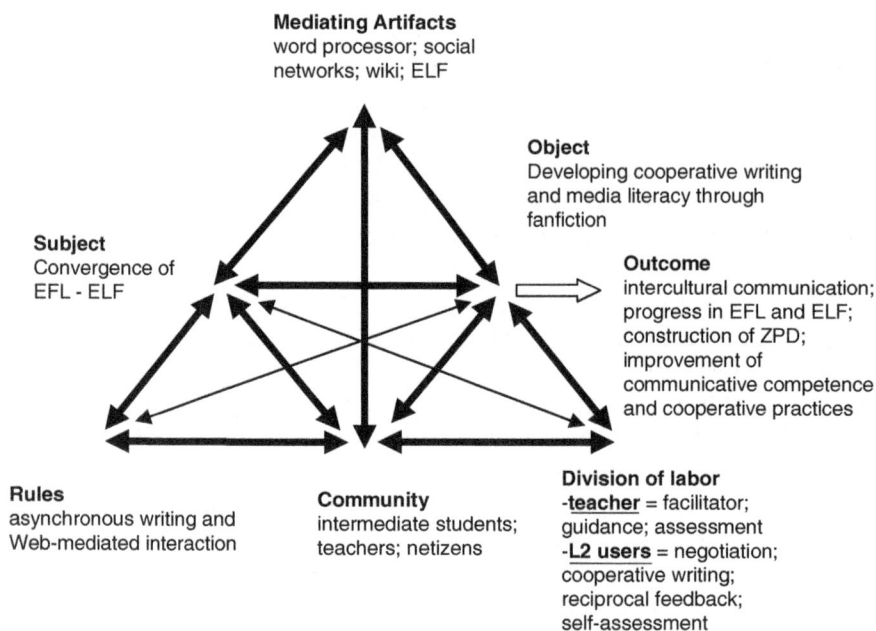

Mediating Artifacts
word processor; social networks; wiki; ELF

Object
Developing cooperative writing and media literacy through fanfiction

Subject
Convergence of EFL - ELF

Outcome
intercultural communication; progress in EFL and ELF; construction of ZPD; improvement of communicative competence and cooperative practices

Rules
asynchronous writing and Web-mediated interaction

Community
intermediate students; teachers; netizens

Division of labor
-**teacher** = facilitator; guidance; assessment
-**L2 users** = negotiation; cooperative writing; reciprocal feedback; self-assessment

Figure 4.1   Teaching/learning activity model

Engeström's (1987) activity theory model in van Lier (2004: 210) and Lantolf and Thorne (2006: 259), and consists of a large triangle made up of smaller triangles. The two-way arrows indicate that the contextual components of a learning activity are interconnected. The white arrow located outside the triangle shows that the interplay of the elements which characterise the ecology of a learning environment contribute to the expected outcome. This, in its turn, may be taken as the starting point of a new learning activity.

Starting from the base of the triangle, the diagram provides a description of the *community* of participants, which included not only the students and their teachers, but also the *netizens* who could access our wiki to read the texts produced by the CoP, or post messages through the open forum that was available on the wiki itself. We then have a description of the modality (*rules*) in which online interaction should be carried out (*asynchronous writing*) and a definition of the different roles assigned to participants. Teachers were supposed to act as *facilitators* of the communicative process involved in Web-mediated cooperative writing. They would *guide* the students when they asked for their support. In addition, teachers and students were constantly involved in a *joint assessment* of the ongoing process, in order to make all necessary adjustments. Moving clockwise, the *subject* of this research consisted in bridging the gap (*convergence*) between the scholastic use of EFL and the use of ELF as an affordance to carry out authentic Internet-mediated communication. The other mediating artifacts that were available were a *word processor, social networks* and a *wiki*. The *object* of our activity plan was to enhance the students' cooperative creative writing and media literacy via the use of ELF, to interconnect distally located classes and produce fanfiction texts. Finally, the *outcome* of this activity plan consisted in fostering intercultural communication within a networked CoP, whereby participants could improve their communicative competence in English through mutual scaffolding in a ZPD.

The teacher survey on ELF

At the end of the two phases of this project, two pencil-and-paper ethnographic questionnaires, based on Dörnyei (2010), were administered to students and their five teachers. The purpose of this ethnographic survey, some of whose results were published in Grazzi (2013: 107–138), was to collect quantitative and qualitative data concerning a) the respondents' use of ELF in online communication from home and from school, b) the respondents' opinions on the use of ELF at school, and c) their opinion on cooperative writing and fanfiction as learning tools.

Let us now focus on the teacher questionnaire, and in particular on Part 4, shown in Table 4.1, which concerns teachers' attitudes towards the use of ELF as an integral part of their syllabuses.

64

Table 4.1 Teacher survey: ELF

Part 4 ELF (English as a Lingua Franca)

9. In this part, you can say how much you agree or disagree with the following statements by simply circling (O) a number from 1 to 6. Please do not leave out any of the items.

Strongly disagree	Disagree	Slightly disagree	Slightly agree	Agree	Strongly agree
1	2	3	4	5	6

1.	ELF refers to the use of standard English as a global language, for international communication.	1 2 3 4 5 6
2.	ELF refers to the pronunciation and intonation of English spoken by L2 users.	1 2 3 4 5 6
3.	ELF is a sort of "broken" English used by L2 users for international communication.	1 2 3 4 5 6
4.	ELF refers to different world Englishes emerging locally and used globally for international communication.	1 2 3 4 5 6
5.	Standard English belongs to native-speakers, while ELF belongs to non-native speakers.	1 2 3 4 5 6
6.	Both native and non-native speakers of English contribute to the evolution of ELF 'glocally'.	1 2 3 4 5 6
7.	Non-native teachers of English should take ENL (English as a Native Language) as their target model.	1 2 3 4 5 6
8.	Non-native teachers of English should take the SUE (Successful User of English) as their target model.	1 2 3 4 5 6
9.	Standard English and native-speaker competence are the appropriate targets of ELT (English Language Teaching).	1 2 3 4 5 6
10.	The main target of ELT is to make learners become SUEs, who are able to use multiple skills in different discourses and communicative contexts, while maintaining their socio-cultural identity.	1 2 3 4 5 6
11.	L2 users gain prestige and have better opportunities if they speak ENL.	1 2 3 4 5 6
12.	Taking ENL as a model of proficiency in ELT reinforces linguistic imperialism and entails the loss of one's socio-cultural identity.	1 2 3 4 5 6
13.	The use of ELF should not be allowed at school as it easily turns into a students' pidgin.	1 2 3 4 5 6
14.	ELF is informed by EFL and is emergent at school when learners carry out authentic communicative activities in their 'glocal' socio-cultural environment.	1 2 3 4 5 6
15.	The students' L1 and socio-cultural identity interfere with the learning of English and cause errors.	1 2 3 4 5 6
16.	The students' L1 and socio-cultural identity are resources that can enrich English and adapt it to their interactive needs.	1 2 3 4 5 6
17.	ELT materials should only present learners with examples of how native-speakers use their different varieties of ENL.	1 2 3 4 5 6
18.	ELT materials should present learners with examples of how ENL and ELF are used by SUEs (including both native speakers of English and L2 users).	1 2 3 4 5 6

The results of this part of the survey show that three out of the five teachers involved in this project consider NS English as the target model in ELT and a key to success for their students. According to them, the successful L2-user is a non-native speaker (NNS) of English who conforms to the norms of SE and also affirms his/her cultural identity. In other words, even though language standards of accuracy and fluency correspond to the NS model, this is hardly perceived as a threat to or limitation of the learner's right to appropriate the foreign language and express his/her sociocultural identity. It is as if learning English essentially consisted in a neutral system of lexicogrammar rules to be acquired as such in order to be able to express oneself correctly in an additional language. Consequently, ELF is conceptualised rather vaguely and the respondents sometimes give contradictory answers: on the one hand they seem to agree (albeit half-heartedly) with the idea that NNSs and language learners contribute to the emergence of English glocally and that the L1 linguaculture can enrich English, but on the other hand they think that the students' native tongue interferes with the acquisition of *proper* English, i.e. SE. In addition, even though respondents agree that ELT materials should present learners with examples of how ENL and ELF are used by both NSs and successful users of English (SUE) (Prodromou 2008: ix), they seem to assume that ELF should conform to NS English norms, and that its diversity from ENL basically consists in the fact that it is spoken by NNSs in international contexts.

As for the other two teachers, one answered only the final question in the grid, therefore that part of her questionnaire was considered irrelevant, while the other provided answers which are absolutely in line with the theories and conceptualisations of ELF that have been presented previously in this chapter.

All in all, the results of this survey indicate that the teachers of English involved in this project recognised the educational potential of NBLT and were favourable to the incorporation of innovative learning activities like cooperative writing and fanfiction into the school syllabus. However, respondents also revealed their resistance to the idea that whenever SUEs are involved in authentic communication in multilingual and multicultural contexts, ELF emerges naturally and becomes an integral part of the nonnative speaker's linguacultural identity.

Discussion

The data provided by the teacher survey indicate that ELF was still perceived to be a controversial issue at the end of this project. Let us now consider some of their pedagogical implications.

First of all, it should be noted that NBLT has become an important resource in contemporary ELT, independently of the ELF-based approach that is presented here. Today, the use of digital materials such as audiovisuals, hypertexts and online dictionaries have become an integral part of English syllabuses, while digital aids such as computers, interactive whiteboards and tablet PCs have become very common devices in the English classroom. Nevertheless, recent research (Matsuda 2012; Vettorel and Lopriore 2013; Bayyurt and Akcan 2014) has pointed out that the reality of ELF is underrepresented in textbooks and Web-based teaching materials, while the traditional EFL-oriented curriculum is still dominant in language education. Not surprisingly, since English teachers have not been well informed about the sociolinguistic phenomena that have determined the emergence of ELF in the age of globalisation, they tend to reject any deviations from NS norms. For this reason, the results of this pilot study support the reconceptualisation of English based on the assumption that EFL and ELF are not mutually exclusive, but tend to converge along a continuum that runs from the NS model of English to the students' natural appropriation and adaptation of this language when learning is situated in a real multilingual and multicultural context. The argument of this chapter, therefore, is that ELF represents a viable option whenever the class is participating in authentic communication online.

Secondly, the techniques required to carry out networked activities like cooperative creative writing and fanfiction are not specific to either EFL or ELF. What varies is the teacher's approach to the learners' performance. While in the case of EFL the teacher has a gatekeeping function that entails the correction of the students' errors and the assessment of their work according to NS-based descriptors of competence, such as those provided by the Common European Framework of Reference (CEFR), in the case of ELF the teacher focuses on the pragmatic relevance of the process that leads to successful communication, such as the effective use of communicative strategies like language transfer and accommodation. From this perspective, the assessment of the whole communicative interaction should involve the teacher and their class in a joint effort to reflect on the process that was carried out by the CoP and on the results that were achieved as regards the improvement of the learners' communicative and intercultural competence.

Finally, the analysis of the texts produced by the students who participated in this project indicates that their shared Italian languacultural background influenced their use of ELF considerably, as shown by cases of reverse unilateral idiomaticity. Hence, it is advisable for teachers to interconnect classes from diverse languacultural backgrounds in order to situate ELF in an international environment where its use as a contact language would be more genuine. To this end, language teachers should promote partnerships with colleagues from other countries and create opportunities for their students to cooperate.

Conclusions

This chapter first traced the theoretical framework that inspired the pilot study that was presented here. The design of this project is centred on a blended approach that connects several distinct areas of applied linguistics – sociocultural theory, educational linguistics, cultural learning, NBLT and others – to investigate research questions about ELT from the perspective of ELF studies.

The basic assumption is that EFL and ELF, which are mutually exclusive, may in fact converge by means of the learner's performance when English is used as a contact language in multilingual and multicultural settings. It is evident from the discussion in this chapter that even if the institutional English curriculum is based on the NS model, learners tend to appropriate and adapt the foreign language to their languacultural identities. They activate a process that leads to the emergence of ELF, which is co-constructed by L2-users through their interaction, as was exemplified by the cases of creative idiomaticity discussed above.

Kramsch (1993: 233) claimed that "learning a language is learning to exercise both a social and a personal voice, it is both a process of socialisation into a given speech community and the acquisition of literacy as a means of expressing personal meanings". She created the metaphor of *third place* to represent the area that "grows in the interstices between the cultures the learner grew up with and the new cultures he or she is introduced to" (1993: 236). Sixteen years later, Kramsch (2009: 200) reformulated this concept to include the sociocultural changes that had taken place in the meantime: "I propose reframing the notion of third place as symbolic competence, an ability that is both theoretical and practical, and that emerges from the needs to find appropriate subject positions within and across the languages at hand."

As we have seen, the Internet provides an open virtual space where communities of *netizens* from diverse languacultural backgrounds are drawn together by their interest in a common pursuit and use ELF as a mediational tool. Fanfiction is a case in point. Therefore, the goal of this project was to take advantage of the opportunities and resources offered by the Web to interconnect distally-located classes and create CoPs engaged in cooperative creative writing. This way, it was possible to go beyond the circumscribed pedagogic environment of the English classroom and reach out to a wider *fandom* that shares the same interest in literature.

The teaching/learning experience that was presented here should help teachers of English to improve their understanding of the potential of network-based activities in language teaching/learning, and at the same time should make them reconceptualise their assumptions of ELF.

In conclusion, this research shows that the integration of ELF-based NBLT in the English syllabus, like fanfiction and collaborative creative writing, should be intended as part of a wider pedagogical design that requires appropriate training programmes, as well as new teaching materials that do not exclude ELF from the panorama of languacultural options that English offers today.

Engagement priorities

1. Mind the gap!
   ELF studies have been thriving at academic level, over the last fifteen years (e.g. books, journals, conventions, research projects, PhD thesis etc.). So far, however, there has been very little dissemination of information at school level and among language educators. What kind of actions would you recommend to fill this gap and raise the awareness of teachers in schools about ELF?

2. ELF and ELT
   If you are a member of a group of high-school or University teachers of English attending a training course, you might be willing to share your ideas about ELF and its pedagogic implications. Here are a few links to interesting videos to stimulate your debate:
   - TESOL International: Interview with Dr. Jennifer Jenkins
     http://youtu.be/Gp96u8UzvV4
   - BBC, David Crystal: World Languages
     http://youtu.be/5Kvs8SxN8mc
   - BBC, David Crystal: The Biggest Challenges for Teachers
     http://youtu.be/ItODnX5geCM
   - TESOL International, Professor Kurt Kohn: 'My English': Second Language Acquisition as Individual and Social Construction.
     http://youtu.be/yCfpD49YhSg
   - FACULTI, Dr. Martin Dewey: Language Studies – English as a lingua franca.
     http://youtu.be/8VzWm8AgVps
   Create a focus group online with your fellow trainees (e.g. on a social network like Facebook) and carry out a discussion on ELF moderated by your teacher-trainer. When your forum is over, work cooperatively and make your own video where you present your shared views about the role of ELF in ELT. This clip could be uploaded onto YouTube and be shared with the wider community of English teachers.

3. ELF and Web-based projects
   This chapter provides teachers of English with examples of Web-based activities for the language classroom where ELF is used as a contact language to carry out cooperative creative writing. Use a similar teaching/learning activity model (see Table 4.2) and design a new Web-based project focused on fanfiction that could be implemented with students from different languacultural backgrounds, at high school or University level.

4. The convergence of EFL and ELF.
   This chapter shows that learners tend to reshape English according to their languacultural identities, as shown by examples of unilateral idiomaticity and semantic transfer. If you are attending a teacher-training course with

colleagues from other schools/cities/countries, create a CoP with students from your classes and interconnect them online via a social network (e.g. create a group on Facebook or create a wiki on Wikispaces.com). Assign the CoP a communicative task (e.g. start a forum to discuss about a range of different topics of their interest; work on fanfiction cooperatively). Collect the texts the CoP has produced and find instances of creative use of language whereby EFL and ELF tend to converge.

Notes

1. Fanfiction is a very popular form of networked creative writing, whereby fans of a particular literary genre produce their own original sequels or new versions of their favourite books.
2. Rogoff (in Wertsch et al. 1995: 150–151) defines *participatory appropriation* as 'the process by which individuals transform their understanding of and responsibility for activities through their own participation. [...] The basic idea of appropriation is that, through participation, people change and in the process become prepared to engage in subsequent similar activities'.
3. The wiki was called *Cooperative Creative Writing and ELF* and was hosted on Wikispaces, a free social platform for writing designed for education, at http://collaborative-writing-elf.wikispaces.com/
4. Quoted from *The Corpus of Contemporary American English*, http://corpus.byu.edu/coca/
5. From Paisà, www.corpusitaliano.it
6. Source: *Cambridge Advanced Learner's Dictionary*.
7. Wikispaces: http://fanfiction-rome-palermo-messina.wikispaces.com/. The students' texts were uploaded to: http://fanfiction-rome-palermo-messina.wikispaces.com/

References

Bayyurt, Y. and Akcan, S. (eds). (2014). *Current Perspectives on Pedagogy for English as a Lingua Franca*. Berlin: de Gruyter Mouton.

Butlin, R. (1987). The German Boy. In *British Short Stories of Today*. London: Penguin Books.

Campagna, S., Garzone, G., Ilie, C. and Rowley-Jolivet, E. (eds). (2012). *Evolving Genres in Web-Mediated Communication*. Bern: Peter Lang AG.

Cook, G. (2000). *Language Play, Language Learning*. Oxford: Oxford University Press.

Crystal, D. (2011). *Internet Linguistics: A Student Guide*. London and New York: Routledge.

Dahl, R. (1959). Parson's Pleasure. In *Kiss Kiss*. London: Penguin Books (1962).

Dörnyei, Z. (2010). *Questionnaires in Second Language Research*. (Second Edition). New York, NY: Routledge.

Engeström, Y. (1987). *Learning by Expanding: An Activity Theoretical Approach to Developmental Research*. Helsinki: Orienta-Consultit.

Gagliardi, C. and Maley, A. (eds). (2010). *EIL, ELF, Global English: Teaching and Learning Issues*. Bern: Peter Lang AG.

Goodyear, P., Banks, S., Hodgson, V. and McConnell, D. (eds). (2004). *Advances in Research on Networked Learning*. Dordrecht, Netherlands: Kluwer Publishers.

Graddol, D. (2006). *English Next*. London: The British Council.

Grazzi, E. (2011). New Forms of Communication on the Web: the Cases of Social Networks and Memes. In G. Di Martino, L. Lombardo, S. Nuccorini (eds), *Challenges for the 21st Century: Dilemmas, Ambiguities, Directions. Papers from the 24th AIA Conference.* Vol. II Language Studies. Roma: Edizioni Q.

Grazzi, E. (2013). *The Sociocultural Dimension of ELF in the English Classroom.* Roma: Editoriale Anicia.

Guth, S. and Helm, F. (eds). (2010). *Telecollaboration 2.0: Language, Literacies, and Intercultural Learning in the 21st Century.* New York, NY: Peter Lang.

Jenkins, H. (2006). *Fan, Bloggers, and Gamers.* New York City, NY: New York University Press.

Jenkins, J. (2007). *English as a Lingua Franca: Attitude and Identity.* Oxford: Oxford University Press.

Jenkins, J., Cogo, A. and Dewey, M. (2011). Review of developments in research into English as a lingua franca. *Language Teaching* 44: 281–315.

Joyce, J. (1914). *Dubliners.* London: Penguin Classics (2000).

Kramsch, C. (1993). *Context and Culture in Language Teaching.* Oxford: Oxford University Press.

Kramsch, C. (2009). *The Multilingual Subject.* Oxford: Oxford University Press.

Lantolf, J.P. and Thorne, S.L. (2006). *Sociocultural Theory and the Genesis of Second Language Development.* Oxford: Oxford University Press.

Matsuda, A. (2012). *Principles and Practices of Teaching English as an International Language.* Bristol: Multilingual Matters.

Mauranen, A. (2003). The Corpus of English as a Lingua Franca in Academic Settings. *TESOL Quarterly* 37(3): 513–527.

Mauranen, A. (2012). *Exploring ELF – Academic English Shaped by Non-native Speakers.* Cambridge: Cambridge University Press.

O'Dowd, R. and Ware, P. (2009). Critical issues in telecollaborative task design. In *Computer Assisted Language Learning* 22(2): 173–188.

Pennycook, A. (2001). *Critical Applied Linguistics.* New York, NY: Routledge.

Prodromou, L. (2008). *English as a Lingua Franca: A Corpus-based Analysis.* London: Continuum.

Rogoff, B. (1995). Observing sociocultural activity on three planes: participatory appropriation, guided participation, and apprenticeship. In J.V. Wertsch, P. Del Rio, and A. Alvarez (eds), *Sociocultural Studies of Mind.* Cambridge: Cambridge University Press.

Seidlhofer, B. (2004). Research perspectives on teaching English as a lingua franca. *Annual Review of Applied Linguistics* 24: 209–239.

Seidlhofer, B. (2011). *Understanding English as a Lingua Franca.* Oxford: Oxford University Press.

Sifakis, N.C. (2014). ELF awareness as an opportunity for change: a transformative perspective for ESOL teacher education. In *Journal of English as a Lingua Franca* 3(2): 317–335.

Sifakis, N.C. and Fay, R. (2011). Integrating an ELF pedagogy in a changing world: the case of Greek state schooling. In A. Archibald, A. Cogo and J. Jenkins (eds), *Latest Trends in ELF Research.* Newcastle-Upon-Tyne: Cambridge Scholars Publishing.

Spolsky, B. (1978). *Educational Linguistics: An Introduction.* Rowley, MA: Newbury House Publishers.

Thorne, S. and Black, R. (2007). Language and literacy development in computer-mediated contexts and communities. *Annual Review of Applied Linguistics* 27: 1–28.

Thorne, S., Black, R. and Sykes, J. (2009). Second language use, socialization, and learning in internet interest communities and online gaming. *The Modern Language Journal* 93: 802–822.

Tomasello, M. (2003). *Constructing a Language*. Cambridge, MA and London England: Harvard University Press.

van Lier, L. (2004). *The Ecology and Semiotics of Language learning: A Sociocultural Perspective* Norwell, MA: Kluwer Academic Publishers.

Vettorel, P. (2014). *English as a Lingua Franca in Wider Networking. Blogging Practices*. Berlin: De Gruyter Mouton.

Vettorel, P. and Lopriore, L. (2013). Is there ELF in ELT course-books? *Studies in Second Language Learning and Teaching* 4(3): 483–504.

Vygotsky, L.S. (1978). *Mind in Society*. Cambridge: Cambridge University Press.

Wenger, E. (1998). *Communities of Practice*. Cambridge: Cambridge University Press.

Wilde, O. (1890). *The Picture of Dorian Gray*. London: Penguin Classics (2003).

5
ELF Oral Presentations in a Multilingual Context: Intelligibility, Familiarity and Agency

Iris Schaller-Schwaner

Introduction

In the Swiss context, oral use of English in research and HE is embedded in a nexus of societal quadrilingualism, varying profiles of individual multilingualism and different forms of institutional and educational bilingualism, to which internationals contribute a further dynamic. High-stakes public speaking in academia can bring tensions and conflicting demands to a head. Oral presentations are thus among the first and most enduring challenges in multilingual academic contexts in which ELF is integrated into an individual's academic socialisation and multilingual repertoire.

A number of factors make oral presentations stressful for speakers: lack of experience in oracy, activation of competing languages, memory and processing overload in ex-tempore style, and insecurity about intelligibility in the interactional vacuum. Interestingly, ELF research has rarely focused on oral presentations, but teaching EAP in and for multilingual situations requires research into what happens in disciplinary contexts when multilingual users of ELF deliver oral presentations to other multilingual speakers in particular institutional conditions.

This chapter focuses on qualitative data, field notes and analysis of evidence-informed reflective teaching in an EAP ELF setting. It describes how an EAP lecturer's ethnographic ELF research on presentations in two disciplinary speech events in a bilingual Swiss university has fed into her pedagogical responses to ELF classroom presentations. Specifically, it focuses on how fluctuations in intelligibility are dealt with both strategically and through pronunciation work in order to promote learner agency and autonomous functionality in 'code-sharing' lingua-franca mode in ELF (Schaller-Schwaner 2010, 2011: 438). It explores how variability in ELF and the role of agency in coping with it require teachers to incorporate both in-depth experience of interactions among speakers from unfamiliar L1 backgrounds and to provide phonemic points of orientation to compensate for lack of such experience as well as for "similect" effects (Mauranen 2012: 28).

The Swiss linguistic landscape will be sketched in the first section. The second section considers ELF in European HE, specifically the author's institutional context, and connections with intelligibility. The next section focuses on ethnographic ELF research on presentations in disciplinary contexts and an EAP ELF classroom, while the final section interprets results and illustrates pedagogical implications for teaching English for Plurilingual Academic Purposes (henceforth EPAP) (Schaller-Schwaner 2009, 2012).

The Swiss linguistic landscape

The local context, partially conditioning how ELF unfolds, is Switzerland's only bilingual university, the University of Fribourg (UFR), situated in western Switzerland in a canton with two official languages: French (the cantonal majority language) and German (the national majority language whose spoken forms, Swiss German varieties, are not readily understood by others). UFR also has large numbers of Italophone students, together with international students and researchers not only from Europe, but also from Asian countries, notably India. French and/or German have been the official teaching languages, but English has become an additional or primary medium of instruction in several Master's programmes.

Most Swiss citizens grow up in *either* German, French or Italian, and only the small minority who speak Romansh become systematically bi- or multilingual (cf. Haas 2010; Werlen et al. 2011). There are 22 monolingual cantons and only four are officially bi- or trilingual. The canton of Fribourg/Freiburg has two official languages. Despite the Latin *Confoederatio Helvetica*, CH, Switzerland historically had no lingua franca (cf. Werlen et al. 2011: 7). In Germanophone areas, Alemannic varieties of German are prestigious and spoken regardless of an individual's social or educational background. Standard German is a school subject whose spoken forms tend to retain a 'foreign' tinge, but diglossia may also bring about multilingual flexibility and awareness (Berthele 2010). In Francophone cantons, dialects carry less prestige and French appears to be taught as formal literacy in a uniform 'central' standard variety. Francophones are less likely to use non-L1s productively in public, or to contribute to whole-class oral work.

UFR is a cantonal bilingual institution that tries simultaneously to protect twin monolingualism and promote individual bilingualism. This has led to different types of institutional bilingualism. Brohy's (2005) tripartite typology of parallel, complementary and integrative bilingualism is discussed elsewhere (cf. Schaller-Schwaner 2011: 425–426). Parallel bilingualism, i.e. twin monolingualism, requires communicative bridges between French and German, while integrative bilingualism requires students to use French and German as well as English receptively and has been most typical of the small but vibrant Science faculty. The sciences' bottom-up inclusion of English presented 'wild/unruly trilingualism' for UFR language management before English became a primary teaching language in MSc programmes in 2005, at which point it became discreetly veiled in UFR's PR media parlance as 'bi(tri)lingualism'.

ELF and intelligibility in European HE

University contexts in Europe comprise monolingual institutions and histori-cally bilingual institutions working and teaching in two languages. They vary in the way additional languages affect the institutional linguistic ecology (see e.g. Veronesi and Nickenig 2009). Individual additional language socialisation for academic purposes used to be an asset, but from the 1970s a 'BTA' (Been To America, cf. Swales 2004: 2) became an informal language requirement for a career in the sciences. Research on how university language practices in Europe have evolved in the last 20 years, including ELF, is found in Haberland et al. (2008), Smit and Dafouz (2012), Haberland et al. (2013) and Doiz et al. (2013).

In Switzerland, academic language skills beyond L1, particularly English, are increasingly required even at Bachelor level. Politically, this is contentious and may disadvantage individuals who studied other national languages at school before English. On the other hand, its use is accelerated by the non-territorial nature of ELF, the dynamic complexity and availability of ELF as a resource (cf. also Hülmbauer 2011) and by earlier, or more varied mobility, faster exchange of information, more ad-hoc languaging for communal disciplinary speech events and more multilingual fluctuation in the language repertoires of local academic communities. It is often overlooked that it is stable, spatially-bound communi-ties, not malleable constellations of interlingual speakers (Hülmbauer 2013), that develop code switching and mixing, or parallel or mediated-simultaneous or unreciprocated language use (cf. also Hülmbauer 2011: 44). Interpersonal encounters involving mobilisation of many different resources are often cited as exemplifying multilingualism because many codes are visible on the surface. Hülmbauer's (2013) and Cogo's (2012) deeper approach allows constellations of intercultural speakers and the intralingual and interlingual resources that flow into ELF encounters to reveal their multilingual saturation.

Returning to specific academic ELF settings, it should be noted that, unlike in the locally motivated, public disciplinary lunch-time speech events this author examined (Schaller-Schwaner 2012: 148–158), consistent ELF use is not predict-able from the official labelling of a programme as English-medium. Varying patterns of moment-to-moment local language use in courses nominally taught in English were found in certain Swedish, Danish and Norwegian set-tings of Bologna-designed 'English-medium' international university courses (cf. Neville and Wagner 2008, Ljosland 2011, Söderlundh 2013). This is balanced by ample evidence from other Nordic university settings operating in ELF (e.g. Björkman 2013, Hynninen 2013, cf. also Mauranen 2003, 2012), indicating that findings from UFR may be useful for others.

At UFR, ELF is as complex and dynamic as elsewhere, but is at times the weakest language locally with the lowest number of fluent speakers and the least institutional support. It may be the weakest link in a student's multilingual repertoire. As an embedded language (Schaller-Schwaner 2008b: 264–265; but cf. Hülmbauer 2011: 44–48), it can be difficult to maintain as an output language. Speakers of oral presentations know that they share other or stronger languages with some members of their audience but also that, if they do not stay in 'code-sharing' lingua-franca mode (Schaller-Schwaner 2010, 2011; cf. Hülmbauer 2011), they will exclude or alienate others, as explained in Schaller-Schwaner (2011: 436), splitting the bilingual audience into addressees and auditors (Bell 1984, 2001) and flouting the genre expectations.

This means that ELF as a practice needs getting used to. Linguistic insecurities or classroom roles such as 'doing being a student' (e.g. Attenborough 2011) need to be tackled in the process of becoming a confident and aware ELF user. Developing multilingual awareness for ELF users means presenters not only having to cope with competing responses from their own complex language repertoires, learning to override them and sticking to English, but also having to deal with language contact phenomena within ELF and monitoring their own output.

Many ELFA users originally learn English as a foreign language at school in largely same-language groups. They are thus used to typical language contact features connected to their own particular linguistic backgrounds and usually find the English of speakers with similar multilingual repertoires easier to process.

Roughly, this corresponds to Mauranen's (2012: 29) notion of "similects", L2 lects of English that "arise in parallel, not in mutual interaction" but do not develop further as speakers of the same L1 have no reason to interact in English. However, at UFR, speakers do interact in ELF to include someone who does not share their L1, to signal disciplinary membership, or to socialise doctoral students into an English-medium spoken academic genre.

For the study of ELF in European HE, the empirical work on ELF intelligibility by Jenkins (2000) remains pivotal. Researching mutual intelligibility and accommodation in interactions among non-L1 users of English in terms of features and processes, Jenkins (2000) proposed the Lingua Franca Core, based on what caused misunderstandings in English among internationals and featuring certain stress patterns, consonants and consonant clusters, vowel lengths, and one central vowel. Jenkins also highlighted that interpersonal accommodation processes and adaption of one's pronunciation to high-stakes situations were crucial for ELF. Jenkins' analysis led to disputes but also to explorations and applications (e.g. Walker 2010) as well as to further research in this area, such as Deterding (2012), which also focuses on (non-overt) misunderstandings when there is no breakdown of communication or no interference with overall comprehension. Partial intelligibility surfaces in the analytical process when a transcriber does not manage to recognise a lexical item or does not hear a word accurately (Deterding 2012: 187).

As regards the ELF academic presentations studied here, partial or non-understanding is usually not overt either. As there is no visible interaction, absence of understanding can go undetected: on the one hand, identifying words in running speech that one cannot interrupt is more difficult, while on the other nobody will notice if the listener has a problem. In addition, intelligibility is affected by shared schematic knowledge. Members of a disciplinary community construct meanings more easily during an oral presentation than someone who depends on actually recognising a word because they are simultaneously building disciplinary knowledge. Pictorial information supports cueing into the existing disciplinary schemata and helps construct them but itself involves degrees of familiarity with specialist semiotic conventions (Danielsson 2014).

Intelligibility as a linguistic construct encompasses recognisability of words and a listener's ability to recognise words or stretches of speech and identify them with sense units (Field 2005). Ethnographically, it is also an emic category and an account of experiential data. For an EAP teacher/researcher and ELF listener who is not a member of the discipline, for example, emic intelligibility entails an element of trying to construct disciplinary knowledge, but also an element of difficulty of transcribing, as shown in Deterding (2012), in which unintelligibility surfaced not during ELF interactions but afterwards when an interlocutor as transcriber did not recognise or misidentified words during transcription. In transcribing ("representing spoken ELF in written form", Breiteneder et al. 2006: 161), one realises the extent to which one cannot identify a word reliably or when one cannot decode the sound sequence heard, that is, associate it with a meaning.

While detailed quantitative tests of intelligibility such as Field (2005) can contribute essential insights into intelligibility as an etic category, the emic point here is informants' own (self-)perceptions of strain, listening effort or frustration with themselves or the presenter, which participants associate with pronunciation. Put differently, lack of or limited intelligibility is not a property of the speech signal alone but is intertwined with factors such as speaker, listener, context, purpose and private or shared assessment of a participant experience. As an emic category, it is usually reported and discursively constructed as 'inability to understand' or 'understanding difficulty', and comprises individual and collective experience of language use as well as the sense people make of it, including attitudes, social perceptions and intentions, personal positionings, or even prejudice.

What familiarity contributes to enhancing intelligibility also seems connected to the interplay of linguistic criteria and an individual's expectations, perceptions, and memory. Speech perception and recognition of spoken language appear to be a highly integrated process in which experience with linguistic properties and experience with 'indexical' properties that are specific to speaker-identity are attended to and retained together (e.g. Szakay et al. 2012, Borrie et al. 2013).

To be conceptually clear about understanding (cf. Pitzl 2005, 2015), ability to transcribe can be seen as one possible operationalisation of intelligibility but does not equal understanding, as Deterding (2013: 11) seems to be suggesting. Real-time listeners orient towards content. Gaps or disturbances are not contemplated, as perceptual fluency is essential, but they register as strain or partial understanding. When transcribing or listening to a recording repeatedly, listeners process differently and declaratively; they have time and become aware of what they hear, of what/why they fail to understand, and of perceptual and productive fluctuations. This is pedagogically relevant, as are doubts about intelligibility, which undermine presenters' confidence and impact their delivery. EAP learners' concern about pronunciation and intelligibility in the interactional vacuum of an oral presentation is a pro-active way of managing understanding. Besides, in planned speech, measures to tackle the transience of spoken words (e.g. explicit structure, visuals, gesture, mobilisation of prior knowledge) can be taken.

Oral presentations in academic ELF contexts

This section first outlines ethnographic work on the emerging use of ELF in two academic speech events in two different faculties of UFR. It then provides a reflective account of the author's classroom practices combined with student data produced in the teaching process.

Ethnographic research on ELF in academic contexts: oral presentations

Ethnographic research on ELF in UFR academic settings (e.g. Schaller-Schwaner 2005, 2008a, 2008b, 2009, 2011) set out to produce evidence of the bottom-up functions of ELF in local academic niches outside language teaching. Essentially following a Swalesian 'situation-first' approach (Swales 1998, 2004: 73), it involved regular attendance at two innovative disciplinary lunch-time speech events (presentation + discussion), one in psychology and one in biochemistry, over more than one year, taking detailed field notes, audio recording, interviewing and observing the disciplinary contexts to produce a 'thick' description of the two genres. The analysis included a differentiation of the local purposes of ELF in these events: as a sine-qua-non and/or a deliberate choice for negotiating the bilingual divide under very specific institutional conditions and vis-à-vis various multi- and bi(tri-)lingual audiences and expectations. The findings suggest that ELF academic speech genres, under partially fluctuating multilingual conditions, fulfil a variety of roles: they are communal, emerging, local, academic disciplinary traditions (cf. Mauranen 2002, 2005, 2006); they constitute tertiary-education, disciplinary and additional-language socialisation; they represent research genres as well as local instantiations of wider discourse communities; they are regular, cumulative manifestations of a collective LSP choice; and they are cohesive practices for local disciplinary colleagues and co-constitutive of the university environment and the institution (Schaller-Schwaner 2008b, 2009, 2011). Each of these factors shape the particular ELF that speakers engage in as organisers or chairs, presenters, (peripheral) participants, audience, teachers, students, visitors, regulars, novices, or experts. The study also shows more and less experienced ELF users differing in their (self-)positionings (in the sense of Davies and Harré 1990 cf. Schaller-Schwaner 2011) but coping with the challenges of orally presenting in English and asking or answering questions in a language that is not necessarily their default mode of interpersonal communication.

One setting, a lunch-time seminar in biochemistry, was attended by all research teams plus graduate students for weekly presentations and discussion. ELF had been in use for about 15 years and was being adopted officially as the primary teaching language of MSc programmes in the Sciences. In weekly Journal Clubs, doctoral students presented recently published research articles. From open-ended interviews about their experience with English, it emerged that the speakers with the least familiar pronunciations and those that displayed least awareness of their multilingual audience, for example, in terms of speed, were most difficult to understand. Speakers of Swiss national languages often found that Indian Englishes required getting used to and individual Indian speakers made remarks that indicated awareness of not only accommodating to European ELF users, but also 'subconsciously' adopting local ways of using words 'from seniors or elders in the lab'. They all relied heavily on visual support and many drew attention to its importance. This ethnographic research was not designed as a study of intelligibility, but the subject of 'difficult understanding' was raised by interviewees and experienced by the author as an observer in some presentations. In addition to interview and observation results, data triangulation was possible through analysis of participants' actions, for example involving visuals, which were essential and used in all presentations.

The other lunch-time event, in psychology, was a peer-event for colleagues from a hitherto linguistically segregated department. The presenters were external and internal junior and senior researchers. The observation took place during the second and third year of its existence so that the use of ELF as a local oral practice was still new to the department and some presenters. As explained in more detail elsewhere (Schaller-Schwaner 2011), of the different Experience-with-English positionings (Davies and Harré 1990) constructed by speakers in ELF lunch-time speech events, in psychology there was one subsumed under 'BTA-Returner' (Schaller-Schwaner 2011: 433) that co-occurred with noticeable hyper-use of a feature that very few learners of English ever assimilate, namely the lengthened ðiː: pronunciation of the definite article as a 'filler' (Roach 2009a: 167). It was used by a new professor to the psychology department, who originated from a country not held in high esteem at that time. He was indexing Britain explicitly and implicitly throughout the first few minutes of his lunch-time presentation as if flagging his 'BTA' – a safe positioning at a tertiary education institution. The local practice was only being established, he was a newcomer himself, so an authenticating feature as an experienced user of English in an L1 context signalled linguistic security from a different reference system in order to give a sense of orientation in a context which had not yet acquired local experience of ELF. Importantly, his use of this feature can be interpreted not as an individual displaying linguistic insecurity but as his agentive way of coping with insecurity.

The mainstream notion of language as a monolingual entity that belongs to its respective cultural community was still prevalent with regard to local language issues and insecurities. Another, established, local chair with plentiful experience as an international presenter was hesitant at first about being recorded and said this constituted 'additional evaluation' and heightened his 'reactivity'. In the local setting, with linguistically segregated chairs offering complete study programmes both in French and in German, he had every reason for heightened reactivity concerning his speech and for feeling evaluated when speaking in public as he was a Germanophone from Germany occupying one of the Francophone chairs and functioning entirely in French. Thus, as a cohesive strategy, conducting the lunch-time seminar in English drew departmental colleagues together, negotiated the departmental language boundary and emphasised disciplinary communality through the use of English. The signs of insecurity were a function not only of English being new but also of the language attitudes and ideologies English was intended to overcome.

Reflective teaching and classroom research: a case study

The second form of research drawn on here is observation and reflection on the author's own classroom practices and the data her courses produce. Its aim is to improve teaching and learning with a more detailed needs analysis, reflecting students' specific academic purposes, and detailed feedback on oral performance.

The research draws on two main sources of data and results. The first of these is course-related. As a teacher, the author always takes personal notes in class when participants introduce each other, writes down observations after class, and jots down suggestions or concerns while negotiating with individuals, pairs or small groups about cooperation and presentation topics. Extensive notes support later adaptation of a new course to what learner needs and profiles appear, as was the case for two C1 Academic English courses drawn on here. Students' oral presentations in class are also occasions for teacher's written notes, on the basis of which detailed face-to-face feedback is given. Written peer feedback is requested from the audience, but goes to the presenters themselves and is shared only on a voluntary basis. Audio recordings of the presentations and subsequent discussions are also provided so that recordings of co-presentations can be listened to together or individually and passages that require attention be focused on. Students can also request a copy of their audio recording for their own purposes.

Data in terms of notes from oral presentations derive from critical moments for the teacher, who is also an ELF listener. They influence feedback to students, and they also result in teacher learning about the dynamic nature of intelligibility in ELF and the role of familiarity. Students can, however, exercise their learner agency through access to their own recordings, becoming aware of what strengths to play on and what weaknesses to attend to.

The second source is data from an ongoing process of reflective pronunciation teaching over many years involving individual work in one-to-one situations coupled with collaborative annotation and note taking, in which students are helped to realise their agency as oral users of ELF.

From the first source, two oral co-presentations are discussed below, each one involving an individual, one Chinese and one Russian, whose oral contributions in class were extremely difficult to understand for the teacher, an ELF listener. This judgment was formed through instances in which not enough words were recognisable from a stretch of speech for the listener to be able to understand more than the general topic before the speaker's intention became clear(er) through (dis)confirmation of the next turn, a form of implicit other-initiated, co-constructed repair (cf. Smit 2010: 211ff.). Its purpose is comparable to Mauranen's (2012: 225) "echoing in search of form", which "is done by somewhat fuzzy matching, as if imperceptibly doing corrective or clarificatory language work". The teacher, as an ELF participant, uses identified or uncertain words from the learner's utterance to trial a partial 'candidate' confirming and developing the topic, thus beginning what might reflect the learner's intention. Then a pause and a quizzical face from the teacher signal that her hypothesis is incomplete and invite other-continuation/help from the speaker. Class participants also cooperate by supplying something they recognised. However, class cooperation happened less frequently in relation to oral contributions by the Chinese and the Russian participants and the teacher sensed a lack of joint achievement.

The Chinese law student was paired off with a Francophone Swiss, while the newly arrived Russian computer science student joined a 'similect' Slavonic group with a Polish and a Czech student. The Russian participant generally spoke at such a speed that it was virtually impossible to develop a hypothesis about what she was saying quickly enough to be able to process what was coming next in order to confirm or disconfirm the original hypothesis. Judging from the help the Polish student was able to offer occasionally, it appeared that the Slavonic-language speaker found her more intelligible. Interestingly, the Russian student took offence when asked to slow down and refused to accept that she was difficult to understand. The analysis below reflects the author's attempt as an ELF listener and as an EAP teacher to come to terms with not understanding an assertively fluent and rhotic course participant.

The respective joint presentations in which the Chinese and the Russian participant were involved reflected the efforts they had made and the way the two speakers had used preparation advice. The Chinese student still had difficult pronunciation, but he and his Swiss partner had produced excellent slides with picture illustrations and textual explanations that included many of the words they felt were difficult to pronounce/understand. Their talk was clearly structured and sign-posting was frequent. They had also rehearsed their co-presentation and they added interactivity by taking turns repeatedly during the presentation, each time recapitulating some of what the other had just said. The peer feedback confirmed the overall fluency, interactivity and topic-relevance of the slides, but almost half the respondents still found the speakers hard to understand, one commenting that pronunciation was not clear. Half of the remaining respondents mentioned two other factors as weaknesses: "watched too much on the screen and not enough to the audience", "standing sideways to the audience ... it would be better to stand face-to-face to the audience".

The peer feedback received by the three Slavonic co-presenters is not on record. They spoke on a topic that clearly interested the audience (lycanthropy) but they sounded under-rehearsed to the author or as if performing at the limit of their capacity, using many words, including proper names, that they had perhaps never pronounced in English, e.g. 'psike for *psyche* (the Czech student) or *Zeus* as 'servʊs with an apical r instead of zjuːs (the Polish student) or 'gari for the first name of *Harry Potter* (the Russian student). The Slavonic threesome's colourful slides were audibly appreciated and they had lifted expressions and whole sentences from a written source. The Russian student, who spoke second, referred to a previous presentation to establish a connection. She was reading from notes but frequently looked up at the audience. She had also slowed down enough for the teacher to take some notes, here complemented by notes from the recording, which revealed that pronunciation was not the only factor in making her difficult to understand. Table 5.1 shows pronunciation variations co-occurring in the same presentation.

While invariable ɪd for -*ed* endings often causes no intelligibility problem, occasional ɪd became confusing in combination with nonstandard features in

Table 5.1   Pronunciation variation during oral presentation

Pronunciation as heard by teacher	Word as interpreted by teacher	Word as intended by presenter	Unexpected realisation/ variation
'ɒpɒsɪt	*opposite*	opposed (of this theory) ['as opposed to']	stress placement; occasional ɪd for –ed, non-standard preposition
feə	*fair*	fear	diphthong quality different
'fʌnəlɪ	*funnily*	finally	monophthong realisation/ shortening of diphthong
'dɪsɪs	*disses*	disease	stress placement; vowel quantity;
'deɪvɪl 'eɪvɪl	intelligible in context	evil devil	two monophthongs of different length replaced by same diphthong;
ɪ'naʊ	not identified initially	enough	triggered by spelling (notorious variability of –ough realisations)
wɒrs bɪ'kɒrs 'ɒrθɒr	*wars becourse orthor*	was because author	rhotic post-vocalic r realised in places where there is none (hyper-rhoticity)

stress placement and/or use of prepositions, for example, when the intended word *opposed* was pronounced 'ɒpɒsɪt and so was heard as *opposite*, and only the recording revealed that she had said *opposed of this theory*. This holds more generally: unexpected realisations of words may have been recognised had the listener not been distracted by nonstandard variations in article use, some interchangeable uses of verbs and nouns and intermittent absence of copular *be*. The most unfamiliar feature for this author was the student's hyper-rhoticity (Hickey 2014: 150): using rhotic post-vocalic r where there is none (etymologically/in the spelling); for example, wɒrs was heard as *wars* instead of *was*, bɪ'kɒrs was heard as *becourse* instead of *because*, 'ɒrθɒr as *orthor* instead of *author*. The teacher had not encountered this before and had not recognised either the words or the phenomenon, a feature of L1 English varieties under pressure from General American (cf. Krämer 2012), or, in terms of stylising, indexing white American speech (cf. Cutler 2014). The teacher was confused as an ELF listener by something unexpected, non-transparent and unilaterally persisting (cf. Seidlhofer 2011: 134–135). For the presenter, however, indexing American pronunciation may have been a safe positioning. Whether it actually was a 'BTA' or a reflection of her ambition to earn one cannot be ascertained, but it was likely her agentive way of coping with the high-stakes situation. Preparing her presentation in a Slavonic-language 'similect' threesome, and co-presenting in it, may have activated more Slavonic features than had she been able to converge with speakers with a different multilingual repertoire communicatively requiring her to adjust her pronunciation interlingually (cf. Jenkins 2000: 169ff., 214–215). It was high-stakes because the student's mid-semester written progress test had been the weakest of the group and the assessment of the presentation was important. Speaking speed was a signal of fluency, which, while not compensating for lack of accuracy, projected competence. However, she appeared reluctant to accommodate to the multilingual ELF context even in an EAP class, which she may have found as taxing as the trilingual context in which she was now studying computer science.

Pedagogical implications for teaching EPAP

The author's research and teaching is based conceptually on the EAP tradition of examining the oral practices and spoken genres instantiated by disciplinary communities to derive content and advice for teaching. In the genre paradigm, Swales (e.g. 2004) and related work (e.g. Weissberg 1993; Aguilar 2003; Zareva 2009; cf. also Mauranen et al. 2010) focus on how the respective disciplines are performed through the spoken discourse forms that its members practise and into which they implicitly socialise students.

In the author's local context, English is by no means the default or only oral language of disciplinary socialisation. In the author's experience, the main teaching effort in relation to oral presentations has to be invested in motivating and encouraging students to speak English (cf. MacIntyre 2007) while standing in front of an audience of peers with same and other (more or less familiar) L1s in this formal academic set-up, and to help them deal with multilingual competition, that is, to maintain English as the output language. Macro processes before the presentation, for example, negotiating relevant topics, selecting engaging content and rehearsing enough to do 'fresh' talk, need to be balanced with micro support. Based on analysis of speaking rate and information content in ELF presentations, Hincks (2010) recommends giving ELF oral presenters more time. However, relaxing the time constraint in class is not sufficient. Bankowski's (2010) oral presentation training for an Asian multilingual academic context makes use of video models but also includes some of the teaching suggestions presented below.

Intelligibility in English for Plurilingual Academic Purposes

ELF means sharing the multilingual work of intelligibility, a point worth reiterating in teaching contexts (cf. Pitzl 2015). Addressing multilingual listeners is a challenge because it involves processing differences for the non-L1 audience (Levis 2007), and because awareness of the audience's other languages will influence a speaker's performance. According to Grosjean's research on speech modes (e.g. 2001, 2008), the slightest indication of more than one

language in the setting changes the bi- or multilingual speaker's mode of operating linguistically. He assumes a situational and behavioural continuum that
triggers activation of languages and language processing mechanisms in the
repertoire, for example, code switching or mixing at one end of the continuum
in full bilingual mode. Activation of the multilingual repertoire is subject to a
'wax and wane' and requires learning control (Grosjean 2001: 16, 18, 20–21).
Even while someone is speaking only one language (Grosjean 2001: 5), other
language resources in the multilingual repertoire, though not intended for
imminent output, are also activated (Grosjean 2008: 18). In monolingual
mode – in a monolingual environment talking about a monolingual topic to
monolinguals – it may become residual, but other-language signals or lingua
franca language choice directed at other multilingual speakers will reactivate
other languages to different degrees, which in turn need to be inhibited or
accessed depending on the communicative demands. This is entailed in the
'code-sharing' lingua-franca mode assumed to operate in ELF as a multilingual
practice (Schaller-Schwaner 2011: 435–439). Expert users of this mode can stay
in the same language and move along the mode continuum as required.

As regards the listener, an explanation of the difference between L1 and L2
audiences goes back to Weinreich's (1953) concept of interlingual identification,
that is, the observation that listeners tend to 'hear' their own phonemes or the
phonemes of their dominant language when confronted with variation. This
means that whatever the actual sound is like phonetically, the listener automati-
cally identifies it as a realisation of the closest dominant phoneme. Plausibly,
L1 English listeners would understand varied and variable pronunciations
of English more easily, given life-long experience with variation in English,
because they process any English in terms of the meaning distinctive elements
of their own English and there is usually a quick match between a realisation
and a phoneme. However, if an individual with a complex language repertoire
but less experience with English is listening in a new ELF setting to an unfamiliar speaker with a different complex language repertoire, matching may be
slower as the incoming language cannot be easily processed via the most dominant phonemes, which of course originally derive from a different language or
interact with it (de Groot 2011: 273–274). In this sense, intelligibility can indeed
be seen as 'a moving target' and highly context-sensitive (Levis 2007).

These questions of intelligibility give rise to a number of teaching implications in relation to oral presentations in ELF. These involve four areas: familiarisation, matching language and visual information, exploiting multilingualism,
and maximising agency. These will be discussed in turn below.

Familiarisation

Less experienced ELF users, who are in the process of expanding their repertoires or learning to manage competing demands on it, will have processing

problems if the first few words they hear prove hard to recognise. Heavier use of bottom-up processing (Levis 2007) may be involved or simply a delay in processing caused by having to unpack unfamiliar realisations. Familiar realisations are faster to process.

Exposure to and familiarisation with the presenter's phonetic form permits the audience to pair familiar and 'new'. The aha-experience, that is, the surprising realisation, helps the audience to adjust their expectations. As Levis (2007) underlines, familiarity supports listeners' ability to process and builds their flexibility and tolerance of variation.

As Table 5.2 shows, teaching can promote familiarisation by encouraging in-depth interactions between speakers from unfamiliar L1 backgrounds.

Matching language and visual information

The advantages of visual information for information processing are well known. In cross-modal processing, facial expression, mouth and lip movement and other visual information is integrated with auditory input and enhances spoken language comprehension by bi- and plurilinguals (Marian 2009: 53–54). Bankowski (2010: 192) underlines how the effectiveness of presentations varies with the appropriateness, relevance and explanation of slides since visuals free up capacity for assimilating meaning from fast speech and unfamiliar realisations of English. In terms of language processing, visual input interacts with the auditory unfolding of a word and disambiguates doubtful sound shapes, excluding implausible lexical options and making the processing load lighter, which is important in terms of speed (Marian 2009: 57). During the listening process, orthography is not only processed as written input, but also activates the auditory shape of a word in phonetic and phonological form (Marian 2009: 59), which a listener already possesses.

Visuals can therefore be exploited in oral presentations to maximise intelligibility. As well as providing students with signposting language (e.g. *What you can see here is…*), teachers could suggest that students put 'uncomfortable' words on slides and pronounce them without turning away from the audience, so that listeners understand what a certain realisation refers to.

Eye contact also aids language processing. As indicated by the critical peer feedback that the Chinese and Francophone co-presenters received despite their visuals, poor eye contact, strained intelligibility and weak audience rapport might be connected. Multilingual speakers should not, however, focus on a familiar member of the audience with the same L1 (or habitual other L2), as eye contact can activate habitual languages to a degree that they become competitive for imminent output, of which more below. Table 5.2 shows what teachers can do in terms of classroom management, awareness-raising and individual feedback (also in one-to-one sessions, cf. below) to promote intelligibility and agency and to avoid priming activation of other languages.

Table 5.2 Pedagogical guidelines and rationale for promoting agency and intelligibility in EAP ELF oral presentations

Guidelines	Rationale
Classroom management	
Use joint presentations and let co-presenters negotiate engaging content	Necessitates productive oral interaction; creates experience of doing ELF
Avoid same L1 or 'similect' pairings; match partners with unfamiliar L1	Communicatively requires interlingual accessibility of pronunciation; promotes familiarisation with variable realisations
Record presentations and make their own presentations available to Ss	Time lag permits students to really listen and hear what the audience hears
Listen to the recording together with presenter(s); negotiate intelligibility	Teacher feedback for attention/noticing; can be verified/rejected by learner
Specific instructions to presenters	
Consider ELF your multilingual resource and/or shared intention; pay attention to disciplinary function; talk to your multilingual audience directly	Sensitises students to their agency; to functional language concepts; promotes development of confidence in ELF; enhances audience rapport/solidarity
Prime yourself for English as an output language, e.g. chat to the chair; avoid eye contact with familiar/same-L1 Ss	Activation level of language for output heightened; prevents triggering habitual interpersonal language choice
Familiarise listeners with your pronunciation by keeping close to your slides/hand-out (for the introduction)	Repeating words from visuals permits identification of unfamiliar realisations with familiar words
Make articulation clear and intelligible, use recognisable pronunciation (check with different L1 speakers for variation)	Focus students on the process of intelligibility, recognisability; variation; the negotiability of ELF as a resource
Speak loud enough despite insecurity, adapt speed to multilingual audience	Multilingual processing is slower due to competition from other languages
Suggestions for 1:1 sessions	
Point out international convergence; guide autonomous functionality in ELF; enable learner to incorporate new articulatory actions	Familiarity with one set of phonemes provides orientation, (meta)knowledge, agency; inceptive adjustment of habitus
Focus on salient phonemes; symbols as reminder of meaning distinctiveness	Visual shape as material anchor of sense of orientation, esp. in vowel space
Target interlingual overlap/insecurity to disambiguate languages by sound shape	Helps maintain language selected for output; articulatory sense 'tags' lexis for retrieval (i.e., identifies it by language)
Practise accommodation as a strategy	Proximity at eye level/individualisation
Use handwriting, calligraphic chart, make transcription/sound 'tangible'	Alternative visual/mental picture to orthography; 'grasping' pronunciation

Exploiting multilingualism

Multilingualism in the class can also be exploited to facilitate intelligibility. When preparing presentations, course participants should be encouraged to work together in pairs or groups of different or dissimilar L1, even where 'similect' speakers seem drawn to each other (e.g. by seating themselves in class as if reflecting the territoriality principle). This is because, when 'similect' pairings occur, accommodation among students may activate shared or similar L1 resources in the language repertoire and 'similect' features (cf. Mauranen 2012: 29–30, 248), thus rendering their pronunciation less accessible to listeners from a different linguacultural background (cf. Jenkins 2000: 172–173, 182–84). Teacher feedback on the resulting presentation should also refer to international convergence, that is, reminders beyond the here-and-now of both monolingual and multilingual reference groups' needs or of genre expectations.

Agency

In terms of agency, passive exposure of learners to variation in order to familiarise them with different realisations is insufficient. What needs to be facilitated by teachers are in-depth interactions between learners from unfamiliar backgrounds when preparing co-presentations. During such interaction students learn to cope with lack of comprehension and develop strategies to overcome it, such as repetition, paraphrasing and echoing (cf. Cogo 2009, Mauranen 2012). Teachers also need to facilitate echoing of unrecognised sound sequences, spelling or writing unintelligible words, joint consultation of reference sources and improving the accessibility of their pronunciation.

In order to maximise student agency, teachers also need to provide feedback to students after the presentation by speaking overtly from the point of view of the listener, thus expressing an 'emic intelligibility' perspective. This can be done by checking word identification with the student or pointing out a more widespread or familiar pronunciation once an unrecognised word has been jointly identified. Learner agency can be enhanced further by giving presenters access to an audio recording of their classroom presentations. This enables them to listen to themselves and put the teacher's observations into perspective; the teacher's view can thus be validated or rejected on grounds negotiated by teacher and students. For most students, the practice of learning through a recording of their presentation, individual one-to-one attention and negotiable feedback is a novelty; but it is crucial if they are to be able to appropriate ELF for their own purposes.

Using these teaching techniques engenders agency in a number of senses: agency in the essential psychological sense (e.g. Bandura 2006), in the linguistic anthropology sense of 'socioculturally mediated capacity to act' (Ahearn 2001: 9), in the sociological sense as the force opposed to structuration in multilingual settings (Jaspers and Verschueren 2011: 1157) and the ELF sense that originates with Widdowson (1994), Brutt-Griffler (1998) and Seidlhofer (2001, 2004; cf. also 2011: 49–50). As illustrated in Schaller-Schwaner (2011), agency can manifest in emic positionings of self-efficacy, confidence and coping, in having enough awareness and experience to imagine or undertake or actually manage the transition from being a learner of a language that belongs to someone else to being a speaker of a 'code-sharing' lingua-franca mode (Schaller-Schwaner 2010, 2011, cf. Hülmbauer 2011) which is one's own to use for one's own local purposes, here specifically Plurilingual Academic Purposes in multilingual settings.

A summary of classroom guidelines for teachers engaged in teaching oral presentation for ELF contexts (cf. Schaller-Schwaner 2013) is set out in Table 5.2 below. It is divided into three sections (classroom management, specific instructions for presenters, suggestions for one-to-one feedback sessions). The recommendations for each section are in the left-hand column and the reasons for the recommendations in the right-hand column.

Teaching pronunciation

Finally we turn to the question of pronunciation teaching. Pronunciation work in EPAP is valued since academic public speaking genres in European contexts are generally formal events that require keeping one's languages apart. In this situation, output in other languages needs to be inhibited. This is essential for learners who have yet to separate languages consistently, but it remains a need in areas of overlap of (academic) lexis between two or more languages.

The one-to-one feedback session is based on the working assumption that language selection from the complex multilingual repertoire is embodied (e.g. Block 2013) and enhanced by pronunciation, that is, articulating the sound shape of one particular language. Since productive oral language use is through the body, a physical somatic sense of which of one's languages one is articulating will be helpful in maintaining language selection, in a way that is similar to what Roach (2009b) refers to as shifting 'gear' in articulatory setting but should rather be called habitus embedded in a body or embodiment. It is argued here that this corporeal articulatory sense can be thought of as what 'tags' language structures (de Groot 2011: 279ff), that is, makes different languages more distinct for retrieval, as phonological systems do not overlap more in areas of similarity between languages.

The above case studies showed that in targeting ELF for output, speakers can be thrown by mispronunciations, stress placement or failure to select the English sound shape of certain words. This causes them momentarily to switch to another of their languages. The triggers for this process are the areas in which the lexicon of their languages overlap: shared academic loan words, such as *analysis, hypothesis* and so on, or Romance-origin formal, academic English words whose orthographic shape is very similar to cognate French words. The effect of this orthographic overlap is cumulative and powerful: contact with English is primarily in written form, particularly in French-medium schools. Reading in EAP is largely orthographic; words without an autonomous English sound shape which might become activated trigger the reader's L1 habitus whenever the word is processed.

Performing and maintaining language selection for speech output thus requires changing one's habitus by consistently performing and incorporating other actions into one's repertoire (cf. Wade 2011). In order to achieve this, learners need repeated experience of these other articulatory actions. How is this to be achieved? Modelling a word or sense unit in a one-to-one situation is often insufficient as it is difficult for some learners to hold complex strings of sounds in their working memory. Since awareness of vowel space is rare, auditory information can be complemented by phonemic symbols as a visual anchor, an alternative to the orthographic visual representation.

In order to understand the need for a visual anchor let us first consider a simple example of a vowel that is salient in the multilingual Swiss context and conspicuous by its absence in many learners. Should the pronunciation of the word *study* be stjuːˈdeɪ, ˈstɒdɪ or stʊˈdaɪ? There is a central vowel in many Englishes that they could helpfully converge on, viz. ʌ. For many educated users of ELF the word is ˈstʌdɪ. Importantly, this central vowel frequently disambiguates French and English (*culture, result, support, occurrence, encourage, suggestion*) as well as German and English (*must, discussion, construct, product, reduction*), that is, the realisation of the vowel as ʌ makes the main segmental (i.e., pertaining to individual sounds, not stress or intonation) difference between French or German and English in these words.

Disambiguation can be thought of as follows: when starting to pronounce the word *culture*, for example, targeting the vowel ʌ helps the speaker to physically anchor themselves into English. This makes stressing the first syllable more likely, as ʌ triggers the retrieval of the English syllable ˈkʌl and the subsequent unstressed syllable tʃə. If there is no ʌ being activated, the learner's lips may round into kyl or kʊl and the subsequent French (ˈtyr) or German (ˈtuːɐ or Swiss variants with a consonantal –r realisation) stress pattern and second syllable are likely to rekindle activation of French or German, respectively. The vowel ʌ can saliently identify a word as English and attract nuclear stress to the appropriate syllable, thus disambiguating the realisation as English and helping maintain English. Experimental evidence that shows a single salient vowel having the strongest short-term priming effect on activation and interaction of linguistic resources in the bilingual mental lexicon (Szakay et al. 2012) suggests that avoiding such priming by targeting ʌ may reduce activation and interaction of resources in the multilingual repertoire.

L2, L3, L4 realisations of a vowel system will be different from monolingual realisations because there is interaction between the user's languages' vowel systems (De Groot 2011: 273–274), and there will be variation depending on the state of a user's repertoire, level of experience and the attention the bi- or multilingual speaker can expend. But learners need to have a version of an English vowel system to work with in the first place and will profit from having a sense of orientation when coping with parallel activation of resources from different languages in their repertoire. When one language is targeted for spoken output, the rest of the repertoire is not switched off.

How can the teacher facilitate visual anchoring? In the one-to-one situation, the visual symbol and the physical sense can be pedagogically linked, and the symbol made 'tangible' by hand movements and manual writing. Phoneme symbols can be noted down on a piece of paper, by the teacher and the learner, or a calligraphic phonemic chart, such as Underhill's (2005), can be highlighted and annotated. Attention should be drawn to the articulators, and handwritten symbols can be used as visual reminders while teacher and learner are accommodating to each other during the individual feedback session.

Overall, it is suggested here that it is phenomenologically appropriate in an ELF approach to oral presentation teaching to explore the potential of an available phonemic inventory of English, which acts both as a set of reference points – abstract in the given social context almost on a par with cardinal vowels – and as a mental scaffold. Phonemic symbols are used by university students for languaging about speech and as a springboard for consolidating knowledge and experience to maintain autonomous functionality in English.

Engagement priorities

To promote further discussion of issues emerging from this chapter, the following questions could be explored:

1. Exploring intelligibility in other contexts: As intelligibility is highly context sensitive, what intelligibility questions do teachers face in their own contexts?
2. Visual anchoring of phonemes: What could be problematic about utilising a chart of phonemic symbols for pronunciation teaching in ELF settings which was originally developed as a chart of RP phonemes? What (dis-) advantages could using an IPA (cardinal) vowel quadrilateral have?
3. Longitudinal familiarity: In a different teaching context years after the original study, this author encountered two local life science students, one Francophone and one Germanophone, who both pronounced *yeast* (a model organism) in a way that sounded like *east*, which the teacher did not recognise initially. One of them, a biochemist, then explained this was

probably the Indian pronunciation, but both asserted that everybody now said *east*. What could this be indicative of?
4. Multilingual awareness: How can individuals enhance their awareness of ELF and of the specific conditions under which users of multilingual repertoires operate?
5. Teacher research: To complement the teacher's own perceptions and judgements, how could action research involving more/other listeners be set up for oral-presentation listening situations? What different ways are there to balance familiarity, emic intelligibility and real-time listening experiences vs. working with recorded audios (and transcription)? How would these compare with various context-independent (etic) experimental designs testing spoken word recognition, of which Derwing and Munro (2009: 479) said that 'no one way is fully adequate'?

Acknowledgements

Sincere thanks to the editors for their engagement with successive revisions of this chapter, to Anthony Clark, Tisa Retfalvi-Schär and Jeannette Regan for their comments, and to Raphael Berthele, Claudine Brohy, Ute Smit, Marie-Luise Pitzl and Thomas Studer for answering specific queries. Any errors committed are the author's.

References

Aguilar, M. (2003). The peer seminar, a spoken research process genre. *Journal of English for Academic Purposes* 3: 55–72.
Ahearn, L. M. (2001). Language and agency. *Annual Review of Anthropology* 30: 109–137.
Attenborough, F. T. (2011). 'I don't f***ing care!' Marginalia and the (textual) negotiation of an academic identity by university students. *Discourse & Communication* 5(2): 99–121.
Bandura, A. (2006). Toward a psychology of human agency. *Perspectives on Psychological Science* 1: 164–180.
Bankowski, E. (2010). Developing skills for effective academic presentations in EAP. *International Journal of Teaching and Learning in Higher Education* 22(2): 187–196.
Bell, A. (1984). Language style as audience design. *Language in Society* 13(2): 145–204.
Bell, A. (2001). Back in style: reworking audience design. In Eckert, P. and J.R. Rickford (eds) *Style and Sociolinguistic Variation*. Cambridge: CUP, pp. 139–169.
Berthele, R. (2010). Dialekt als Problem oder Potential? Überlegungen zur Hochdeutschoffensive in der deutschen Schweiz aus Sicht der Mehrsprachigkeitsforschung. In Bitter Bättig, F. and Tanner, A. (eds) *Sprachen lernen- Lernen durch Sprache*. Zürich: Seismo, pp. 37–52.
Björkman, B. (2013). *English as an Academic Lingua Franca. An Investigation of Form and Communicative Effectiveness* (Developments in English as a Language Franca). Boston/Berlin: De Gruyter Mouton.
Block, D. (2013). Moving beyond 'lingualism': Multilingual embodiment and multimodality in SLA. In May, S. (ed.) *The Multilingual Turn: Implications for SLA, TESOL, and Bilingual Education*. New York & London: Routledge, pp. 54–77.

Borrie, S. A., McAuliffe, M. J., Liss, J. M., O'Beirne, G.A. and Anderson, T. J. (2013). The role of linguistic and indexical information in improved recognition of dysarthric speech. *Journal of the Acoustic Society of America* 133: 474–482.

Breiteneder, A., Pitzl, M.-L., Majewski, S. and Kimpfinger, T. (2006). Voice Recording – Methodological Challenges in the Compilation of a Corpus of Spoken ELF. *Nordic Journal of English Studies* 5(2): 161–188. Available at http://hdl.handle.net/2077/3153 (accessed 6 June 2015).

Brohy, C. (2005). Overt bilingualism, covert multilingualism? Official languages and 'other' languages in a bilingual French-German university. Paper presented at the 'Bi- and multilingual universities: challenges & future prospects' Conference. 1–3 September 2005, Helsinki University.

Brutt-Griffler, J. (1998). Conceptual questions in English as a world language. *World Englishes* 17(3): 381–392.

Cogo, A. (2009). Accommodating difference in ELF conversations: A study of pragmatic strategies. In Mauranen, A. and Ranta, E. (eds) *English as a Lingua Franca: Studies and Findings*. Newcastle upon Tyne: Cambridge Scholars Publishing, pp. 254–273.

Cogo, A. (2012). ELF and super-diversity: A case study of ELF multilingual practices from a business context. *Journal of English as a Lingua Franca* 1(2): 283–313.

Cutler, C. A. (2014). *White Hip Hoppers, Language and Identity in Post-modern America*. (Routledge Studies in Sociolinguistics 8). New York & Abingdon, Oxon: Routledge.

Danielsson, K. (2014). Text talk as a means of enhancing learning in secondary education. Multimodal meaning-making in the classroom. Paper presented at the AILA World Congress Brisbane Australia, 15 August 2014.

Davies, B. and Harré, R. (1990). Positioning: The discursive production of selves. *Journal for the Theory of Social Behaviour* 20(1): 44–63 Available at http://www.massey.ac.nz/~alock/position/position.htm (accessed 13 August 2014).

de Groot, A. M. B. (2011). *Language and Cognition in Bilinguals and Multilinguals. An Introduction*. New York & Hove: Psychology Press.

Derwing, T. M. and Munro, M. J. (2009). Putting accent in its place: Rethinking obstacles to communication. *Language Teaching* 42(4): 476–490.

Deterding, D. (2012). Intelligibility in spoken ELF. *Journal of English as a Lingua Franca* 1(1): 185–190.

Deterding, D. (2013). *Misunderstandings in English as a Lingua Franca. An Analysis of ELF Interactions in South-East Asia*. (Developments in English as a Lingua Franca) Boston/Berlin: De Gruyter Mouton.

Doiz, A., Lasagabaster, D. and Sierra, J. M. (eds) 2013. *English-Medium Instruction at Universities*. Bristol etc.: Multilingual Matters.

Field, J. (2005). Intelligibility and the listener: The role of lexical stress. *TESOL Quarterly* 39(9): 399–423.

Grosjean, F. (2001). The bilingual's language modes. In Nicol, J. L. (ed.) *One Mind, Two Languages: Bilingual Language Processing*. Oxford: Blackwell, pp. 1–22.

Grosjean, F. (2008). *Studying Bilinguals*. (Oxford Linguistics) Oxford: OUP.

Haas, W. (ed.) (2010). *'Do you speak Swiss?' Sprachenvielfalt und Sprachkompetenz in der Schweiz. Nationales Forschungsprogramm NFP 56*. Zürich NZZ Libro Verlag.

Haberland, H., Lønsmann, D. and Preisler, B. (eds) (2013). *Language Alternation, Language Choice and Language Encounter in International Tertiary Education* (Multilingual Education 5). Dortrecht: Springer.

Haberland, H., Mortensen, J., Fabricius, A., Preisler, B., Risager, K. and Kjaerbeck, S. (eds) (2008). *Higher Education in the Global Village. Linguistic and Cultural Practices in the International University*. Roskilde, Denmark: University of Roskilde: Department of Culture and Identity.

Hickey, R. (2014). *A Dictionary of Varieties of English*. Malden, MA and Oxford: Wiley Blackwell.

Hincks, R. (2010). Speaking rate and information content in English lingua franca oral presentations. *English for Specific Purposes* 29: 4–18.

Hülmbauer, C. (2011). English as a Lingua Franca (ELF): The mode and its implications. In Jørgensen, J. N. (ed.) *A Toolkit for Transnational Communication* (Copenhagen Studies in Bilingualism 64). Copenhagen, Denmark: University of Copenhagen, Faculty of Humanities, pp. 43–68.

Hülmbauer, C. (2013). From within and without: The virtual and the plurilingual in ELF. *Journal of English as a Lingua Franca* 2(1): 47–73.

Hynninen, N. (2013). Language regulation in English as a Lingua Franca: Exploring language-regulatory practices in academic spoken discourse. Doctoral dissertation (monograph), University of Helsinki. Available at http://urn.fi/URN:ISBN:978-952-10-8639-7 (accessed 6 June 2015).

Jaspers, J. and Verschueren, J. (2011). Multilingual structures and agencies. *Journal of Pragmatics* 43: 1157–1160.

Jenkins, J. (2000). *The Phonology of English as an International Language: New Models, New Norms, New Goals*. Oxford: Oxford University Press.

Krämer, M. (2012). *Underlying Representations* (Key topics in phonology). Cambridge: CUP.

Levis, J. M. (2007). Guidelines for intelligibility, Paper presented at the International TESOL Conference Seattle, WA. Slides available at http://jlevis.public.iastate.edu/intelligibility.ppt (accessed 14 August 2014).

Ljosland, R. (2011): English as an Academic Lingua Franca: Language policies and multilingual practices in a Norwegian university. *Journal of Pragmatics* 43(4): 991–1004.

MacIntyre, P. D. (2007). Willingness to communicate in a second language: Understanding the decision to speak as a volitional process. *The Modern Language Journal* 91: 564–576.

Marian, V. (2009). Audio-visual integration during bilingual language processing. In Pavlenko, A. (ed.) *The Bilingual Mental Lexicon. Interdisciplinary Approaches*. Bristol etc.: Multilingual Matters, pp. 52–78.

Mauranen, A., Pérez-Llantada, C. and J. M. Swales (2010). Academic Englishes: A standardised knowledge? In Kirkpatrick, A. (ed.) *The World Englishes Handbook*. London and New York: Routledge, pp. 634–652.

Mauranen, A. (2002). 'A Good Question'. Expressing evaluation in academic speech. In Cortese, G. and Riley, P. (eds) *Domain-specific English: Textual Practices Across Communities and Classrooms*. Frankfurt: Peter Lang, pp. 115–140.

Mauranen, A. (2003). The corpus of English as Lingua Franca in academic settings. *TESOL Quarterly* 37(3): 513–527

Mauranen, A. (2005). English as a Lingua Franca: An unknown language? In Cortese, G. and Duszak, A. (eds) *Identity, Community, Discourse. English in Intercultural Settings*. (Linguistic Insights 2) Bern etc.: Peter Lang, pp. 269–293.

Mauranen, A. (2006). Speaking in the discipline: Discourse and socialisation in ELF and LN. In Hyland, K. and Bondi, M. (eds) *Academic Discourse Across Disciplines*. (Linguistic Insights 42) Bern etc.: Peter Lang, pp. 271–294.

Mauranen, A. (2012). *Exploring ELF. Academic English Shaped by Non-Native Speakers*. (Cambridge Applied Linguistics) Cambridge etc.: CUP.

Neville, M. and Wagner, J. (2008). Managing languages and participation in a multilingual group examination. In Haberland, H., Mortensen, J., Fabricius, A., Preisler, B., Risager, K. and Kjaerbeck, S. (eds) *Higher Education in the Global Village. Linguistic and Cultural Practices in the International University*. Roskilde, Denmerk: University of Roskilde: Department of Culture and Identity, pp. 149–174.

Pitzl, M.-L. (2005). Non-understanding in English as a lingua franca: Examples from a business context. *Vienna English Working Papers* 14(2): 50–71.

Pitzl, M.-L. (2015). Understanding and misunderstanding in the *Common European Framework of Reference*: what we can learn from research on BELF and Intercultural Communication. *Journal of English as a Lingua Franca* 4(1): 91–124.

Roach, P. (2009a). *English Phonetics and Phonology*. 4th ed. Cambridge: CUP.

Roach, P. (2009b) English phonetics and phonology glossary (A little encyclopaedia of phonetics). Available at http://www.cambridge.org/servlet/file/EPP_PED_Glossary.pdf?ITEM_ENT_ID=2491706&ITEM_VERSION=1&COLLSPEC_ENT_ID=7 (accessed 15 August 2014).

Schaller-Schwaner, I. (2005). Ecological niches, emergent genres or emergent communities of practice? English as an academic Lingua Franca at the French-German bilingual University of Fribourg-Freiburg. Paper presented at the Conference on Bi- and Multilingual Universities -challenges and future prospects, University of Helsinki, 1–3 September 2005.

Schaller-Schwaner, I. (2008a). ELF in academic settings: Working language and edulect, prestige and solidarity. Paper presented at the ELF Forum: The First International Conference of English as a Lingua Franca, Helsinki University, 6–8 March 2008.

Schaller-Schwaner, I. (2008b). Everything is like something: What is this like? On finding a tertium comparationis for L3/L4 English used as an academic lingua franca at Freiburg-Fribourg University. In Gibson, M., Hufeisen, B. and Personne, C. (eds) *Multilingualism: Learning and Instruction. Selected Papers from the L3 Conference in Freiburg/CH.* (Mehrsprachigkeit und multiples Sprachlernen 5) Baltmannsweiler: Schneider Verlag Hohengehren, pp. 255–272.

Schaller-Schwaner, I. (2009). Under the microscope: English for Plurilingual Academic Purposes. In Veronesi, D. and Nickenig, Ch. (eds) Bi- and Multilingual Universities: European Perspectives and Beyond: Conference Proceedings Bolzano-Bozen, 20–22 September 2007. Bozen-Bolzano, Italy: Bozen University Press, pp. 245–263.

Schaller-Schwaner, I. (2010). ELFA in the eye of the beholder: multilingual or mono-lingual practice? Paper presented at the 11th International CercleS Conference Helsinki University, 2–4 September 2010.

Schaller-Schwaner, I. (2011). The eye of the beholder: Is English as a Lingua Franca in academic settings a monolingual or multilingual practice? *Language Learning in Higher Education (Journal of CercleS)* 1: 423–446.

Schaller-Schwaner, I. (2012). Researching English as a Lingua Franca and teaching English for Plurilingual Academic Purposes. In Blons-Pierre, C. (ed.) *Apprendre, enseigner et évaluer les langues dans le context de Bologne et du CECR. Sprachen lernen, lehren und beurteilen im Kontext von Bologna und dem GER.* Bern etc.: Peter Lang, pp. 141–167.

Schaller-Schwaner, I. (2013). A Swiss ELF workshop on giving academic presentations, paper presented at the ELF 6 Conference University of Roma Tre, 4–7 September 2013.

Seidlhofer, B. (2001). Closing a conceptual gap: The case for a description of English as a Lingua Franca. *International Journal of Applied Linguistics* 11(2): 133–158.

Seidlhofer, B. (2004). Research perspectives on teaching English as a Lingua Franca. *Annual Review of Applied Linguistics* 24: 209–239.

Seidlhofer, B. (2011). *Understanding English as a Lingua Franca.* Oxford: Oxford University Press.

Smit, U. (2010). *English as a Lingua Franca in Higher Education. A Longitudinal Study of Classroom Discourse* (Trends in Applied Linguistics 2). Berlin and New York: De Gruyter Mouton.

Smit, U. and Dafouz, E. (eds) (2012). *Integrating Content and Language in Higher Education. Gaining Insights into English-Medium Instruction at European Universities* (AILA Review 25). Amsterdam/Philadelphia: Bejamins.

Söderlundh, H. (2013). Language choice and linguistic variation in classes nominally taught in English. In Haberland, H., Lønsmann, D., Preisler, B. (eds) *Language Alternation, Language Choice and Language Encounter in International Tertiary Education.* (Multilingual Education 5) Dordrecht: Springer Netherlands, pp. 85–102.

Swales, J.M. (1998). *Other Floors, Other Voices: A Textography of a Small University Building.* Mahwah, NJ: Lawrence Erlbaum Associates.

Swales, J.M. (2004). *Research Genres: Explorations and Applications.* Cambridge: CUP.

Szakay, A., Babel, M. and King, J. (2012). Sociophonetic markers facilitate translation priming: Maori English GOAT – a different kind of animal, *U. Penn Working Papers in Linguistics* 18(2): 137–146.

Underhill, A. (2005). *Sound foundations.* 2nd ed. Oxford: Macmillan.

Veronesi, D. and Nickenig, C. (eds) (2009). Bi- and Multilingual Universities: European Perspectives and Beyond: Conference Proceedings Bolzano-Bozen, 20–22 September 2007. Bozen University Press. Available at http://www.unibz.it/it/library/Documents/bupress/publications/fulltext/9788860460240.pdf (accessed 6 June 2015).

Wade, L. (2011). The emancipatory promise of the habitus: Lindy hop, the body, and social change, *Ethnography* 12(2): 224–246.

Walker, R. (2010). *Teaching the pronunciation of English as a Lingua Franca.* Oxford: Oxford University Press.

Weinreich, U. (1953). *Languages in Contact. Findings and Problems.* New York: Publications of the Linguistic Circle of New York.

Weissberg, B. (1993). The graduate seminar: Another research process genre. *English for Specific Purposes* 12: 23–35.

Werlen, I., Rosenberg, L. and Baumgartner, J. (2011). *Sprachkompetenzen der erwachsenen Bevölkerung in der Schweiz.* Zürich: Seismo.

Widdowson, H. G. (1994). The ownership of English. *TESOL Quarterly* 28(2): 377–388.

Zareva, A. (2009). Informational packaging, level of formality, and the use of circumstance adverbials in L1 and L2 student academic presentation. *Journal of English for Academic Purposes* 8: 55–68.

6
Language Awareness and ELF Perceptions of Chinese University Students

Ying Wang

Introduction

Language awareness (LA) has long enjoyed a high status in language education (see Carter 2003, Hawkins 1992). In a broad sense, LA encapsulates 'knowledge about language' or justified truth about language (see Carter 2003: 64). With a traditional focus-on-form orientation (see Richards and Rodgers 2001), LA 'could be glossed as a sensitivity to grammatical, lexical, or phonological features, and the effect on meaning brought about by the use of different forms' (Hales 1997: 217). Following this, ways have been explored to help second language (L2) learners to attend to features and rules of the English used by its monolingual native speakers in the undertaking of English language teaching (ELT). For instance, Callies and Keller (2008: 249) note that 'native speakers do not use linguistic structures randomly' and make a case for the role of explicit instruction in helping German learners of English to notice linguistic devices used by native English speakers (NESs) for highlighting information in discourse. While many studies on LA are traditionally confined to grammar (e.g., Andrews 1997: 149; Svalberg 2001; Valeo 2013), recent LA research has expanded beyond linguistic forms to cover areas such as pragmatics, culture and pedagogy (e.g., Cross 2010; Murray 2010; Porto 2010). Despite various research interests, the traditional LA approach is mainly focused on knowledge about the English used by NESs and connected with the conventions generated in the monolingual context of NESs. This appears to be limited through the lens of English as a lingua franca (ELF), a research field emerging in response to the globalisation of English.

Research into English from the perspective of English as a global lingua franca has widened the scope of language awareness research to include the relationship of non-native speakers (NNESs) with English by addressing their identification with their L1 cultural group, their appreciation of other NNES cultures and their collaboration with their intercultural interlocutors on the equal footing. In addition, ELF research offers evidence for the performativity of NNES variation in intercultural settings and challenges the assumption that NNES variation from native English hinders intercultural communication. In a nutshell, new knowledge about English challenges the traditional approach to LA centred on native English awareness and ELF awareness is now a new area that needs to be explored for the purpose of ELT.

Following this, this chapter addresses student awareness of ELF, that is, English in its new form to which the current sociolinguistic reality has given prominence. The chapter explores whether and how ELF awareness can be developed in classrooms, based on a focus group study on Chinese university students in the Chinese context. The study reveals Chinese students' attitudinal dynamics and perceptual change. Factors that might cause changes are investigated and contexts in which the observed changes take place are inspected. The findings thus allow possible suggestions to be made as to how teachers can 'do' an ELF-aware classroom in China. The chapter concludes by discussing the relevance of this study for other teaching and learning contexts.

ELF awareness and language attitude

With the momentum of seeking to integrate the implications of ELF research into ELT, ELF awareness is attracting scholarly attention. Dewey (2012) inspects teacher attitudes towards ELF and thus offers some sketches of ELF-aware teachers, which are related to knowledge of English in relation to its sociolinguistic contexts and issues arising with the spread of English. Those issues include the spread of English, the ownership of English, 'the diffusion of English and functions of the language', 'a critical awareness of the unsuitability' of the NES-NNES dichotomy and understanding of concepts like ELF, World Englishes, English as a global language and so on (Dewey 2012: 150). Nonetheless, Dewey claims that being aware of the existence of ELF in the world is far from enough for teachers to be empowered in changing their teaching practice from a native English orientation to an ELF orientation.

Sifakis (2014: 323) goes further to see the importance of 'a particular mindset that endorses change and a working understanding of current realities regarding the use of English internationally'. He suggests the need to consider 'what *specific* knowledge, skills, and attitudes' should be included in 'such a mindset', but comments that 'there is relatively little information on this' (Sifakis 2014: 323, original emphasis). He recommends Jenkins (2003, now an updated version 2015) to be a good start.

Jenkins (2015) covers an overview of issues concerning English in its development. Among the topics – the historical, social and political context of English, the issue of who uses English, Standard English ideology and the future of global Englishes – are useful guidance for the examination of awareness of ELF. These inquiries challenge the centre-periphery relationship between NESs and NNESs and the authority of NESs in English. In addition, ELF research offers useful reference to the understanding of how English works today (e.g., Cogo and Dewey 2012; Jenkins 2000; Mauranen 2012; Seidlhofer 2011; studies reported in Mauranen and Ranta 2009; studies reported in the *Journal of English as a Lingua Franca*). That is, conformity to established norms of English does not necessarily lead to communicative success, whilst non-conformity to established norms of English proves to function well in intercultural contexts. This is relevant for my study, which investigates whether the participants link communicative effectiveness with conformity to Standard English. Further, English is used by NNESs in their own way to serve the function of identification (e.g., Jenkins 2007; Kalocsai 2009). NNESs' first languages and cultures are accepted as part of their repertoires to index their identities. This motivates me to attend to Chinese users' perception of English in relation to Chinese and Chinese culture in their own usage of English.

Language attitude is a crucial part of ELF awareness. Basically, knowing what is happening in the world of English does not necessarily link to the acknowledgement of the legitimacy of ELF (e.g., Dewey 2012; Jenkins 2007; Seidlhofer 2011). Acknowledging ELF often involves the challenge to the exclusive native English orientation in ELT. This is reflected in both Dewey (2012) and Sifakis (2014). Both see the importance of the willingness to challenge native English orientation in ELT. Sifakis (2014) proposes to adopt a transformative perspective for teacher education so as to develop ELF-aware teachers. The perspective relates to an attempt to 'understand and change the individual' (Sifakis 2014: 326). That is, through the transformative perspective-based education, teachers are expected to challenge and ultimately move away from an exclusive focus on native English. Although dealing with different groups of individuals, Sifakis's (2014) discussion lends support to this study, which looks into the inner world of individual students and explores ways to develop their understanding of the legitimacy of ELF and various Englishes, such as Chinese speakers' own English in particular. Further, while language attitude is a key issue in the investigation of the legitimacy of Englishes (Bamgboṣe 1998; Jenkins 2007), empirical research reveals the ambivalence in language users, and learners and teachers' attitudes towards ELF (e.g., Dewey 2012; Jenkins 2007; Ranta 2010; Wang 2013). Disagreement is found between English that is used and English that is desired. In light of this, I examine Chinese students' language attitudes in order to attempt to understand the factors driving the attitudes in support of English diversity.

Based on the works discussed above, I explore ELF awareness with a focus on knowledge of ELF in its sociolinguistic reality and appreciation of ELF in its own right. The first factor involves linguistic inquiry into what English is and how English works in its current time and space. In this respect, it is important to consider 'the wider social, political or cultural factors relevant' to ELT (Cogo and Dewey 2012: 170). That is, knowledge of English should include not only linguistic aspects but also socio-cultural and socio-historical aspects of the language.

The second factor points to attitudes related to the phenomenon of ELF, which is different from the one traditionally accepted English. By investigating these two aspects, this study offers suggestions as to what can be enhanced or be intervened in order to transform a native English orientation to an ELF orientation.

Exploring language awareness and student perceptions among Chinese university students

Despite the increased use of English by Chinese speakers in intercultural communication as a consequence of globalisation, NESs are not necessarily the major communication partners of Chinese speakers and NES communities are no longer the main communities that Chinese speakers aim to align with. Rather, Chinese speakers are in contact with ELF both in global communication and in local realisations with other Asian interlocutors.

However, this trend is not being addressed by current ELT practices in China. As Wen (2012: 371) observes, 'almost all the students are still learning English as a foreign language (EFL) in the traditional way, based on standardised native speaker norms and all the teachers teach this model of EFL, too.' By investigating Chinese university students' LA, this chapter explores ways to help them cope with the gap between English inside and outside the classroom and to make informed choices about their English.

Focus groups with Chinese students

The study was carried out using a specific focus group (hereafter FG) methodology (see Wang 2012) involving group discussions of information taken from Crystal (2008), Deterding (2006), Jenkins (2003) and Xu (2008) concerning the spread of English, the concept of ELF, the difference between ELF and EFL, and some features emerging in Chinese speakers' English (see Appendix 1). FGs allow the investigation of dynamic interactions among group members regarding 'focused' issues, taking the form of group discussion with the presence of a moderator (Berg 2007; Bryman 2001; Hennink 2007). By using FGs, I could examine how participants supported, challenged and influenced each other in terms of views about issues related to ELF in a socially co-constructed context. Altogether four FGs were conducted over tea and biscuits in a social centre. The size of each group was between eight and 11 participants, depending on the participants' willingness to participate. While it is impossible to present the whole set of data which depicts the panorama of students' attitudinal development, this chapter focuses on the attitude of Jiajia, a third-year English major in a eight-person FG, while the field work was conducted. The group included four English majors and four non-English majors. The moderator gave a brief induction before the group discussion, with the focus on the spread of English and the phenomenon of Chinese speakers' own way of using English.

Jiajia's attitude went through some changes from the start of group discussion until the end. In the exploration of 'what' was seen to be changed and unchanged, the analysis of 'how' the changes took place and 'how' unchanged aspects were maintained brought to the fore factors which were seen to operate in Jiajia's LA development. Certainly, it is dangerous to treat the sequence of Jiajia's attitudinal profiles throughout the group discussion as marking a linear development of ELF awareness. Yet the study of Jiajia's attitude offers pedagogical implications regarding how an ELF-aware attitude can be developed and, more practically, what intervening activities can be used to raise such awareness.

A case study of attitude change

During the case study, attention was paid not only to what the interactants drew on to make, maintain or reject an argument, but also to how the interactants engaged in the discussion. By examining the resources that Jiajia and her peers drew on in their interaction, I found three main factors facilitating LA development, that is, exposure to linguistic extracts, intercultural experience and ELF-related knowledge input. Through the analysis of the roles played by Jiajia, the moderator and Jiajia's peers in FG social interaction, I found that self-exploration, moderator influence and peer influence all had impacts on Jiajia's LA development.

In terms of timespan, Jiajia's FG engagement exhibited gradual accumulation in LA. At the beginning of the FG, Jiajia revealed a lack of LA, holding a firm belief that Chinese speakers should pursue conformity to native English. As group interaction proceeded, she started to realise Chinese speakers' need for cultural identity in English. Then she became more tolerant towards nonconformity to native English, acquiring a new understanding of intelligibility in English. Later, she challenged NES–NNES power relations. Afterwards, the FG witnessed her questioning the relevance of NESs for NNES–NNES communication. Despite these changes, Jiajia continued to view the ideal model of English in classrooms as native English, revealing that there was still an obstacle to a complete change in attitude. This section presents snapshots of these critical moments, using a single extract as an example of each.

A lack of LA

The beginning of the FG highlighted native English monolingualism, which was reflected in Jiajia's claim that Chinese university students should make efforts to assimilate to the monolingual native English code (see extract 1).

Extract 1

(1) Jiajia: [...] we should try our best to approximate [*the* English used in] native English speaking countries [...] when you communicate with your interlocutors, you can't force them to fit in our Chinese way of thinking. In order to be quicker, to take shorter

> time before you get things done, before you reach agreements on contracts, or before you complete whatever project, you DEFINITELY need to FIT IN.
> (2) Dan: So a common standard is necessary for communication.
> (3) Jiajia: Only if we follow ONE standard can we possibly communicate more easily.

A lack of LA was visible here. Firstly, NESs were considered as Chinese speakers' major intercultural interlocutors. This assumption aligns with the traditional view of EFL in Chinese speakers' use of English and overlooks the emerging role of ELF in NNES-NNES communications, which is becoming increasingly prominent against the backdrop of English globalisation. Secondly, approximation to native English was taken as necessary for intelligibility. This demonstrated a belief in English as fixed systems, which can be prescribed to NNESs according to NESs' use of English in NES contexts where the systems are originally generated, and a denial of language users' need to adapt forms according to contexts and interlocutors. Thirdly, she emphasised uniformity with native English and put the 'communicative burden' (Lippi-Green 1994: 187) on NNESs entirely and solely, by highlighting NNESs' responsibility to 'fit in' with their NES counterparts' way of using English and excluding NESs from a commitment to adapt to the communicative contexts (turn 1). This one-way communicative commitment reinforced an unequal NES-NNES power relation. In short, the FG started with Jiajia having little knowledge of the changing role of English and the nature of how English works in real life contexts as well as an inability to critically analyse the existing NES-NNES power relation.

Reflection on Chinese culture in English

The first identifiable change in Jiajia's attitude was brought about by a reflection on Chinese culture in relation to English and foregrounded her self-discovery of the limitation of native English for Chinese speakers' cultural expression. While her adherence to native English was mainly expressed on the abstract level earlier (see extract 1), Jiajia shaped her argument for the first time in response to the moderator's invitation to comment on examples of Chinese speakers' English listed in the hand-out (see extract 2).

Extract 2

(1) Jiajia: [...] possibly, different cultures, different nations, even those English speaking nations, would have their own things to be added to English when they have contacted English for some time, so something, some usage should be accepted, like some of the examples listed here [in the hand-out], but for other variations, you'd better avoid. An example just came up to me. That is *long* [Chinese Pinyin, 龙, dragon], we had once discussed the

translation of this matter [on our translation course], an important symbol in Chinese culture. If you translate this matter into *dragon*, I personally can't agree. Many people have suggested using *long*, Chinese pinyin of this matter, because *dragon* and *long* have different cultural connotations. *Long* is auspicious in Chinese culture and relates to Chinese divinity, but *dragon* represents evil in foreigners' eyes. I think examples like this are acceptable, although they don't conform to native English. But if everybody [i.e., every Chinese speaker] uses English in the way, say, extra vowel at the end of the word, or any unclear English, the effects of communication will be hindered. If they [i.e., 'errors'] don't convey your national culture, don't help your cultural expression, they should be avoided.

In this extract, Jiajia engaged with given linguistic data on the handout and recalled her previous exchange with her teacher and peers regarding the comparison of Chinese and native speakers' ways of referring to Chinese culture matters. She categorised given examples as culturally relevant or irrelevant in considering the acceptability of instances of Chinese speakers' English. The attitudinal change emerging in her self-exploration seemed to suggest the benefits of concrete language data in stimulating reflection on non-conformity to native English in terms of its value for Chinese speakers to express Chinese culture.

However, Jiajia's consideration of the appropriateness of native English for Chinese speakers was limited to lexical aspects of English, as exemplified by *long* (龙, dragon). Other aspects of English, including accent, which have been closely associated with identity by sociolinguists (e.g., Jenkins 2007; Labov 1966; Lippi-Green 1994), were considered by Jiajia as irrelevant to culture and identity. This knowledge gap suggests some need for expert intervention or support.

Reconsideration of intelligibility

A second change features Jiajia's reconsideration of intelligibility. Whilst previously Jiajia had seen non-conformity to native English as the threat to intelligibility (see extract 1), she came to realise that intelligibility was not bound to conformity to a pre-determined code but depended on interactive practices between interlocutors (see extract 3).

Extract 3
(1) Ding: I have some work experience [...] as far as I observe, I just feel Easterners and Westerners use different organs to produce sounds, so I just feel our biological differences must lead to our

differences in pronunciation. In my opinion, errors that don't affect communication, communication between interlocutors are acceptable. I had a French customer, his English is like, er, although Chinese speakers' English is far from standard, his pronunciation, their pronunciation is even scary. I think his English is all right because communication is not affected, I mean we could get the business contract signed [...] communication comes first, language is a tool, it is acceptable when communication is not hindered.

(2) Jiajia: I agree with you. I mean, two interlocutors, just like you and your French customer, you both can compromise, you could understand what he meant. But if I am working as an English teacher, if I am teaching students, I can't let it go if the students produce the same sound for *slow* and *snow*, I can't accept that teachers don't teach nasal sound, I would correct them [i.e., errors]. But if you're using English in real life situations, it is all right as long as agreement can be reached between two interlocutors.

As seen in this extract, discussion of intercultural encounters seemed to make a difference in language attitude. Ding drew on his observation and experience to explain his linguistic tolerance. By contrast, Jiajia did not mention any linguistic experience to endorse her argument for uniformity to native English prior to Ding's persuasion. Comparing Jiajia and Ding, it is inferable that the lack of experience of ELF communication creates a myth of intelligibility, whereas linguistic experience helps to resolve the myth.

This extract also highlights the impact of peer interaction on Jiajia. On the one hand, Ding started his turn and projected himself as a knower and an experienced user of English, by announcing his observation and experience and suggesting a critical analysis of 'errors'. On the other hand, Jiajia drew on Ding's life experience, treating him as a source of information about intelligibility in relation to forms. Informed by Ding's experience, Jiajia came to accept that the right to decide what forms to be used and to judge which forms were appropriate belonged to interlocutors in communicative settings rather than native speakers off-site.

It is interesting to see Jiajia's hesitation at this point. While Jiajia accepted Ding's view of 'errors' in real life experience, she narrowed down her interest in native English to classroom settings exclusively. She ascribed the communicative success between Ding and the French colleague to their 'compromise', a word suggesting the result as less desirable on both sides. After her explanation of the need to learn 'correct' forms of English, however, she returned to an endonormative perspective and ended her turn. The hesitation seemed to imply a struggle in re-evaluating the importance of native English in response to Ding's life example, which challenged her adherence to native English.

Questioning NES-NNES power relations

Extract 4 illustrates another striking change, revealing Jiajia's questioning of NES-NNES power relation in English.

> *Extract 4*
>
> (1) Jiajia: [...] If they [i.e., NESs] could accept our way of using English, the promotion of our English would need less effort. But their acceptance is influenced by the rest ONE POINT SEVEN BILLION SPEAKERS [i.e., NNESs]-
>
> (2) Jing: -But [...] if you write these on your examination answer sheets, how do you think teachers would react?
>
> (3) An: [...] As she [i.e., Muka] said, native speakers don't accept these, so, so these are still wrong at the present. But just like what happened to *long time no see*, which has been accepted by them. It is possible for *give you some colour to see see* to be accepted. Then it won't be wrong any more.
>
> (4) Muka: So the norm providers are always native speakers.
>
> (5) Jiajia: [...] They are norm providers. But they are not dictators, they are not the boss, they can't make us do this or that. They need to communicate with us. We were talking about native speakers as a big group [that we hope to join]. But what about individual native speakers who come to China. They need to do business with us. In order to communicate with us, won't they accept this kind of English? You can't deny the possibility that more and more native speakers turn to accept this kind of English over time ... We might never use this kind of English for our exams, as we know these are wrong. But written forms are not our major forms of communication. In oral communication, the errors in oral English are possible to be accepted.

This extract demonstrates the extent to which Jiajia took in the knowledge input, that is, the stimuli, provided by the moderator. She saw the numerical significance in terms of the issue of who would decide the future of English. She coped with challenges posed by her peers (i.e., Jing and Muka) who emphasised NESs' authority and reminded her of the risk that non-conformity to native English would be penalised in the educational system. While she tried not to challenge the traditional view of NESs' role as norm providers, she appealed for NNESs' role in English change and pointed out power struggle between NNESs and NESs. She rejected the view of Chinese speakers of English as passive receivers of English distributed by NESs (*they [i.e., NESs] can't make us do this or that*). She also understood that the pursuit of native English suited the purpose of being integrated with a native English speaker community (*we were talking about native speakers as a big group [that we hope to join].*) and suggested they consider NESs' needs to communicate with Chinese speakers for the purpose of business transaction outside native English community (*But what if individual native speakers come to China. They need to do business with us.*). The changing perspective implied an awareness of the changing role of English for Chinese speakers from a foreign language to a lingua franca. Her expression of NESs' needs to orient towards Chinese speakers was the complete opposite of her earlier insistence on Chinese speakers' needs to 'fit in' with NES identity. At this point, Jiajia became aware of Chinese speakers' linguistic right to use of English. Further, she addressed the issue of language assessment and made a strong claim that forms of English being tested according to native English norms were not appropriate for real life communication.

In short, extract 4 suggests the value of explicit knowledge input in the form of FG stimuli in encouraging Jiajia to reflect on the issues frequently discussed in the ELF literature, such as the changing role of English, the numerical significance of NNESs vis-a-vis NESs in the future change of English, communicative function of non-conformity to native English, NNESs' agency in the spread of English, and the status quo that native English prevailed.

Challenging the relevance of NESs for NNESs

Another indicator of Jiajia's LA development was the challenge to the relevance of NESs for NNES–NNES communication (see extract 5):

Extract 5

(1) Muka: But at the end of the day, it is still native speakers who decide, approve or disapprove. Only THEIR approval can make our use acceptable [...]

(2) Jiajia: [...] I went to English Corner in my first year of university and met an Indian guy. I personally think his English was very bad, very non-standard, and very unpleasant [...] in that situation, I communicated with him [...] but when he was talking with me, I just didn't feel that I could understand him. In that situation, shall I find a British speaker and ask him to judge our English and tell us what we should do between us?

This extract reveals the role of intercultural encounters. Jiajia drew on her life experience of intercultural encounter to challenge Muka's claim that NESs had power in gatekeeping Chinese speakers' English. The question Jiajia raised (*shall I turn to a British speaker and ask him to judge our English and tell us what we should do between us?*) was obviously a rhetorical question. In her encounter with an Indian speaker of English, it was neither practical to find a NES for reference nor necessary to have a third person involved in their negotiation.

Using this example, Jiajia seemed to suggest that NESs' power, maintained by language policy, was irrelevant to NNESs' use of English in practice. This inference was supported by the point Jiajia made earlier (see extract 3) and later (see extract 6) that interlocutors were not committed to fixed linguistic norms existing prior to their entry into particular communicative context but ready to adapt according to their on-site communicative needs. By comparing Muka and Jiajia in terms of how they argue for their own positions, the influence of linguistic experience on their language attitude became more salient. Muka kept claiming the authority of native English but never mentioned linguistic experience throughout the FG, whereas Jiajia frequently reflected on her own linguistic experience or used the experience of others such as Ding.

Extract 5 also unveils the role of the moderator's induction, that is, the stimuli. Jiajia's rhetorical question mirrored the question mentioned by the moderator in relation to Jenkins' (2007) discussion of ELF-related issues: why should NNESs refer to NESs in intercultural communications where NESs are often absent? It was possible that the stimuli facilitated Jiajia's reflection on her intercultural experience.

Unchanged belief about English in education

Despite the increasing LA, Jiajia's belief regarding what kind of English should be pursued in classrooms remained unchanged, as illustrated in extract 6.

Extract 6
(1) Ruo: [...] language is developing [...] why can't we have others learn our language? I don't mean Chinese, I mean, our English is developing, they should accept us, Chinese speakers' English, so that we learn from each other rather than we simply passively learn from them
(2) An: [What] you [said is] scaring. I'm going to be a teacher, you're suggesting no standard, no standard for teachers to teach-
(3) Lan: -A standard is needed for English teaching
[Two turns omitted]
(4) Ding: I have sympathy for her [i.e., An's] concern. She's talking about something related to education, but we're talking about something used for communication [...] the concept that [the moderator's name] mentioned applies to communication. Different things-
(5) Jiajia: -So we don't have disagreement. Nobody is going to abandon the standard. But when two persons are using English for communication, they have their internal agreement regarding how much they can deviate. We share this idea. This concept doesn't affect teaching. We teach standard [English], and we compromise while communicating.
[Ruo and Ding echo, nodding]

The group went through discussion and reached the consensus that Standard English was to be taught in classrooms, while 'compromise' was needed in their use of English outside the classroom. This strongly correlates with Ranta's (2010) finding about Finnish students' language attitude that 'real' English is their macro goal maintained by schools, while their micro goal is English that helps them to achieve their real life purposes out of school.

In this FG context, 'compromise' seems to have double connotations. On the one hand, with the focus on the situation where English is used, Jiajia seems to claim the inappropriateness of Standard English. This is supported by the expression 'internal agreement', which seems to suggest accommodation to communicative contexts. On the other hand, Jiajia seems to suggest compromising with the principle maintained by education that Standard English is to be pursued. In this sense, it could be argued that the agreement consolidates a hierarchy that Standard English was good, while Chinese speakers' English was less good.

Peer interaction was the highlight of extract 6, which showcases how Jiajia and her peers jointly constructed their understanding of ELF-related issues. A tension first rose between the supporter (Ruo) of Chinese speakers' own English and the challengers (An and Lan), revealing different views in terms of what kind of English was to be taught in classrooms. Then Ding suggested drawing a line between English learnt in classrooms and English used in real life outside classrooms and 'fixing' ENL and Chinese speakers' own English to different domains. His suggestion resolved the tension and was welcomed by the group.

While this extract illustrates that 'collaborative interactions enable students to construct hypotheses about language and surpass what they might have been able to do on their own' (Dagenais et al. 2008: 148), the hypothesis about English co-constructed in extract 6 was noticeably based on Ding's misinterpretation of the concept of ELF. Ding not only called attention to the moderator's message that ELF conceptualises English used as the chosen code for communication, but also noted that the moderator did not explicitly mention the implication of ELF for pedagogy. Simply because the moderator did not specify, Ding inferred that the concept of ELF was irrelevant to pedagogy. This reveals a form of 'false language awareness' in Ding (Svalberg 2001: 200) and implies the need for feedback on the group understanding of ELF or support from an expert so as to develop true knowledge of English.

Pedagogical implications

The FG study recalls previous research on consciousness-raising and gives an idea of what content can be integrated into a LA class and how a LA class can be conducted addressing the particular case of ELF. In the first place, this study suggests that exposure to linguistic data motivates reflection on cultural identity in relation to English. Exposure to linguistic examples is welcomed in traditional LA research for the sake of raising awareness of native English conventions (e.g., Bowker 1999; Dodigovic 2003). From an English as an International Language (EIL) perspective, Flowerdew (2012) suggests that the use of corpora can raise the awareness that English is not just native English. Further, Jiajia's LA development confirms the importance of personal experience in shaping attitudes. Moreover, the input of explicit knowledge about the global spread of English helps to raise ELF awareness. Explicit knowledge is found to have an immediate impact on L2 learners' consciousness of linguistic features (e.g., Butler 2002; Ellis 2004; Hu 2011) and language skills (e.g., Cross 2010; Ruan 2014; Zhang 2010). In this study, it motivated Jiajia to recall her intercultural experience and to reflect on how English worked in real life situations. As a result, she questioned the default role of ENL as the only model for Chinese speakers.

This study sees the relevance of traditional themes of pedagogy, such as learner exploration, peer interaction and teachers' role, for LA development. Basically, Jiajia's transformation from an adherent to NES monolingualism to a questioner of the relevance of NESs for NNESs is a journey of self-exploration. She drew on her own linguistic experience and engaged in her peers' arguments, while she formed her attitude gradually through the FG. From a cognitive perspective, Wells (1999) claims that speakers benefit from the process of verbalising their understanding in dialogic interaction in terms of knowledge construction. Based on sociocultural theory, Dagenais et al. (2008) find that group discussion offers opportunities for the participants to collaborate in making sense of socio-linguistic phenomenon, foster discursive co-construction of new knowledge about linguistic diversity, and develop a critical stance on the hierarchy of languages. This study confirms the value of peer interaction in LA raising, manifesting how the FG members shared their own knowledge and experience with their peers to co-construct views of English and their own English.

To some extent, the FG moderator's role resembled that of a teacher (see Richards and Rodgers 2001). She served as the primary source of knowledge about ELF and provided examples of Chinese speakers' English. She organised the FG and created an atmosphere that was easy for the participants to express their opinions. She also encouraged the participants to speak and facilitated the group discussion to move on. She planned the task and sequenced the questions to be discussed. However, the moderator offered no feedback or support when misunderstanding occurred or when the FG appeared to need help from an expert. This study reveals the difficulty in developing the acceptance of Chinese speakers' non-conformity to native English in a context where teacher guidance was absent.

In addition, the FG study features discussion in the participants' first language. While it is good to organise English-medium discussion, it might be good for the teacher to focus on the purpose of boosting student understanding by encouraging them freely to express their ideas in their first language if it is preferred.

Raising ELF awareness in university classrooms

According to Bolitho et al. (2003: 251), teachers need to consider LA development by helping learners to 'gain insights into how languages work' and encourage them to 'discover language for themselves' (Hawkins 1984 in Bolitho et al. 2003: 251). Current study shows the influence of student exploration and reveals the need for teacher support. According to Murray (2010: 293), learners benefit from both inductive approach-informed activities that 'break away from simplistic explanations of form-function correspondences' and a deductive approach-based appreciation of general principles that underlie speech acts. Following this, a guided LA approach is proposed, integrating teacher support and student exploration and including the aspects as discussed in the rest of this section.

Providing explicit knowledge

Sifakis (2014) considers the primary task for ELF-aware teacher education to be the introduction to ELF-related literature. In the same vein, students can benefit from knowledge in this respect. A considerable body of literature offers sources of knowledge about the spread of English, covering the historical, political and sociocultural contexts of the spread of English, the statistics of users of English around the world, and the variation of English as a consequence of its spread (e.g., Crystal 2003; Graddol et al. 2007). Among others (e.g., Cogo and Dewey 2012; Jenkins 2007), a comprehensive discussion of ELF as a concept can be found in Seidlhofer (2011), which poses fundamental challenges to the idea of native English as the only reference of English and reconsiders conventional concepts, such as nativeness, language, culture, and community. Students can be introduced to the literature and guided to explore issues discussed in it.

It is also important to help students understand the issue of linguistic right in the discussion of linguistic diversity. It would be helpful to introduce university students to different perspectives on the spread of English and different Englishes so as to promote critical analysis of native English and other kinds of English. Critical voices can be found in Phillipson (1992) and Pennycook (1994) with regards to the spread of English. The Quirk–Kachru debate in *English Today* journal provides good resources to provoke reflections on different forms of English (Kachru 1991; Quirk 1990). While it is still a popular view that 'the true repository of the English language is its native speakers' (Trudgill 2002: 151), Jenkins' (2014) book offers in-depth discussion of the complexity of English language policies and practices in academic ELF discourse and points to the need for a total change of mind-set regarding native English as the exclusively preferred English.

Using authentic ELF data

Flowerdew (2012) sees a few advantages to using corpora to support language learning from an EIL perspective. As he points out, a wide range of corpora proves that 'real' English is not just native English and corpora representing various Englishes can help students to understand multilingualism in reality. He also hypothesises that a diversity of corpora allow for more cultural assumptions than those exclusively associated with native English. He further notes that language learners' needs and wants should be respected, and so they should not be exposed to mainstream native English exclusively. While these points certainly provide support to the value of authentic ELF data, the limitations of Flowerdew's suggestion need to be considered in order for authentic ELF data to be effective for ELF awareness development. Firstly, noticing the diversity features does not necessarily lead to positive attitude to English that does not conform to mainstream norms (e.g., Dewey 2012; Galloway and Rose 2014). Secondly, teachers cannot assume how students perceive their needs or wants. A body of research shows a wide spread of aspiration for native English and some studies reveal that students perceive a need for native English in the era of ELF (e.g., Groom 2012; Kuo 2006; Timmis 2002). Wang (2013) looks into the complexity of language attitude and finds that aspiration for native English relates to the symbolic power, whereas English that does not conform to native English is motivated by needs for cultural and communicative effects. The point is that teachers need to help students to identify their needs and wants for English that is relevant to their context of use.

To utilise ELF corpora for the purpose of ELF awareness, teachers first need to select and present authentic ELF data that is appropriate to the class. A few ELF corpora offer authentic ELF data, including Vienna-Oxford International Corpus of English (www.univie.ac.at/voice/) and the ELF academic corpus (http://www.helsinki.fi/englanti/elfa/elfacorpus). Traditional ELT corpora are usually presented in order to show similarity of linguistic features and to prescribe usage on that basis. ELF corpora, on the other hand, should be presented in order to show diversity of features and be used descriptively not prescriptively.

More importantly, teachers can use questions to facilitate student understanding of ELF-related issues and to guide students in consulting their own needs and wants for English that is relevant to their context. Possible questions include:

- What is your purpose of learning and using English? What kind of English do you think would suit your purpose?

- What do you think makes a successful communication? Is your view relevant to the contexts in which you might use English?
- Are there any features of this ELF data which fit in or conflict with your views of good English? What are the implications of the comparisons for your language learning and practice?
- What do you think of the speakers' use of English? Do you like their way of using English? Why?
- Do you think that the speakers have achieved their purposes? If yes, how? If no, what do you think are possible reasons?

This approach will boost student understanding of the nature of ELF communication and further free them from the reliance on prescribed rules of Standard English. However, teachers need to make it explicit that the use of ELF data does not encourage students to imitate the patterns emerging in the data but helps them to discover the strategies underlying successful communication. To assist students, the teacher can have students work in groups to evaluate the acceptability of given examples of English and discuss the criteria behind their judgement. Then, the teacher checks student explanations of their criteria. Attention can be paid to whether and how students draw on the information that the teacher provides prior to their discussion. Feedback can be offered if misunderstandings occur or if students struggle to make sense of the abstract concept.

Increasing intercultural encounters

As Garrett (2010) notes, personal experience provides a major source of attitude formation. Nevertheless, experience can lead to positive or negative attitudes. Jenkins (2007) finds that teachers associated negative attitudes towards ELF with their unpleasant experience of being criticised about their own English. In light of this, simply reflecting on linguistic experience does not necessarily lead to better LA. In Galloway and Rose's (2014: 9) research on student awareness of ELF, they find that student exposure to various Englishes was 'less successful' in having students understand how ELF works in real life than eliciting their own 'stereotypes and prejudices' about Englishes. They further suggest that 'with careful guidance, listening journals can be a useful tool' to help students understand that ELF is more relevant for them than native English. Bearing in mind the importance of teacher guidance, teachers can draw on students' cultural and communicative experiences, encourage them to reflect on those and analyse the reasons for communicative breakdown, and how the students feel about the use of English in their communicative contexts.

Secondly, listening and reading materials can be selected from those generated in a diversity of English, including both native English and non-native English, for students' listening and reading tasks. Alternatively, students can be asked to write for an imaginary readership which includes both NESs and

NNESs or which includes NNESs only. This task can help students to think about what kind of English is appropriate to serve the target readers from different first language backgrounds and why.

Necessarily, teachers should keep checking student understanding through-out different activities and offer feedback when needed to avoid 'false' LA. No matter what activities are conducted, teachers' language attitudes play a crucial role in student LA. Thus, teachers need to focus on meaning and content pro-duced in student performance rather than linguistic forms used by students for different learning tasks. By doing this, teachers can release students from the worry that non-conformity to native English would be penalised. Moreover, teachers serve as role models for students and thus their linguistic behaviour can influence students' language attitudes.

Conclusions

This study attends to consciousness-raising of English in its sociocultural context of globalisation and explores possible ways of raising ELF awareness among Chinese university students by identifying positive factors and difficul-ties in their LA development. It leads to the proposal of a *guided LA approach*, which highlights both teacher intervention and student exploration and offers suggestions about what an ELF awareness class should include. While focused on Chinese university students, the findings resonate with other studies on consciousness-raising among participants from other cultural backgrounds. The proposal made on the basis of Chinese students' ELF awareness-raising is thus not culture-specific but relevant to classrooms in other settings.

Teachers need to be aware of ELF before they can organise awareness-raising activities. In this regard, research reveals that some teachers are aware of ELF but confined by the native English-focused ELT system (see Dewey 2012; Jenkins 2007). This is true for China. As Wen notes (2012: 372), 'some teach-ers, although they are in support of ELF conceptually, do not know what to do when the old system of English teaching that has been really powerful, remains untouched'. Nevertheless, while individual teachers cannot change the whole teaching and testing system that is deeply influenced by native English mono-lingualism, they can help students to make a critical analysis of what different Englishes can offer them and what they need by learning and using English so as to make an informed choice. On the other hand, raising ELF awareness does not suggest the exclusion of native English in language classrooms but draws attention to the diversity of English including both native and non-native Englishes. It is the hope of this chapter that the struggle and hesitation between exornormative and endonormative orientations (see Wang 2013) in association with the incomplete knowledge of English in current sociolinguis-tic reality can be resolved by increasing awareness of ELF and, in turn, Chinese students can be empowered and informed in making their own choice of language and using various linguistic resources with confidence.

Engagement priorities

This chapter has explored possible ways of developing student LA. Dewey (2012: 167) finds that teachers struggle with 'the duality' that means that on the one hand they are responsible for addressing student needs for ELF use while on the other they also have to follow institutional requirements that are bound by 'norm-based accounts of language and language testing'. His suggestion is to promote 'awareness of the sociolinguistics of English' among teachers (Dewey 2012: 167). Therefore, the following questions might deserve further discussion by English language teachers or teachers who use English as a medium of instruction:

1. This study reveals the conflict between what ELF researchers believe and what students are concerned with. While researchers believe that non-native speakers have a right to use English in their own way, participants in this study were concerned with questions that were exclusively oriented towards native English. How do you think that teachers, who have to take into account both linguistic research and students needs, can best address this conflict?
2. This study reports some positive effects of ELF encounters on the participants' language attitudes. Importantly, however, ELF does not mean 'anything goes'. How do you think students would react to the data showing unsuccessful intercultural encounters? How would you as teachers react to the data showing unsuccessful intercultural encounters? How could you help your students analyse the data and develop students' critical understanding of English-related issues?
3. This study focuses on Chinese university students. Do you think the discussion in this chapter based on a focus group context is applicable to other age groups or other contexts that you have encountered or might encounter in your teaching? If so, to what extent?

Appendix 6.1   Focus group handout

Statistics of English users in the world

Görlach(2002): 370 million native English speakers, 220 million second language English speakers, 240 million other speakers of English

Jenkins(2003): 337,407,300 native English speakers, 235,351,300 second language English speakers.

Jenkins (2009): 329,140,800 native English speakers, 430,614,500second language English speakers.

Crystal (2008): 2 billion English users around the world

Examples of Chinese speakers' English

- Extra vowel: and /ændə/.
- Nasalised vowels
- /ʒ/ pronounced as /r/
- indistinguishable between /v/ and /z/
- indistinguishable between /l/ and /n/
- Stress on final pronouns

Syntax: *This morning I bought a book.*
             Before I left the office, I had finished the work.
Pragmatic: *Have you eaten?*

Appendix 6.2 Transcription conventions (adapted from Jenkins 2007 and VOICE website)

[	Overlapping speech starts
Full stop.	To indicate termination
[...]	Author's gaps
CAPITAL	In a louder voice
[author's commentary]	Author's commentary
Hyphen-	Interruption, the beginning of interrupter's turn
Utter-	Abrupt cut-off, unfinished utterance

References

Bamgboṣe, A. (1998). Torn between the norms: Innovations in world Englishes. *World Englishes* 17(1): 1–14.

Berg, B. L. (2007). *Qualitative research methods for the social sciences.* 6th ed. Boston, Mass.; London: Pearson Education Allyn & Bacon.

Bolitho, R., R. Carter, R. Hughes, R. Ivanič, H. Masuhara and B. Tomlinson. (2003). Ten questions about language awareness. *ELT Journal* 57(3): 251–259.

Bowker, L. (1999). Exploring the potential of corpora for raising language awareness in student translators. *Language Awareness* 8(3–4): 160–173.

Bryman, A. (2001). *Social research methods.* Oxford: Oxford University Press.

Butler, Y. G. (2002). Second language learners' theories on the use of English articles: An analysis of the metalinguistic knowledge used by Japanese students in acquiring the English article system. *Studies in Second Language Acquisition* 24: 451–480.

Callies, M. and Keller, W. R. (2008). The teaching and acquisition of focus constructions: An integrated approach to language awareness across the curriculum. *Language Awareness* 17(3): 249–266.

Carter, R. (2003). Key concepts in ELT: Language awareness. *ELT Journal* 57(1): 64–65.

Cogo, A. and Dewey, M. (2012). *Analyzing English as a Lingua Franca: A corpus-driven investigation.* London; New York: Continuum.

Cross, J. (2010). Raising L2 listeners' metacognitive awareness: A sociocultural theory perspective. *Language Awareness* 19(4): 281–297.

Crystal, D. (2003). *English as a global language.* 2nd ed. Cambridge: Cambridge University Press.

Crystal, D. (2008). Two thousand million. *English Today* 24(1): 3–6.

Dagenais, D., Walsh, N., Armand, F. and Maraillet, E. (2008). Collaboration and co-construction of knowledge during language awareness activities in Canadian elementary school. *Language Awareness* 17(2): 139–155.

Deterding, D. (2006). The pronunciation of English by speakers from China. *English World-Wide* 27(2): 175–198.

Dewey, M. (2012). Towards a post-normative approach: Learning the pedagogy of ELF. *Journal of English as a Lingua Franca* 1(1): 141–170.

Dodigovic, M. (2003). Natural Language Processing (NLP) as an instrument of raising the language awareness of learners of English as a second language. *Language Awareness* 12(3–4): 187–203.

Ellis, R. (2004). The definition and measurement of L2 explicit knowledge. *Language Learning* 54: 227–275.

Flowerdew, J. (2012). Corpora in language teaching from the perspective of English as an international language. In Alsagoff, L., McKay, S. L., Hu, G. and Renandya, W. R. (eds), *Principles and Practices for Teaching English as an International Language*. New York and London: Routledge, pp. 226–243.

Galloway, N. and Rose, H. (2014). Using listening journals to raise awareness of Global Englishes in ELT. *ELT Journal* 68(4): 386–396.

Garrett, P. (2010). *Attitudes to language*. Cambridge: Cambridge University Press.

Görlach, M. (2002). *Still more Englishes*. Amsterdam: John Benjamins Publication.

Graddol, D., Leith, D., Swann, J., Rhys, M. and Gillen, J. (eds). (2007). *Changing English*. London: Routledge.

Groom, C. (2012). Non-native attitudes towards teaching English as a lingua franca in Europe. *English Today* 28(1): 50–57.

Hales, T. (1997). Exploring data-driven language awareness. *ELT Journal* 51(3): 217–223.

Hawkins, E. (1992). Awareness of language/knowledge about language in the curriculum in England and Wales: An historical note on twenty years of Curricular Debate. *Language Awareness* 1(1): 5–17.

Hennink, M. M. (2007). *International focus group research: A handbook for the health and social sciences*. Cambridge: Cambridge University Press.

Hu, G. (2011). Metalinguistic knowledge, metalanguage, and their relationship in L2 learners. *System* 39(1): 63–77.

Jenkins, J. (2000). *The phonology of English as an international language: New models, new norms, new goals*. Oxford: Oxford University Press.

Jenkins, J. (2003). *World Englishes: A resource book for students*. London; New York: Routledge.

Jenkins, J. (2007). *English as a Lingua Franca: Attitude and identity*. Oxford; New York: Oxford University Press.

Jenkins, J. (2009). *World Englishes: A resource book for students*. 2nd ed. London; New York: Routledge.

Jenkins, J. (2014). *English as a Lingua Franca in the international university: The politics of academic English language policy*. London; New York: Routledge.

Jenkins, J. (2015). *Global Englishes: A resource book for students*. 3rd ed. London; New York: Routledge.

Kachru, B. (1991). Liberation linguistics and the Quirk concern. *English Today* 25: 3–13.

Kalocsai, K. (2009). Erasmus exchange students: A behind-the-scenes view into an ELF community of practice. *Apples – Journal of Applied Language Studies* 3(1): 25–49.

Kuo, I. C. (2006). Addressing the issue of teaching English as a lingua franca. *ELT Journal* 60(3): 213–221.

Labov, W. (1966). *The social stratification of language in New York City*. Washington, DC: CAL.

Lippi-Green, R. (1994). Accent, standard language ideology, and discriminatory pretext in the courts. *Language in Society* 23: 163–198.

Mauranen, A. (2012). *Exploring ELF: Academic English shaped by non-native speakers*. Cambridge: Cambridge University Press.

Mauranen, A. and Ranta, E. (2009). *English as a Lingua Franca: Studies and findings*. Newcastle upon Tyne: Cambridge Scholars Publishing.

Murray, N. (2010). Pragmatics, awareness raising, and the Cooperative Principle. *ELT Journal* 64(3): 293–301.

Pennycook, A. (1994). *The cultural politics of English as an international language*. London: Longman.

Phillipson, R. (1992). *Linguistic imperialism*. Oxford: Oxford University Press.

Porto, M. (2010). Culturally responsive L2 education: an awareness-raising proposal. *ELT Journal* 64(1): 45–53.

Quirk, R. (1990).Language varieties and standard language. *English Today* 6(1): 3–10.

Ranta, E. (2010). English in the real world vs. English at school: Finnish English teachers' and students' views. *International Journal of Applied Linguistics* 20(2): 156–177.

Richards, J. C. and Rodgers, T. S. (2001). *Approaches and methods in language teaching*. 2nd ed. Cambridge: Cambridge University Press.

Ruan, Z. (2014). Metacognitive awareness of EFL student writers in a Chinese ELT context. *Language Awareness* 23(1–2): 71–69.

Seidlhofer, B. (2011). *Understanding English as a Lingua Franca*. Oxford: Oxford University Press.

Sifakis, N. C. (2014). ELF awareness as an opportunity for change: A transformative perspective for ESOL teacher education. *Journal of English as a Lingua Franca* 3(2): 317–335.

Svalberg, A. M. L. (2001). The problem of false language awareness. *Language Awareness* 10(2–3): 200–212.

Timmis, I. (2002). Native-speaker norms and international English: a classroom view. *ELT Journal* 56(3): 240–249.

Trudgill, P. (2002). *Sociolinguistic variation and change*. Edinburgh: Edinburgh University Press.

Valeo, A. (2013). Language awareness in a content-based language programme. *Language Awareness* 22(2): 126–145.

Wang, Y. (2012). Chinese speakers' perceptions of their English in intercultural communication. Unpublished doctoral thesis, University of Southampton.

Wang, Y. (2013). Non-conformity to ENL norms: A perspective from Chinese English users. *Journal of English as a Lingua Franca* 2(2): 255–282.

Wells, G. (1999). *Dialogic inquiry: Towards a sociocultural practice and theory of education*. New York: Cambridge University Press.

Wen, Q. (2012). English as a lingua franca: A pedagogical perspective. *Journal of English as a Lingua Franca* 1(2): 371–376.

Xu, Z. (2008). Analysis of syntactic features of Chinese English. *Asian Englishes* 11(2): 4–31.

Zhang, J. L. (2010). A dynamic metacognitive systems account of Chinese university students' knowledge about EFL reading. *TESOL Quarterly* 44(2): 320–353.

7

ELF-Aware In-Service Teacher Education: A Transformative Perspective

Yasemin Bayyurt and Nicos C. Sifakis

Introduction

Recent work in the field of English as a Lingua Franca (henceforth ELF) has been focused on defining, delineating, and clarifying the nature of ELF. While some work has addressed issues of teacher education and training (see below for a review), we have yet to see a comprehensive proposal that aims both to educate English as a Foreign Language (henceforth EFL) or English as a Second Language (henceforth ESL) teachers about ELF and to engage them in developing, teaching, and evaluating ELF-aware lessons in their own teaching context.

In this chapter we will present the findings from a teacher education project that attempts to do just that. This project, based on a proposal of Sifakis (2007) and located at Bogazici University in Istanbul, aims (a) to educate in-service teachers from Turkey and Greece about ELF concerns and (b) to urge them to develop and teach ELF-aware lessons. One of the project's original features is that it is entirely distance-oriented. It does not require teachers to attend face-to-face seminars in which they are told about ELF; instead, they read selections from the literature on global English, ELF, and English as an International Language (henceforth EIL), and respond to questions that prompt them to reflect on issues linking what they have read with their own teaching experience. Their responses are collected online for sharing and discussion in a Forum specially designed for the project. In the second phase of the project, the teachers develop, teach, and evaluate newly created lessons based on their understanding of ELF. We will summarise the theoretical background of the project, present some key findings, and discuss implications for ELF-aware teacher development programmes.

ELF implications for the EFL classroom and for teacher education

A powerful message coming from ELF research is that we live in a world that can be described as increasingly post-EFL insofar as EFL is native-speaker-oriented in its norms (Standard English), curricula, testing orientations, and attitudes resulting from the desire to emulate native speakers of English. This post-EFL paradigm is oriented to the processes and practices found in non-native-speaker interactions. What also becomes clear from the literature is that the post-EFL world is dauntingly complex, both in interactional contexts and teaching-learning contexts.

It is probably for reasons closely linked to post-EFL complexity that early ELF research shied away from any extended examination of the implications that ELF-related research has for English for Speakers of Other Languages (henceforth ESOL) classrooms. Seidlhofer characterised an attempt to link ELF research with the EFL/ESL classroom as 'premature [...] before certain prerequisites have been met' (Seidlhofer 2004: 209). Since then, however, some major descriptions of ELF include at least some references to the EFL/ESL classroom (see, e.g., Jenkins 2007: 241; Seidlhofer 2011: 196–198) and more recent ELF research has continued to suggest implications for pedagogy. For example, in a paper on pronunciation negotiation strategies in an ELF context, Matsumoto (2011) concludes by prompting teachers to familiarise learners with successful ELF interactions and goes on to suggest that learners should be provided 'with opportunities for discussion of the differences between NS-NNS interaction and ELF interaction, and on differences in ELF speakers' accents' (Matsumoto 2011: 110). Potential learner awareness of successful ELF interaction is one result of ELF research conducted in specific contexts. Mauranen mentions the benefits for learners and users engaged in academic ELF interactions, as well as for interpreters, translators, and text editors, of an understanding of processes enhancing explicitness (2012: 235). Fernández-Polo (2014) discusses the use of the phrase 'I mean' in conference presentations given by ELF speakers and points out the benefits of making ESP learners' aware of the processes behind successful and problematic explicitation strategies in ELF interactions. Seidlhofer (2009) discusses the way ELF users co-construct idiomatic expressions as a means of both communicating effectively and establishing a shared affective space.

Other implications for pedagogy have been suggested from studies of ELF corpora, such as the VOICE corpus (Hülmbauer 2010; Pitzl 2012) and the ELFA corpus (Mauranen and Ranta 2009; Metsä-Ketelä 2012; Carey 2013). Further suggested implications may be found in studies that do not have an overt ELF orientation, but nevertheless address issues worth considering in interactions between non-native users – see Lindemann and Subtirelu (2013), for example, for a discussion of the effect that social factors have on perceptions of L2 speech.

However interesting and enlightening the studies' insights, ELF researchers remain largely uninterested in the ways in which teachers can make use of them, and pedagogical implications of their research, though hinted at, remain largely unexplored. The reasons may be summarised as follows: 'We do not believe it is our place to tell teachers what to do, but that it is for English Language Teaching (henceforth ELT) practitioners to decide whether/to what extent ELF is relevant to their learners in their context' (Jenkins 2011: 492).

Notwithstanding the reluctance of ELF researchers to explore pedagogical implications, there have been some attempts to link our growing understanding of ELF to teacher education. For example, Sifakis (2007) put forward a proposal for a transformative teacher education component that targets EFL teachers' convictions and established practices about teaching, learning, and language use through an action research roadmap. Blair (2015) outlines the basics of a pedagogy that prioritises the 'post-native' model of learner multicompetence and focuses on informing teachers and learners about the variability and diversity of English. Dewey (2012) offers an evaluation of teacher qualification programmes and finds them problematic in terms of the real impact of ELF on their claims about language accuracy, correctness, context, and teacher autonomy.

Central to any examination of the implications of ELF research for teacher education is a concern for teachers' perceptions and attitudes towards ELF and ELF-related issues. So far, a contrasting picture has emerged: on the one hand, there is a willingness to find out more about ELF and non-native speakers' successful interaction strategies; on the other hand, there is confusion about what needs to be done to integrate the teaching of such strategies into established, EFL-bound practices. For example, a study of Greek state school EFL teachers showed that their awareness of the need to prepare learners to communicate with other NNSs did not deter them from the traditional EFL practice of teaching Standard, or native English (Sifakis and Sougari 2005). Other studies (Matsuda 2009; Sifakis 2009) have recorded teachers' resistance to a more pluralistic understanding of English. Bayyurt's (2006) study of Turkish EFL teachers' perceptions of culture revealed the predominance of traditional EFL practices while finding little awareness of the changing status of English. Llurda (2009) highlighted the function of non-native teachers as promoters of English as an international language in a pedagogical context that is still largely norm-dependent. As Jenkins has shown (Jenkins 2007, 2011: 307), implementation of an ELF-aware pedagogy is largely dependent on the shifting of teachers' and learners' attitudes.

For any radical changes in ELT pedagogy to occur, they must first be considered and reflected upon in the mind-sets of individual teachers. For Widdowson, the usefulness of ELF is in helping us 'to consider its effect as a catalyst for change in established ways of thinking' (2012: 5). Similarly, Seidlhofer argues for the need to replace a 'normative mind-set' with the recognition that norms are 'continually shifting and changing' (2008: 33–34). Dewey argues for the need for teachers 'to re-examine current methodology and practice in context-relevant ways' (2012: 141). And, according to Park and Wee, teachers 'should proceed to question some of the more deeply rooted assumptions [they] hold about language' (2011: 368).

Towards an ELF-aware teacher education

In light of the above, what is needed is an approach that will help teachers to appreciate (a) principles that arise from ELF research and (b) how these principles might have a bearing on their own teaching context. Such an approach would start teachers on a reflective journey in which they think critically about established teaching practice and their convictions concerning English as a medium of communication.

In this chapter, we present insights from a teacher education project (called the English as a Lingua Franca-Teacher Education (ELF-TEd) project, http:// teacherdevelopment.boun.edu.tr/) that attempted to do exactly that. The project was headed by the authors and its first phase was carried out during the 2012–2013 school year at Bogazici University in Istanbul, Turkey. It involved EFL teachers from Turkey and from Greece who were interested in finding out more about ELF and the impact their discoveries might have on their teaching. The project had two phases. In the first phase, we asked participants first to read excerpts from the published literature on ELF, EIL, and World Englishes (henceforth WE), and then to respond to questions aimed at helping them to reflect on implications for teaching. In the second phase, we asked them to design lessons or sets of activities that employed what they had learnt about ELF. Subsequently, they were expected to teach and record these lessons, and then, as a final step, write their reflections on the whole experience.

The reflective process is based on a proposal by Sifakis (2007). It is intended to make teachers conscious of their deep convictions about Standard English, the role of native speakers, the importance of mutual intelligibility in interactions involving non-native speakers, and their own role as feedback providers in the classroom. The suitability of the transformative framework (Mezirow 1991; Mezirow and Associates 2000) lies in the fact that it prompts participants to consider what Mezirow calls a 'disorienting dilemma', namely, a psychological situation triggered by a life experience or event on which participants can build a critical mechanism that will help them, with input from their colleagues, to confront and ultimately change their established 'frames of reference'. In the ELF-TEd project, the disorienting dilemmas were stimulated by the readings provided and the questions that were asked.

At the core of the ELF-TEd project is the notion of 'ELF-awareness'. We did not require teachers to accept the ELF 'gospel', nor did we merely inform them about ELF and related issues. Instead, we exposed them to those issues, prompted them to think about them, and asked them to connect what they were learning to their own context for teaching. For this reason, it was essential that they design, teach, and evaluate lessons that embodied their engagement with the issues. As a result, it was hoped, participants would take a step toward becoming 'ELF-aware' teachers, in the sense that they would be fully aware of constraints on their teaching and autonomous about using their knowledge of ELF to the advantage of their learners.

Twelve teachers participated in the study (11 from Turkey and one from Greece). Four taught in primary schools, three in Turkey and one in Greece, four in secondary schools, and four in a university. In this chapter, we analyse the perceptions of three non-native secondary school English language teachers throughout the different stages of the project in order to see how these perceptions relate to classroom practice. The three teachers worked in three different state schools – two in Istanbul and one in Sakarya. They taught English to ninth and tenth graders (14–16 years old). Perin taught in Sakarya, a one-and-a-half hour drive from Istanbul. Gamze taught at a highly competitive Anatolian High School in Istanbul, and Sude taught at a less competitive high school, also in Istanbul. Gamze, with more than 20 years of teaching experience, was the most experienced of the three. Perin and Sude had been teaching for between five and ten years. Perin was in the process of completing an MA programme, whereas Gamze and Sude already had MA degrees. None of the teachers had any prior knowledge of ELF. Perin responded to 55 questions, almost half of the questions on the project portal based on the readings on ELF and ELF related publications that were assigned weekly; Gamze and Sude responded to all 118 questions. All three teachers prepared, implemented, and evaluated lesson plans and participated in discussion sessions in which they shared their plans and evaluations.

The first phase of the ELF-TEd project lasted eight months, from 1 October 2012 to 31 May 2013. Every two weeks we had face-to-face focus-group meetings with the teachers where we discussed issues arising from their reflections. Perin missed two of these meetings, but Gamze and Sude, besides contributing actively to the website, attended all of them.

Procedure

We used two methods of data collection: online and face-to-face. At the start of the project, teachers were asked to upload their brief autobiographies on the project's portal. They then uploaded their reflections-responses to the questions based on the readings on the project portal (www.teacherdevelopment.boun. edu.tr). Before face-to-face meetings, they would receive email prompts that prepared them for the meetings, to which they also responded via email. In the final stage of the project, they uploaded their lesson plans, together with reflections on how each lesson went. The data collected from the face-to-face meetings included focus-group interviews and group discussions that focused on prompting teachers to report their experience of their transformative process.

We used content analysis and thematic analysis to uncover meaning in the participants' responses to questions, their reflections after the trial lessons, and their self-evaluations. According to Braun and Clarke (2006), thematic analysis is a qualitative analytic enquiry used for 'identifying, analysing, and reporting patterns (themes) within data. It minimally organises and describes your data set in (rich) detail' (2006: 79). Mayring (2004) describes content analysis as 'systematic examination of communicative material. [...] What is essential, however, is that the communicative material should be fixed or recorded in some form' (2004: 266). In this study, thematic analysis was used to identify categories found in the data, and content analysis was used to examine the written, spoken, and visual data in relation to the categories. Content analysis can be applied to recorded material, open-ended responses to interview questions, survey questions, and so on.

Two broad thematic categories emerged from the content analysis of portal entries, teachers' reflections, and focus group interviews: one involving issues concerning native/non-native speakers of English, and one regarding emerging topics in the pedagogy of ELF in secondary school classrooms. In the first category, teachers focused on the sub-themes of intelligibility, communities of practice, and the ownership of English, whereas in the second category, their reflections focused on ELF-aware language teaching methodology and ELF-aware language teaching materials.

Teachers' reflections

Although other data resources were also examined, due to space restrictions we will present only our analysis of the teachers' uploaded responses to questions. The data will be analysed in the light of the themes that are described above, that is, the components of nativeness/non-nativeness issues and ELF-aware pedagogy. The first category includes teachers' comments on the use of English in and out of their language classes, on the facilitating function of intelligibility in communications in and out of their language classes, and on the ownership of English, whether it belongs to native speakers only or to both native and non-native speakers. Focus group interview data includes teachers' reflections on answers shared on the web site and on their ELF-aware lesson plans.

How do teachers perceive the nativeness/non-nativeness issue and implications that arise from it for their own teaching context? For our participants, the global character of English is a powerful mechanism of communication that should be appreciated by learners, as the following extracts from teacher responses show:

> To me as a teacher, in class, power is the ideas that the students have. English is the medium to share the ideas all around the world, so my aim is

to give importance to the comprehension side of this global language. (P1: Gamze, question 2)

When students do not be aware of the globalization of English, they have a tendency of criticizing their peers, even their teachers and regional English speaker teachers for not using standard English especially, their pronunciations. [...] There are different varieties of English all over the world and teachers of English even the ones who are native speakers should have knowledge of different varieties of lexis, discourse, grammar and pronunciations [...] students should be aware of all these variations. (P2: Sude, question 2)

However, teachers are practical too, when thinking about the practical implications for their teaching context. It is important for learners to have an awareness of the powerful ways in which English can help them grow as citizens of the world, but they need to understand that what is important is the successful use of English in this global context. In other words, global English should not be equated with an 'anything goes' attitude:

It is not possible to teach all the varieties of English, so we absolutely need some basic standard forms. (P5: Perin, question 2)

What this quotation also implies is that the global character of English needs an alternative pedagogical model, one that would not prioritise standard varieties of English, but one that would still integrate a rule-based system of English that would combine successful communication patterns across many different global settings involving non-native interlocutors. As the following teacher acknowledges, this is easier said than done:

The idea of ELF is a really great change in pedagogy as well. [...] This could be an encouraging thing for the people who cannot speak English in order not to make errors. I have a student in my class. She is a 10th grader. I cannot encourage her to speak. Her father is a judge. Finding correctness may take place in her family, but two weeks ago when the foreign students did an interactive lesson, she reacted them and answered some questions which I asked her to do. This helped her see that ELF is available in communication. (P1: Gamze, question 43)

What this means, essentially, is that learners should first understand and then accept, in their hearts, that they are ELF speakers. This is difficult, as attitudes and deeper convictions about what is desirable and achievable (in the form of the native speaker model of standardness) will contradict reality. It is for this reason that learners' exposure to real, successful (not in the sense of 'correct') interactions involving non-native interlocutors in different global contexts is of paramount importance. As the following excerpt shows, our participants understand this well:

> I agree with the misconception of 'only NNS is accented'. There are some different accents in my own language (L1), too. Each language has some different accents. Speaking with accent does not mean lack of intelligibility. And, the misconception (NNS is responsible for communication problems) is especially important. Actually, most of the NNSs are fed with the same resources. And these are the books and other audio-lingual materials printed and published by the NS's countries. Native speakers are the ones who fed themselves with different sources like, their families, friends, social environments, cultures, and so on. In this case: How could NNS be responsible for communication problems? (P2: Sude, question 40)

A powerful way of becoming aware of the perils of deeply held convictions about the importance of native speaker standard norms in the teaching of English is relating them to what teachers and learners know very well, that is, their L1. The following quotation was a reflection from a teacher in response to a question following the reading of two articles from the ELF literature on intelligibility. What it shows is that thinking about our own context can help unlock these convictions and, subsequently, unblock teachers and learners from realising the true potential of successful ELF communication:

> What is interesting for me is that the monolingual norms are undesirable in some contexts such as pronouncing the words according to RP. To tell the truth, this is new for me, and proves me the power of ELF [...] At this point, I consider my mother tongue. [...] Most of the people in Turkey do not use Istanbul Turkish even if they are educated, so different regions use different ways of speech. That can be quite possible in English as well. If this is the truth, we cannot insist on that merely the native speakers represent what is intelligible. (P5: Perin, question 40)

What our findings show is that different teachers respond differently to the implications of ELF regarding the teaching of specific norms. For example, for the following teacher, exposure to the rich variety of Englishes in the world does not imply the need for a clear rule-based system that should be used in this alternative pedagogical mode mentioned above:

> Quite the contrary to the custodians of the language, I believe, if there is, diversity, there is richness. While I am reading Widdowson's article I start to think about the reason why most Turkish teachers give importance to

teaching grammar. Could it be the respect to the owners of the language, could it be a way to teach Standard English by 'showing symbolic of solidarity'. Could it be a way to introduce the culture of the owners? Maybe showing us that English is an international language may help us giving less importance to grammar. We may find ways to show that English serves the communicative and communal needs of us, the speakers. (P1: Gamze, question 26)

When prompted to think about their role as custodians of English for their learners (following their reading of Widdowson's 1994 article on the ownership of English), this teacher offers a very concise perspective regarding the ownership of English when non-native speakers are involved:

I'm not a 'custodian' of English, but I feel myself as a person who has privilege of ownership of English, because I have used and taught it for years. [...] If this language has a right to invade everywhere in my country, I should have a right to own it. [...] Having this awareness is very important to adopt our changing role? (P2: Sude, question 26)

In response to the same issues, the following teacher goes even further:

To begin with, I can state that the author's view about the 'ownership' of English is simply the fact that no nation owns it. That is, if it is an international language, we cannot discuss the issue of who owns it? Instead, we can affirm that it is the language of the people all over the world. (P5: Perin, question 26)

For this teacher, since English is an international language, it is owned by the people who use it all around the world. What these perspectives show us is that, as English grows as a global language, it becomes a globally mobile language, occurring in various forms and blending with various languages in diverse contexts. As a result, the English that people use might have little similarity to its original form, whatever that might have been (Blommaert 2012). As Gamze states in the first quotation, diversity is richness.

What also arises from these teachers' engagement with the ELF-TEd project is that their growing self-awareness as non-native speakers boosts their self-confidence as teachers (on the issue of non-native speaker teachers' self-confidence see (Bayyurt 2006, 2012; Llurda 2009; McKay and Bokhorst-Heng 2008) This is something that has not been previously documented in ELF studies of teachers. One way that this becomes evident is that, as the following quotation shows, teachers are described as having fewer limiting beliefs than their learners:

Teachers seem to be moving away from native-speaker norms faster than students are: It's something which I know from my own experience, because most of my students are still in the pursuit of having a British accent or an American accent. (P2: Sude, question 71)

Learners seem to find the ELF perspective less agreeable than teachers, even if they are aware of the global uses of English. This finding coincides with the expectations of the parents of young learners in primary schools, as seen in the primary teachers' data from this same ELF-TEd project (Bayyurt and Sifakis 2013, 2015).

When non-native EFL teachers become ELF-aware, they realise that they not only have a rightful claim to English, much like its many native speakers around the world, as we have seen; but also their knowledge of the local languacultural context renders them more capable teachers:

> As for changing role of my own, all those readings gained me self-confidence. Put differently, I have always thought that native speaker teachers are better than non-native speakers even though I have read some articles related to global English. I have never questioned the issue of who is better. But, now I'm very confident of myself that I teach the English which is useful for my students. I may not teach perfect English to a Pakistani student because I do not have any idea about his/her cultural norms and life. However, I know my students and their life, their way of learning English, so I'm sure I can teach better than any other native speaker teacher or non-native speaker teacher who is not Turkish'. (P5: Perin, question 26)

This is an important acknowledgement, especially as it draws from the Turkish EFL context. In Turkey, during the past decade, there has been a tendency to hire non-native English language teachers from other countries in Europe, Asia, and elsewhere in the world to teach at private schools besides native English language teachers. What the above quotation makes clear is the teacher's perspective regarding the advantages of hiring teachers who share the same L1 with the learners.

With regard to developing ELF-aware lessons for their own learners, our participants are specific about the need for a transformative perspective to established EFL practices:

> When it comes to the need for transformation in ELT methodology, we can say that the current methodology does not suit to these aims and approaches to some extent. For instance, many course books do not exemplify any activity that may give the chance to practice interaction strategies. For my own teaching context, I can affirm that these goals are realistic because my students learn English in a foreign language context, and they need to communicate with people from all over the world. Henceforth, it is

better for them to focus more on intelligibility rather than correctness. (P5: Perin, question 38)

However, the same teacher acknowledges that the ELF literature does not offer specific advice for teaching practice, which is something teachers need once they have become ELF-aware:

In my opinion, the teaching part is the most important for me as may be antici-pated. First things first, there is not any clear explanation on how to teach. The comments are too general, so they are not practical. I think we talk about theory of how to teach ELF rather than the practice of ELF teaching. As for the goals and approaches, I agree with them. We should focus on intelligibility, textual competence and interaction strategies. (P5: Perin, question 38)

Similarly, for this teacher:

It is my contention that teachers need some ELF AWARE activities to help them to overcome subjective hindrances to use in class. Our state high school yearly plan given by the ministry includes global issues. The plans are made based on CEFR Descriptors. A guidebook could be prepared for the teachers to help them understand how they adapt ELF to classroom teaching. This guidebook could be a website or a Moodle. (P1: Gamze, question 71)

As already stated, in this project we were not focused on providing teachers with ready-made ideas or recipes for activities that could be used in their teach-ing context. We wanted to see how they would develop their own orientation of ELF-aware activities that would be appropriate for their learners and broader teaching context. While certain teachers struggled to come up with original ideas for ELF-aware activities, others were more creative with delineating a precise pedagogical approach, based on their readings of the ELF literature:

I will include different varieties of English to the curriculum and I will welcome when they produce new forms. I will not correct their mistakes immediately and I will inform all the students about the importance of it. The students also must be open-minded about their peers' different styles. I will prepare some extra materials for the quick learners. (P2: Sude, Question 111)

Discussion

Our aim in this project was to raise teachers' awareness of ELF and to research the extent to which such awareness could lead to ELF-related classroom

practice. What our project has shown so far is that teachers found their experience of engaging with the ELF literature through the system of responding to
reflective questions rewarding. Those questions helped to draw their attention
to particular ELF-related concerns, such as the role of the use of standard varieties of English (e.g., British English, American English, and so on) in the foreign
language classroom, the role of the native and non-native speakers in different
communicative contexts, the issue of the ownership of English by its different
users, the function of intelligibility in NNS–NNS interactions, or the role of the
non-native speaker teacher in an Expanding Circle context like Turkey.

These issues are hard to deal with in the first place, but the progression of
the articles teachers had to read, combined with the corresponding open-ended
reflective questions, managed not only to facilitate them in their appreciation
of those ELF issues but also, more importantly, to help them make sense of
those issues with reference to their own context. This is not a minor achievement considering the fuzziness of the ELF concept for many a researcher, let
alone teacher. From this perspective, the project has succeeded in helping
teachers appreciate the complexity of the ELF construct and, what is more,
personalise it for their own teaching context.

Could it be argued that our participants showed a transformation in their
perspectives about the roles and functions of the English language in today's
world? To answer this, we have to consider the extent to which the teachers
have shown a substantial change (a) in their established convictions about
English and (b) in their habitual patterns of teaching.

What we have found so far from this study is that teachers showed change
but that this change was slow and depended on a series of constraints that
had to do both with the individual teacher and with the broader context in
which they work. Constraints that were related to individual teachers can be
linked to their personality; for example, the extent to which they were more
or less open to change as individuals, not merely as teachers. Constraints that
were context-related also had a psychological impact to the extent that we were
able to see teachers' self-perception of their professional roles as teachers and
their corresponding willingness to bring about change in their teaching habits.
Having said that, it must be stressed that the greatest change that we have
documented in this project concerned teachers' own self-perceptions as non-
native speakers of English. We have seen a transformation from a mentality of
a speaker feeling 'subordinate' to a 'superior' native speaker to a mentality
of a speaker feeling equal to, if not better equipped than, native speakers to
deal with the needs of a communicative situation involving other non-native
speakers (also see Park 2012). The point at which the transformation happened
in the project was when the teachers realised the implications that the function of English as an international language has for millions, if not billions, of
non-native speakers around the world.

With regard to implications for actual teaching practices, two distinct suggestions and two major problems seem to arise from the project participants' responses. The first suggestion concerns teachers' role as correctors of learners' speech. This is one of the roles that EFL teachers consider very highly, especially in Expanding Circle contexts, and it is clear from the ELF-TEd participants' responses that ELF-aware teachers should stop indiscriminately correcting all of their learners' 'wrong' English. For our participants, there is a place and a time for correction, and it is not a practice that should be thoughtlessly extended throughout an entire lesson. On the contrary, it is important that teachers are very careful with providing corrective feedback and should find ways to make their feedback more relevant to the constraints of the different communicative situations that arise with each different activity. What our ELF-aware teachers have understood from their engagement with the ELF literature is that learners should be prompted to grow as ELF users. For this to happen, it is necessary for them to be allowed to express themselves freely, if not all the time, at least some of the time. ELF-aware teachers should become conscious of the need to develop in their learners the capacity to communicate intelligibly with other speakers, despite the inevitable existence of errors.

The second implication for ELF-aware instruction is the primacy of the cultural component in foreign language teaching. By 'culture' here we do not mean the major cultural distinctions between languages and ethnicities, but the 'small cultures' or personality facets of each individual learner (Holliday 1999). Our participants understand that the function of English as a global language implies that every communicatively successful speaker (native or non-native) essentially owns the language and that, for this ownership to occur in speakers' minds, it is important that these speakers are allowed to exhibit their own personal cultural characteristics, instead of engaging in tasks that require them to be someone else (e.g., a stereotypically idealised native speaker). These characteristics can have many guises, for example through learners' own pronunciation or through their use of lexis from their mother tongue, or from languages that they happen to share with other speakers. In the ELF-aware instructional paradigm, the concept of 'foreignness' is not helpful as it 'indicates distance' (Ehlich 2009: 27) and should give way to the concept of 'ownership': after all, learners use English all the time outside their EFL classroom, for example, playing games online with co-players from all over the world. In this regard, it is useful to consider the pedagogical proposal for Expanding Circle contexts that Fay et al. (2010) have put forward: they suggest ways of tailoring textbook activities to make the best of the individual cultural characteristics of learners in ways that make use of English not as an inter-national but as an intra-national language (i.e., as a vehicle of communication for learners of different cultural backgrounds in the same classroom), thereby raising learners' multicultural awareness through English (MATE).

This brings us to the two problems, or obstacles, that can potentially hinder ELF-aware lessons. The first problem is related to the perceptions of learners and other stakeholders (e.g., parents, directors of study, etc.) concerning the role of English language teaching in Expanding Circle contexts like Turkey. These perceptions are typically oriented towards the native speaker and Standard English norms. Teachers realise that they have to struggle with these mind-sets (provided their own mind-set is already transformed, of course), and this is something that must be seriously taken into consideration in developing ELF-aware lessons. Not everyone is equally open to this new perspective, which means that teachers should make the transition from conventional EFL to ELF-aware lessons as slowly and seamlessly as their context allows (also see Sifakis 2009).

The second problem is related to the lack of appropriately designed ELF-aware teaching materials. This has been documented before in the relevant literature (e.g., Jenkins 2007; Seidlhofer 2011; Sifakis 2009). The problem that our participants see with this is that they and their learners have been used to implementing commercially available courseware and that integrating ELF-aware activities in such a context would imply two things. First, that teachers would have to design original ELF-aware activities that would either extend existing textbook activities or function as stand-alone activities beyond the textbook, or both. Secondly, that teachers would have to get used to experimenting more and more with practices that may seem entirely novel and at times even unwelcome to them and their learners, such as applying the less strict approach to correction suggested above. In the former case, going beyond the textbook might imply to learners and other stakeholders that the teacher is deviating from the established syllabus. In the latter case, a more rigorous and time-consuming training process is necessary that would make teachers more aware of the impact of their teaching and instil in them the necessary self-confidence to develop and evaluate appropriate ELF-aware activities for their context. This is another reason why the transformative process towards the ELF-aware classroom can be slow and painstaking.

It becomes increasingly clear from our experience in this project that ELF-aware instructional practices are entirely in line with current concerns about the importance of applying a post-method pedagogy (Kumaravadivelu 2001). This means that what is appropriate for local contexts is the development of locally developed instructional materials. It also means that teachers should not blindly endorse a particular teaching methodology but have an informed awareness of many different methodologies and work up the competence to select and fine-tune the instructional approach that best fits their local context.

It is very probably for this reason that our ELF-TEd participants have perceived their ELF-aware training as an opportunity to widen their scope and knowledge about new developments in ELT. This enabled them to think about their language teaching context and the place of foreign language teaching in the Turkish educational system. In other words, teachers found their engagement with ELF both an opportunity to receive new information about fascinating issues concerning the English language and a springboard for growing professionally as reflective teachers. Their involvement with ELF and the ELF-related literature led them to think about their own teaching in context, pertinent aspects of the curriculum, and their native-speaker-centred course books (also see Sifakis 2014, Sifakis and Bayyurt forthcoming).

Conclusion

In this chapter we have presented a pilot study of an in-service ELF-aware teacher education project that engaged teachers in reading excerpts from the ELF and WE literature, reflecting on their perceptions about related concerns, and developing, teaching, and evaluating original ELF-aware lessons for their learners. The aim of the project was to make teachers 'ELF-aware', that is, prompt them to engage with the important issues raised in the ELF literature and allow them to draw their own conclusions regarding the nature of the ELF construct and the implications for their teaching context. We have described the findings of the project, based on the responses of participating Turkish ESOL teachers.

What our study has conclusively shown is that ELF teacher education is worthy of investigation because it draws teachers' attention to a reality they may not have been previously aware of. Our ELF-TEd project aimed to move a step forward in relation to Jenkins's detachment of ELF research from teaching (Jenkins 2011 – see Introduction), by linking the two through the creation of a 'safe' environment, where teachers can make sense of the ELF literature and enter the transformative process of becoming ELF-aware speakers, teachers and materials designers. This process can be quite powerful for teachers and learners alike, as the following quotation shows:

> For me ELF-aware teacher is giving importance to communication and respect to other cultures. [...] In my classroom practice, ELF-awareness has changed my students' attitude towards using a foreign language. As a non-native English speaking teacher I feel much better and relaxed in using the language. (Gamze, e-mail interview, 7 April 2013)

In the next decade, ELF teacher education will become an important issue not only for ELF theoreticians and educational practitioners but also for ESOL practitioners. As we have seen, the strength of ELF research, together with the broader World Englishes literature, lies in its potential to challenge deep-seated convictions about the functions of the English language, the roles of its users and the pedagogical implications that this phenomenon can have (Bayyurt and Sifakis 2013, 2015).

We will continue with the ELF-TEd project for the next few years to see how teachers from different parts of the world perceive and respond to this ELF-aware teacher education approach. Learner reactions to these ELF-aware applications present yet another issue which needs further investigation. It would be interesting to see how learners who live in countries of the Expanding Circle and use a lot of English in their everyday life (while online-gaming, Skyping, etc. with other people around the world) respond to their teachers' ELF-aware interventions in the EFL classroom.

Engagement priorities

In this chapter we have described a teacher training project that attempts to introduce in-service teachers working in the EFL field to the so-called ELF construct. We have used the term 'ELF-aware teaching' to refer to teachers' involvement in understanding ELF-related concerns and their trying out and evaluation of activities with their learners that implement such an understanding. What we have also shown in this chapter is that ELF-aware teacher education has had transformative effects on the teachers involved in the project. What follows is a series of points to consider when engaging in ELF-aware teaching and teacher education.

1. As a first step, read as much as you can about ELF, seeking published books, peer-reviewed journal papers, and chapters. As you read, make notes of your reflections. What are your attitudes toward ELF discourse? To what extent do you consider such discourse helpful and/or problematic? It is vital that you offer reasons for your perspectives. There are no right or wrong answers here, as long as you are fully aware of your own attitudes towards ELF and potential shortcomings of current EFL pedagogical practices (e.g., over-correction of learners' errors, too much emphasis on teaching to a test, etc.). In what ways would an ELF-aware pedagogy be helpful for your learners?
2. As a second step, you need to find out as much as you can about your learners' beliefs and attitudes about English and its function in the world today. Enquire into the extent to which they use English outside of the EFL class (e.g., playing online videogames and engaging with co-players). Find out about whether they are happy with the EFL perspective of the class and ask them if they would not mind you integrating elements of ELF (e.g., examples of successful non-native discourse) into the lessons. Conduct similar surveys of every other stakeholder (parents, sponsors, headmasters, etc.).
3. If your teaching context allows it and you are confident about the value of introducing your learners to ELF-aware input and pedagogy, start experimenting with activities or entire lessons that are ELF-aware. These lessons

would be very different from context to context, but they are likely to have, among other things, a focus on spoken discourse, a teaching perspective that favours differentiated instruction and a pedagogical orientation that is not correction-centred. Continue to experiment and reflect on the efficacy of these lessons and activities and always poll your learners about their efficacy. We would like to stress that ELF-aware instruction does not imply a downright rejection of EFL practices but attempts to give the EFL class (and its typically Standard English orientation) a much more authentic sense of real world English usage. Whether you will be transformed or not as a result of these experimentations is, again, something that will depend on many things, your learners, the target situation, parents, sponsors, available teaching materials, and, most importantly of all, your own predisposition.

Acknowledgements

We would like to thank Boğaziçi University Research Projects, project number 8000, and the Turkish Ministry of National Education for their support in realising this project as a valuable contribution to the academic world. We would also like to thank all the teachers who took part in this project.

References

Bayyurt, Y. (2006). Non-native English language teachers' perspective on culture in English as a foreign language classrooms. *Teacher Development* 10(2): 233–247.

Bayyurt, Y. (2012). Proposing a model for English language education in the Turkish socio-cultural context. In Bayyurt, Y. and Bektaş-Çetinkaya, Y. (eds), *Research Perspectives on Teaching and Learning English in Turkey: Policies and Practices* Frankfurt: Peter Lang, pp. 301–312.

Bayyurt, Y. and Sifakis, N. (2013). Transforming into an ELF-aware teacher. Paper presented at *Conference on New Frontiers in Teaching and Learning English*, Verona University, Italy, 15 February. Available at http://prin-confs-2013.dlls.univr.it/prin/download/teachingLearning/verona_presentation_14_february_2013.pdf.

Bayyurt, Y. and Sifakis, N. (2015). Developing an ELF-Aware Pedagogy: Insights from a Self-Education Programme. In P. Vettorel (ed.), *New Frontiers in Teaching and Learning English*. Cambridge: Cambridge Scholars Publishing, pp. 55–76.

Blair, A. (2015). Evolving a post-native, multilingual model for ELF-aware teacher education. In Bayyurt, Y. and Akcan, S. (eds), *Current Perspectives on Pedagogy for ELF*. Berlin: De Gruyter Mouton, pp. 89–101.

Blommaert, J. (2012). Sociolinguistics and English Language Studies. *Working Papers in Urban Language & Literacies* 85: 1–17.

Braun, V. and Clarke, V. (2006). Using thematic analysis in psychology. *Qualitative Research in Psychology* 3(2): 77–101.

Carey, R. (2013). On the other side: Formulaic organizing chunks in spoken and written academic ELF. *Journal of English as a Lingua Franca* 2(2): 207–228.

Dewey, M. (2012). Towards a post-normative approach: Learning the pedagogy of ELF. *Journal of English as a Lingua Franca* 1(1): 141–170.

Ehlich, K. (2009). What makes a language foreign? In Knapp, K. and Seidlhofer, B. (eds), *Handbook of Foreign Language Communication and Learning*. Berlin: De Gruyter Mouton, pp. 21–44.

Fay, R., Lytra, V. and Ntavaliagkou, M. (2010). Multicultural awareness through English: A potential contribution of TESOL in Greek schools. *Intercultural Education* 21(6): 579–593.

Fernández-Polo, F. J. (2014). The role of *I mean* in conference presentations by ELF speakers. *English for Specific Purposes* 34: 58–67.

Holliday, A. (1999). Small cultures. *Applied Linguistics* 20(2): 237–264.

Hülmbauer, C. (2010). *English as a Lingua Franca Between Correctness and Effectiveness: Shifting Constellations*. Saarbrücken: VDM-Verlag Müller.

Jenkins, J. (2007). *English as a Lingua Franca: Attitude and Identity*. Oxford: Oxford University Press.

Jenkins, J. (2011). Accommodating (to) ELF in the international university. *Journal of Pragmatics* 43(4): 926–936.

Kumaravadivelu, B. (2001). Towards a post-method pedagogy. *TESOL Quarterly* 33(4): 537–560.

Lindemann, S. and Subtirelu, N. (2013). Reliably biased: The role of listener expectation in the perception of second language speech. *Language Learning* 63(3): 567–594.

Llurda, E. (2009). Attitudes towards English as an international language: The pervasiveness of native models among L2 users and teachers. In Sharifian, F. (ed.), *English as an International Language: Perspectives and Pedagogical Issues*. Clevedon: Multilingual Matters, pp. 119–134.

Matsuda, A. (2009). Desirable but not necessary? The place of World Englishes and English as an international language in English teacher preparation programs in Japan. In Sharifian, F. (ed.), *English as an International Language: Perspectives and Pedagogical Issues*. Clevedon: Multilingual Matters, pp. 169–189.

Matsumoto, Y. (2011). Successful ELF communications and implications for ELT: Sequential analysis of ELF pronunciation negotiation strategies. *Modern Language Journal* 95(1): 97–114.

Mauranen, A. (2012). *Exploring ELF: Academic English shaped by non-native speakers*. Cambridge: Cambridge University Press.

Mauranen, A. and Ranta, E. (eds) (2009). *English as a Lingua Franca: Studies and Findings*. Newcastle upon Tyne: Cambridge Scholars Publishing.

Mayring, P. (2004). Qualitative content analysis. In U. Flick, E. von Kardoff and I. Steinke (eds), *A Companion to Qualitative Research*. London: Sage, pp. 266–269.

McKay, S. L. and Bokhorst-Heng, W. D. (2008). *International English in its Sociolinguistic Contexts: Towards a Socially Sensitive EIL Pedagogy*. London: Routledge.

Metsä-Ketelä, M. (2012). Frequencies of vague expressions in English as an academic Lingua Franca. *Journal of English as a Lingua Franca* 1(2), 263–285.

Mezirow, J. (1991). *Transformative Dimensions of Adult Learning*. San Francisco: Jossey-Bass.

Mezirow, J. and Associates (eds) (2000). *Learning as Transformation*. San Francisco: Jossey-Bass.

Park, G. (2012). 'I am never afraid of being recognized as an NNES': One teacher's journey in claiming and embracing her nonnative-speaker identity. *TESOL Quarterly* 46(1): 127–151.

Park, S.-Y. J. and Wee, L. (2011). A practice-based critique of English as a Lingua Franca. *World Englishes* 30(3): 360–374.

Pitzl, M.-L. (2012). Creativity meets convention: Idiom variation and re-metaphorization in ELF. *Journal of English as a Lingua Franca* 1(1): 27–55.

Seidlhofer, B. (2004). Research perspectives on teaching English as a Lingua Franca. *Annual Review of Applied Linguistics* 24: 209–239.

Seidlhofer, B. (2008). Of norms and mindsets. *Australian Review of Applied Linguistics* 31(3): 1–7.

Seidlhofer, B. (2009). Accommodation and the idiom principle in English as a Lingua Franca. *Intercultural Pragmatics* 6(2): 195–215.

Seidlhofer, B. (2011). *Understanding English as a Lingua Franca*. Oxford: Oxford University Press.

Sifakis, N. C. (2007). The education of the teachers of English as a Lingua Franca: A transformative perspective. *International Journal of Applied Linguistics* 17(3): 355–375.

Sifakis, N. C. (2009). Challenges in teaching ELF in the periphery: The Greek context. *ELT Journal* 63(3): 230–237.

Sifakis, N. C. (2014). ELF awareness as an opportunity for change: A transformative perspective for ESOL teacher education. *Journal of English as a Lingua Franca* 3(2): 315–333.

Sifakis, N. C. and Bayyurt, Y. (forthcoming). Educating the ELF-aware teacher: Insights from ELF and World Englishes in teacher training. *World Englishes*.

Sifakis, N. C. and Sougari, A.-M. (2005). Pronunciation issues and EIL pedagogy in the periphery: A survey of Greek state school teachers' beliefs. *TESOL Quarterly* 39(4): 467–488.

Widdowson, H. G. (1994). The ownership of English. *TESOL Quarterly* 28(2): 377–389.

Widdowson, H. G. (2012). ELF and the inconvenience of established concepts. *Journal of English as a Lingua Franca* 1(1): 5–26.

8
The Pedagogical Implications of ELF in a Domestic Migrant Workplace

Kellie Gonçalves

Introduction

Linguistic studies on the pedagogical aspects of ELF in professional and business contexts has largely focused on 'white collar' workplace settings and BELF. In this chapter I discuss the pedagogical aspects of EIL since they are appropriate for teaching domestic workers and ELF speakers within a local, domestic labour context among Portuguese and Spanish-speaking domestics and their Anglophone clients in a multilingual cleaning company in New Jersey, U.S. This project is situated within a broader theoretical framework of mobilities and globalization within the 21st century (Urry 2000; Adey 2010; Kramsch 2014) and concerned with the 'consequences of globalization' (Bauman 1998) and the 'turbulence of modern migration' (Papastergiadis 2000), both of which point to transient and dynamic individuals and the complexity of language learning and use of the target language, English.

Domestic workers' accounts of language practices among the densely-tied social networks (Milroy 1987 [1980]) within their local community reveal that individuals do not rely on English in their private, daily lives since their ethnic enclave accommodates to Portuguese and Spanish-speaking residents (Gonçalves 2012). As a result, English serves as an additional language of wider communication for these workers and inevitably influences their investment in the target language (Norton 2000; Block 2007), which also correlates to the amount of time they have resided in the U.S. and their experiences of learning English within traditional and formal classroom settings. For the domestic workers who use ELF in the workplace, insecurities about their language skills indicate that comparisons to native speaker norms (Jenkins 2007; Cogo 2010) are still very much alive. Moreover, domestic workers' language practices do not always coincide with how their language use is perceived by co-workers, language brokers and their English-speaking clients, many of who assess their skills positively.

This chapter explores the communicative practices and ELF perceptions of Portuguese-speaking domestic workers interacting with their Anglophone clients. The chapter is structured as follows: In the first section I discuss how ELF is understood in relation to migration and the workplace. I then explore the communicative practices of migrant domestic workers employed by a cleaning company, using examples of interview data with the workers and company clients. I conclude the chapter by outlining the pedagogical implications and recommendations for ELF-based teaching to migrant domestic workers in the future.

Understanding ELF, migration and the workplace

ELF communication is understood to involve both speakers who may or may not be considered 'bilingual' as well as native speakers. Studies of language practices and ELF use within business contexts have focused primarily on 'white collar' workplace settings and emphasize the need to develop international communicative competence among speakers of different L1 backgrounds (Poncini 2004; Louhiala-Salminen et al. 2005; Planken 2005; Kankaanranta and Louhiala-Salminen 2007, 2010; Rogerson-Revell 2008; Ehrenreich 2009; Planken and Nickerson 2009; Pullin Stark 2009; Cogo 2012). Many of these studies also provide suggestions for facilitating professional communication in different workplace contexts, that is, being able to write information effectively, delivering persuasive oral presentations, and utilizing key business and economic terminology (cf. Kankaanranta and Louhiala-Salminen 2007).

However, not all workers who use ELF have access to institutions of higher education or strive to use English for 'professional' reasons. This is particularly true of the object of this study – the migrant domestic worker ELF learner and user.

Migrant domestic workers and ELF

According to Papastergiadis (2000: 10) 'the modern migrant no longer conforms to the stereotypical image of the male urban peasant. Women in manufacturing, electronic assembly lines and domestic workers are now at the front line of global migration'. Most studies carried out with domestic workers are found within the fields of women studies, cultural studies and sociology (Rollins 1985; Chang 2000) and tend to be one-sided in that they consider domestic workers' views and experiences only (Ruiz 1987; Hondagneu-Sotelo 1990; Parreñas Salazar 2001; Romero 2002). Rollin's (1985) study looked at both domestic workers and employers from a sociological perspective, and more recently, outside of the U.S., Lan (2006) conducted a study of Filipina domestic workers in Taiwan in which both domestic workers and clients were interviewed. Despite the positive effects of mobility and globalization within the 21st century, domestic workers suffer from both economic and social inequalities, and live what Blommaert (2010: 3) has termed 'un-globalized lives' since they do not reap the same benefits as elite society members. Moreover, such individuals' linguistic and communicative resources may lack semiotic mobility within their daily contexts, one of which is the workplace. In other words, the language resources that individuals have access to, or are denied access to, are inevitably tied to notions of inequality and power, that is, access to standard varieties or 'advanced multimodal and multilingual literacy skills' (Blommaert 2010: 5).

All of the studies listed above are concerned with economic inequality, immigration policies, ethnicity, race, and exploitation of domestic workers within the global economy (Anderson 2000), yet none of them explicitly look at language use and communicative practices between domestic workers and their employers[1], nor do they look at the teaching and learning of communicative skills. This chapter will explore these issues from a pedagogical ELF and EIL perspective, by examining data from interviews with domestic migrants.

Communicative practices of domestic migrant workers

The communicative practices of domestic migrant workers will be discussed using examples from semi-structured interviews that were carried out[2] with 18 Portuguese and Spanish-speaking domestic workers (residents of the Ironbound neighbourhood), 21 English-speaking visitors to the area, as well as three bilingual Portuguese/English visitors. The interviews[3] raised the following questions related to language practices and language teaching:

1. What language(s) are used within domestics' home, community and workplace networks?
2. How do domestics perceive and assess their own ELF abilities within their workplace contexts?
3. What are the pedagogical implications for language teaching within the context of domestic migrant workers?

I discuss the first two questions below, I present data involving the domestic workers and their clients. The third question is discussed at length in the final section of this chapter, which deals with the pedagogical implications of the data for teaching domestic migrant workers.

Table 8.1 illustrates the multilingual nature of the cleaning company where the 18 domestic migrant workers were employed.

The table shows that 7 domestic workers are bilingual though their language proficiency varies considerably. For the most part, domestic workers' claims of language knowledge and use, such as understanding and comprehending English and being able to use it with English-speaking clients, did not coincide with the assessment of the company owner, driver, or clients. Many of the

Table 8.1 Cleaning company – language combinations (domestic and non-domestic workers)

Languages		N.speakers
Domestic workers		
Bilingual	European Portuguese & English	3
	Luso-Brazilian Portuguese & English	2
	Spanish & English	2
Monolingual	European Portuguese	7
	Luso-Brazilian Portuguese	2
	Spanish	2
	Total	18
Non-domestic workers		
Trilingual	Luso-Brazilian Portuguese, English, Spanish	1
Monolingual	English	1
	Total	2

domestic workers were modest about their communicative abilities in English and often undervalued and even belittled their skills, which were often compared to NS speakers of English.

As regards to the non-domestic workers, the trilingual company owner, Magda, serves as the main language broker (Del Torto 2008) between the domestic workers, the driver, and the clients, while the driver, Jill, is a monolingual English speaker who claims that she understands certain Spanish and Portuguese lexical items, but is by no means proficient in any other language besides English.

As regards to the language skills of the clients, the majority were monolingual English speakers, three claimed to be competent bilinguals in English and Spanish, English and Arabic, and English and French.

Perceptions and language use within the domestic workers' local community

Newark and more specifically, the Ironbound neighbourhood, is largely regarded as a Portuguese-speaking enclave. The following extract comes from Dona Aura, a European Portuguese-speaking domestic who has resided in the U.S. for 25 years and describes the Ironbound as multilingual and multiethnic. As a result, her day-to-day activities and communicative practices are 'always' carried out in Portuguese (line 4):

(1)
1. Dona Aura: Sim, lá em Newark é quase tudo, (XXX) praticamente é TUDO português.

português, espanhol, brasileiro.
(Yes, there in Newark it's almost everything (XXX) practically
EVERYTHING is Portuguese, Portuguese, Spanish, Brazilian)
2. Kellie: mhm (1.0) Então o seu dia-a-dia é mais o português?
(So your day-to-day is more Portuguese?)
3. Dona Augusta: Ya, SEMPRE o português.
(Yeah, ALWAYS Portuguese)

For Dona Aura, practically everything in the Ironbound neighbourhood is
Portuguese (turn 1). As a result, she does not need to carry out any daily tasks
in English but can resume them all in Portuguese (turn 3). Dona Aura's experiences of being able to use Portuguese on a daily basis confirms what all of the
domestic workers in this study stated about the Ironbound neighbourhood,
namely that because of its multiethnicity and multilingualism, individuals
residing there can use their L1s, in this case European Portuguese or Spanish, in
interactions where English is not necessary. In fact, the only function English
serves within their community is as an additional language of wider communication for interactions in which English is optional but by no means compulsory.
There are numerous shops, restaurants, and supermarkets located within the
Ironbound in which shop assistants do not speak English at all.

Communicative practices in the workplace: domestics, clients, and language brokers

In this section I discuss the communicative practices carried out by domestics,
their Anglophone clients and multilingual language brokers. In extract (2),
I asked Paloma, a European Portuguese-speaking domestic worker who has
resided in the U.S. for over ten years, if she felt her English level was sufficient
for the job:

(2)
1. Kellie: e então você acha que o teu nível de inglês é suficiente para o
trabalho?
(and so do you think your English level is sufficient for your work?)
2. Paloma: não não é (no, no it's not)
3. Kellie: não é? Por que? (it's not, why?)
4. Paloma: porque pronto, porque às vezes *a gente* quer se falar mais coisas ou
as mulheres às vezes querem nos falar a nós *a gente* não consegue (.)
a gente pronto *a gente* **hello, good morning** ou **bye-bye** ou assim
mas (.) o essencial mesmo não sabe e, quer e não consegue emas
pronto, mas *a gente* pra mim acho que se *a gente*, souber falar o
essencial por exemplo, **hello, good morning**, o mais importante,
ser simpático pra mulheres pra falar (.) pronto o essencial, de ser

educado assim (because well, because sometimes we want to be able to speak more or the women sometimes would like to say more to us and we aren't able to (.) we well we hello, good morning or bye-bye like that but (.) the essentials really we don't know it's, you want to but you're not able to, but anyway, we for me I think if we could speak the essentials for example, hello, good morning, the most important thing, is to be nice to the women to speak (.) well the essential is to be polite)

In extract (2) Paloma admits that despite living in the U.S. for over ten years, her English is not sufficient for the job (turn 2). In explaining her situation and willingness to be able to actually converse more with clients, she continually makes use of the inclusive 'we' (*a gente*, turn 4, italics) to index that all the domestic workers have a difficult time communicating with clients. Her comment subtly suggests that domestic workers do not receive extensive or enough L2 input during their working hours in order to acquire the communicative skills that would allow them to use the target language with their clients. Her use of code-switching within this extract, in which individual lexical items such as *hello* (turn 4, bold italics) and fixed phrases and salutations such as *good morning* and *bye-bye* are inserted into her talk, suggests that Paloma has a small inventory of English structures that are employed for greeting Anglophone clients. This type of code-switching is what Matras (2009: 111) refers to as 'situations of superficial or minimal bilingualism' for individuals who have 'a rudimentary knowledge of another language'. This example also highlights that within this specific workplace context, domestic workers are being exposed to particular registers and structures that are continually being repeated, but not to a full range of language practices and styles necessary to meet certain desired social practices. Although Paloma may not 'master' English, she can draw on her multilingual repertoire in order for her communicative goals to be met.

In another interview, Bianca, a 62-year old Portuguese domestic worker from mainland Portugal, who had at the time of our interview been residing in the Ironbound since 1988 and working at the cleaning company for 23 years, claims that despite the considerable time she had spent in the U.S. she does not feel comfortable speaking English with clients, especially when she has to talk to them on the phone. Despite her position as 'driver' and her proficient English skills, Bianca conveys her dissatisfaction with the way she actually addresses her Anglophone clients because of her pronunciation:[4]

(4)
1. Bianca: que eu devo falar, se eu for trabalhar na casa de uma senhora americana como essa senhora Katie Jones

(I should speak, if I go to work in a home of an American woman like this woman Katie Jones)

2. Kellie: mhm
3. Bianca: é o nome dela, eu acho que devia chamar por *mrs* Jones não é?
(it's her name, I think I should call her Mrs Jones right?)
4. Kellie: mhm
5. Bianca: mas como eu fui habituada a chamar só *mrs* Katie acho que não está bem, tá muito feio pra mim eu não me sinto confortável a chamar pra ela *mrs* Katie nem como o marido achamar Mr Mike
(but since I already got used to calling her Mrs Katie I think it's not good, it's very ugly for me I don't feel comfortable calling her Mrs Katie and not even with her husband saying Mr Mike)
6. Kellie: mhm
7. Bianca: eu não sinto eu sinto que está errado mas eu não sei falar de outra maneira
(I don't feel, I feel that it's wrong but I don't know how to say it differently)
8. Kellie: então você fala *mrs* Katie ou cê fala Mrs Jones?
(so do you say Mrs Katie or do you say Mrs Jones?)
9. Bianca: *mrs* Katie (Mrs Katie)
10. Kellie: e ela importa? (and does she mind?)
11. Bianca: até hoje nunca disse que se importava, mas eu acho que estou a fazer feio devia dizer *mrs* Jones
(until today she hasn't said that she minds, but I think I'm doing something ugly, I should say Mrs Jones)
12. Kellie: cê podia também falar *mrs* Jones (you could also say Mrs Jones)
13. Bianca: mas já acho= (but I already think)
14. Kellie: =por que você não fala *mrs* Jones? (why don't you say Mrs Jones?)
15. Bianca: não sei se tá se está bem, pronunciado
(I don't know if it's, if it's pronounced well)

In extract (4), the use of Bianca's code-switching of the addressee form *Mrs Katie* (turn 5), using her client's first name rather than the usual surname that follows, can be regarded as an instance of stylistic choice and one that has a special conversational effect (Matras 2009). However, when asked about her choice of inserting a first name rather than a surname as the usual lexical option, she admits to knowing that it is wrong (turn 7), but also admits to not knowing how to pronounce *Jones* (turn 15). This may be due to Bianca's awareness of how these phonemes in both English and European Portuguese are pronounced differently. In Standard English, the phoneme [dʒ] is pronounced as a voiced palatal affricate, which is pronounced as a post alveolar stop in Portuguese and often considered to be an allophone of /d/ when used with loanwords (Parkinson 1988). It appears therefore that Bianca is aware of the phonological transference from her L1 that would occur if she were to pronounce *Jones* with a voiced alveolar stop. Rather than mispronouncing a client's name, Bianca makes use of her full linguistic repertoire or in Cook's (1999) terms 'multicompetence' and resorts to being creative with her addressee forms among her Anglophone clients by employing their first names rather than their surnames. Despite being able to be creative with English and have her communicative goals met, Bianca focuses on what she perceives to be the negative aspects of her English skills, which in her opinion are her pronunciation abilities. What is striking within this context is that for years Bianca's interlocutors have also never once 'corrected' Bianca's addressee forms (turn 11), but instead abided by the 'let it pass principle' (Firth 1996) since the intended communicative message was successfully understood.

In extract (5) Bianca further describes another communicative exchange with a client, Mrs Willows, in which she admits to using English but not being satisfied with her communicative efforts because they are not 'correct' (line 7):

(5)
1. Bianca: mas pro exemplo Kellie na sexta-feira na última sexta-feira deste mês (.) eu deixei uma menina numa casa aí depois a senhora chamou-me a dizer *'oh Bianca it's Mrs Willows' 'oh hi Mrs Willows, how are you?' 'oh, I'm ok but my, I'm not with Mira today I **called for Magda** yesterday'* ok ela chamou pra Magda à Magda deixou uma mensagem só que a Magda não teve tempo, envolvida com uma casa nova não escutou a mensagem e ela tinha tido um acidente e não precisava lá da Mira e eu disse *'ok, I **call for Magda** and she call you back'* sei que não tá, não tá correto mas ela entendeu então depois eu entrei em contacto com a Magda e a Magda falou comigo e disse 'ok então vá lá buscar a Mira porque eu não posso lá ir Bianca'

(so for example Kellie on Friday, the last Friday of this month (.) I left a girl at a house and the woman called me and said, *'oh Bianca it's Mrs Willows' 'oh hi Mrs Willows, how are you?' 'oh, I'm ok but my, I'm not with Mira today I **called for Magda** yesterday'* ok she called Magda and left a message but Magda didn't have time, she was occupied with a new house, didn't hear the message and she had had an accident and didn't need Mira and I said *'ok, I **call for Magda** and she call you back'* I know that it's **not correct** but she understood me and afterwards I got into contact with Magda and Magda told me 'ok, so go and get Mira because I can't go there now Bianca'.

In this extract, Bianca re-constructs an entire conversation she had with an Anglophone client by code-switching and conscious use of her L2 within the reported speech clauses (see highlighting in italics). Once again, Bianca's ability to draw on her full linguistic repertoire allows her to use this discourse-related switching creatively, which functions as a special conversational (Matras 2009) and dramatic effect (Holt 1996, 2000), while simultaneously expressing her involvement in talk (Tannen 1989). Bianca is able to assess her own English use and perhaps even the grammatical features employed, such as the insertion of the preposition *for* in the constructions *called for Magda, call for Magda* (see bold italics) or the omission of the future *will* in *she call you back* (see italics), which she claims are 'not correct' (see italics). And while these are not features of Standard English, Bianca is still able to use English in order for her communicative needs to be understood and mutual intelligibility (Jenkins 2000; Seidlhofer 2001) between her and her clients to be successfully achieved.

In another interview, Mrs O'Reilly, an Anglophone client who has been using the cleaning service for roughly 12 years and has had Bianca cleaning her home for nearly a decade, assesses Bianca's speaking skills and communicative practices differently to Bianca herself. In fact, she claims that Bianca's communicative competence in English is 'not a problem' and that Bianca 'does speak English quite well':

(6)

1. Kellie: erm and how is your communication with Bianca (.) how would you describe it?

2. Mrs O'Reilly: I would say it's very good, erm, because she does speak English QUITE well you know? so I would say it's not a problem (.) I remember maybe I had someone else for a while and maybe she was out for a little while, and I did have someone else (.) and she did not speak English that well so Magda had to come with her for a while, erm until she got her (XXX), but I had some (1.0) the children were still home, then, and they, some of them spoke Spanish

3. Kellie: mhm

4. Mrs O'Reilly: so we were able to leave notes, you know? the-, and my husband can speak a little bit of Spanish (.) he's lost a lot of it, but erm he would be able to write a note or two you know so we never really had a problem, as far as that was concerned

5. Kellie: and with Bianca you imagine, erm she speaks (1.0) she's good at English? do-is it- is it I mean, she's also able to produce it?

6. Mrs O'Reilly: OH YE::S, she can speak it all so YES she can produce it cause she will have a conversation with me, she'll ask about

the children or you know I've been through a couple of surgeries this past year and she's very concerned (1.0) erm she
always talked to me about it you know? and you know and
speak about it and see how I'm doing you know? and she
can tell when my grandchildren are around immediately
you know? she will say 'your grandchildren were here' ...
you know? 'cause she'll find toys under the couch and everything else

In extract (6), Mrs O'Reilly assesses Bianca's communicative practices and
English-speaking skills much more positively than Bianca herself does. While
Bianca claims that she can greet customers and speak to them about 'basic' topics concerning the cleaning service, Mrs O'Reilly's depiction about Bianca's use
of English is much more elaborate and advanced than Bianca's initial claim. For
Mrs O'Reilly, Bianca can have conversations about different topics and genres
ranging from her grandchildren to her overall well-being regarding her various
surgeries (turn 6). For Mrs O'Reilly, communication with Bianca is deemed
successful through face-to-face interaction as well as written correspondence
(turn 4). In addition to communicating with Bianca in English, Mrs O'Reilly's
husband has also been able to communicate with Bianca in Spanish (turn 4).
In fact, the different types of communicative practices that occur between
Mrs O'Reilly, her husband and Bianca, whether they are in English, Spanish,
oral, or written communication, are considered to work and have never once
proved to be problematic (turn 4).

Bianca's communicative practices with her clients, as well as with Jill the
Anglophone driver, do not coincide with what Bianca actually states about
her own ELF skills and communicative abilities. In my interview with Jill, who
often has to communicate with Bianca when Magda is away, Jill states the
following:

(7)
1 Jill: I have to deal with Bianca on a daily basis when Magda's gone (1.0)
2   and erm Bianca everyday knocks on the door because if there's a
3   problem and she has to tell me what the problem is (.) Bianca's prob-
4   lem IS (.) IS her insecurity about her English and I tell her that, I said,
5   "Bianca, I UNDERSTAND EVERYTHING YOU'RE SAYING TO ME" and
6   you know? like over Christmas one of her insecurities, I felt (.) if she
7   wouldn't have felt so insecure, we could've resolved some problems
8   faster, you know? Like, making erm, I had to rearrange a lot of clients,
9   you know? a lot of customers, but because Bianca was SO afraid of (.)
10   having to, she made me WAIT until her daughter Anita got home, so
11   I would speak to Anita but I would have KNOWN what Bianca was

12   saying to me because she really, her English is better than she thinks
13   and she understands EVERYTHING I'm saying to her

For Jill, communicating with Bianca is a daily endeavour when Magda is away (line 2) because Bianca is responsible for the weekly schedule and for arranging any unforeseen changes with other drivers. For Jill, communication with Bianca is not as easy as it could potentially be. This becomes clear when Jill states that the main problem Bianca has in terms of her English is her 'insecurity' (line 4). Regardless of Jill's encouragement concerning Bianca's English (line 5), Bianca is not comfortable conversing with Jill in English when changes with clients occur. This is made manifest when Jill insists that problems could have been resolved faster (line 8) had Bianca conversed with her directly rather than waiting for her daughter Anita to function as the language broker (lines 10 & 11).

In discussing the challenges of teaching ELF, Sifakis (2009: 231) mentions that 'instilling confidence' among ELF learners and users within NNS interactions is indeed a major obstacle. Within the context of the cleaning company, domestic workers like Bianca, who have more responsibilities than others, also have to gain the confidence necessary in order to overcome the fear that keeps them silent. They need to be aware that English within the context of their workplace is a language that functions for instrumental and communicative purposes to be employed between them and their clients rather than a language of identification (House 2003).

Pedagogical implications for teaching migrant workers

Several themes and issues emerging from the interviews in relation to ELF, language learning and individuals' perceptions of their own or co-workers communicative abilities have pedagogical implications for ELF in a migrant workplace context. For the domestic workers, most of whom reside in the Ironbound, the need to use English outside of work for daily activities like going to the supermarket, is not necessary. The tight-knit and ethnic enclave of the Ironbound neighbourhood allows its residents to use their L1s, whether European Portuguese, Luso-Brazilian Portuguese, or Spanish, in most social interactions (Gonçalves 2012). As a result, the amount of English input residents receive is not substantial enough for learners who desire to acquire and learn more of the target language to actually do so within their local community. This inevitably influences domestic workers' investment in English because communicating in English is problematic only within the workplace.

With regards to the domestic workers' communicative needs in English, the examples discussed in this chapter exemplify two different cases of ELF users and English L2 learners. They are both at very different proficiency levels and, regardless of the amount of time they have resided in the U.S., they are not satisfied with their ability to speak and use English within their workplace contexts. Domestic workers like Paloma and Bianca, for example, who have been living in the U.S. between 10 and 25 years, perceive their performance very differently from their co-workers and clients. The negative perceptions they have of their own English language use continues to affect their investment in English. For Paloma, her desire as an L2 English speaker would be to have extensive input concerning different registers and English constructions that would enable her to speak more with her Anglophone clients. Bianca, whose English is assessed much more positively by a language broker and long-time client than she would like to admit, fears speaking English because she is afraid she will not be understood correctly due to her pronunciation and use of wrong grammatical structures. Nevertheless, my own observations as well as those of clients indicate that Bianca is able to draw on her 'multicompetence' and be creative with English in order for her communicative needs to be met.

From my interviews, it became clear that most domestic workers were constantly comparing their English skills and abilities to those of native speakers. And while many researchers like McKay argue that 'the prevalent assumption that the goal of English language learning is to achieve native like competence in English must be put aside' (2003a: 7), this assumption is still very much alive among language learners and users themselves. Perhaps we first need to reinforce an alternative assumption among learners and English language professionals (cf. Canagarajah 1999; Seidlhofer et al. 2006) by taking an approach to language teaching and learning that emphasizes language for proficient communicative and instrumental purposes (Sifakis 2009; MacKenzie 2014). This may be challenging within traditional EFL classroom settings, as Kramsch (2014: 299) has recently stated:

> While the monolingual NS has been contested as a target model for FL learners, the purity ideal embodied in the authentic NS still remains intact for FL educators. To be sure, they acknowledge the increasing variations and nonstandard manifestations of the language as it is used in real life, but their teaching is pegged to the pure linguistic standard established by the national gatekeeping academies monitored by NSs.

It makes sense, therefore, in a migrant working context, which is an area where ELF usage and EIL pedagogy overlap, that specific pedagogical areas be addressed regarding teachers' knowledge base, approach and teaching methods, and choice of materials, as well as the learning context. I will discuss each of these areas in turn based on my findings, stating what implementing these recommendations involves on the part of teachers and students alike, while simultaneously acknowledging some of the difficulties in applying such changes.

Teachers' knowledge base

With regard to teachers' knowledge base, the interviews from domestic migrant workers support the argument that ELF teachers should also be speakers of learners' L1s. This means not using an exclusive exonormative native speaker model or an endonormative nativized model (Kirkpatrick 2007), but rather a hybrid model, which encompasses tenets of both. While teachers may indeed be native English speakers, they should also be multilingual speakers in that they are proficient in their students' L1s. In this context, teachers may have English as their L1 but should be proficient in a Portuguese or Spanish variety as well. In other words, the learning environment could be a 'hybrid heteroglossic reality of the world outside' (Kramsch 2014: 300). For teachers, sharing the knowledge of their students' L1 should be viewed as an advantage (Cook 2002) in that they too have had to learn another language. In this way, teachers are experienced language learners, who may inevitably be more sensitive and empathetic towards students facing potential learning difficulties (Medgyes 1994). Finding multilingual ELF teachers may prove to be somewhat challenging, but it is certainly possible considering that 35% of Newark's inhabitants are Hispanic (Newark City Data 2014).

Teachers' approach

Rather than employing the use of English only in the teaching and learning environment, the use of multilingualism or translanguaging (Garcia 2009; Creese and Blackledge 2010; Canagarajah 2011) should be encouraged and promoted. Canagarajah (2011: 2) describes translanguaging for multilinguals as follows:

> Languages are part of a repertoire that is accessed for their communicative purposes; languages are not discrete and separated, but form an integrated system for them; multilingual competence emerges out of local practices where multiple languages are negotiated for communication; competence doesn't consist of separate competencies for each language, but a multicompetence that functions symbiotically for the different languages in one's repertoire; and, for these reasons, proficiency for multilinguals is focused on repertoire building – i.e., developing abilities in the different functions served by different languages – rather than total mastery of each and every language.

Although English is in fact the target language, resorting to students' L1s should not be avoided by teachers or students (Kramsch 1997; Cook 2001). ELF teachers need to be open about utilizing different languages in the learning environment and be convinced that multilingualism rather than monolingualism will foster and promote a better and positive learning atmosphere among their students.

Previous studies looking at EIL teaching that have taken a multilingual and multicultural approach, such as the multi-competence and L2 user model (Cook 2001) or 'appropriate pedagogy approach' (Kramsch and Sullivan 1996), have reported successful findings in different parts of the world (cf. Kramsch and Sullivan 1996 in Vietnam, McKay 2003b in Chile and Creese and Blackledge 2010 in England). The two distinct teaching advantages of a multilingual approach for the migrant workers observed is in the area of grammar teaching and in instilling confidence among students. My interviews revealed that learners often became frustrated when trying to learn English in the classroom because they were not able to understand teachers' instructions or grammatical explanations. Multilingual teachers can and should make use of students' L1 and 'return to translation' (Kramsch 2014: 306) in order to explain grammatical rules and constructions. As language professionals, we take grammatical knowledge, for example word classes, for granted, but many of the domestic workers interviewed did not know what a preposition or adjective was in Portuguese or Spanish, let alone in English. There would be little point in explaining complicated grammatical structures in migrants' L2 when they were not even familiar with the grammatical terminology in their own L1.

The second advantage is motivational. If students lack confidence regarding their language abilities, they will probably be hesitant to practise and use their L2 English with other NNSs or NSs. The advantage of promoting multilingualism within the learning context is that it encourages them to experience language learning as 'play' (Kramsch and Sullivan 1996) and use the target language more freely without worrying about 'correct' pronunciation or grammar. This will boost students' confidence level, which in turn will increase their desire to practice their English outside class with other NNSs with a different L1 from their own.

What would taking a multilingual approach to the teaching of domestic migrants involve? It would certainly include the use of code-switching, which has been widely documented (Hornberger 2002, 2005; Lin 2005; Martin 2005; Shin 2005; Arthur and Martin 2006; Creese and Blackledge 2010). Within an ELF setting, code-switching should be encouraged since it not only indexes bilinguals' ability to use two codes interchangeably for different reasons, such as showing involvement in talk, but signals their personal identities and relationships with their interlocutors (McKay and Bokhorst-Heng 2008). By using two codes interchangeably within a teaching and learning context, teachers are signalling to their students that all languages are equal and being able to draw on one's full linguistic repertoire promotes creativity and learning. According to Martin (2005: 89), allowing students to code-switch during lessons allows students 'creative, pragmatic and "safe" practices [...] between the official language of the lesson and a language which the classroom participants have a greater access to'. Code-switching would be a particularly useful strategy with migrant workers because my findings show that code-switching is something which domestics are particularly adept at when communicating in their L1. For example, in my data domestic workers reproduce entire conversations between themselves and their clients, as indicated in extract (6) when Bianca used code-switching to replicate her conversation with Mrs. Willows. Encouraging migrant workers to code-switch in the classroom is therefore likely to be highly productive, tapping into a communicative practice which is already enjoyed and valued in the domestic workers' community.

Teaching migrant workers should also include applying Firth's (1996) 'let it pass' principle to classroom interaction as well as his 'make it normal' concept, which entails using an unknown phrase or word in one's own speech production. Domestics are already experiencing the 'let it pass' principle in their conversations with target speakers and is exemplified in my data when Bianca addresses a client as *Mrs Katie* or *Mr Mike* rather than using their surname. This so-called 'mistake' has and continues to be 'passed' by *Mrs Katie* and *Mr Mike* since neither of them has ever attempted to correct Bianca. As long as information is conveyed successfully, learners do not necessarily have to be 'corrected', but as Firth suggests 'perceived problems must be dealt with immediately, rather than being allowed to pass' (1996: 250).

In a setting such as this, learning activities should also be tailored to domestic workers' specific needs. This means that students need to be able to tell their teachers what they want and need to learn. In some ways, this reflects Breen's approach to learner autonomy referred to as the 'process syllabus' (Breen 1984) and implies that students and teachers need to negotiate the curriculum (Cook 2001: 232). Teachers would need, for example, to concentrate on different interactional patterns of learners and emphasize certain repair strategies concerning breakdown in communication since this is a theme many domestic workers and ELF learners in general are concerned with (McKay and Bokhorst-Heng 2008).

Finally, teachers need to encourage creativity. This can be done in conjunction with Firth's (1996) 'let it pass principle' and even code-switching (Martin 2005), as discussed above in relation to Bianca's use of *Mrs Katie*, an addressee form that from its initial use has been mutually intelligible to the addressee and creative on Bianca's part. Initially, Bianca's intention was not to mispronounce her client's name and thus produce a way to address her client in which she felt most comfortable. This led to her use of *Mrs Katie* and *Mr Mike*, which she continues to use. This example of being creative in an L2 is important for several reasons. First, it demonstrates different levels of a learner's L2 knowledge. In order to even produce *Mrs Katie*, or *Mr Mike*, Bianca needed to be aware of formal addressee forms in Standard English as well as specific phonemic pronunciation. Second, it indexes an L2 learner's confidence level with 'playing' with an L2 and being creative with it. By inserting *Katie* and *Mike* rather than *Jones*, Bianca was well aware that such a construction was 'wrong', but confident that her addressees would understand her. Indeed, this was the case and continues to be so. Being creative with language in this way should be promoted and 'passed' by teachers since it may allow learners to feel more at ease within the learning environment as well as with target language speakers in authentic settings.

Context and setting

From my interviews, many domestics claimed that they had either stopped attending formal language courses or not begun taking them at all, due to the times of the courses, the place where courses were offered, and their content. For the individuals in this study, attending a language class at night was not possible due to familial obligations and the fact that they were tired after a physically strenuous workday. They claimed that once their official workday was done and their families were attended to, they no longer had the time, energy, or concentration required to attend night classes. The domestic workers in this study that were enrolled in language courses took them on the weekends, although this still entails a certain amount of dedication and commitment on the part of learners and teachers alike (Creese and Blackledge 2010).

Ideally, domestic workers would be taught in a comfortable setting that need not resemble a traditional classroom setting but a place where ELF learners and users feel safe. This could be a local community centre, church, café, or even someone's home. The place should be centrally located within the Ironbound neighbourhood since most of the domestic workers in this study do not have their own means of transportation. This means that, from a logistical perspective, classes have to be conveniently located in order for them to be attended. This should not be difficult to achieve since classes could take place in a public setting on a weekly basis or even rotate settings every week, that is, in someone's home one week, in a café another, and so on. Having a flexible learning environment also signals to learners that learning is not done in a classroom setting only, but in everyday spheres of life. Promoting such a learning environment shows that both teachers and students are willing to be open-minded and flexible. For teachers, this would require working with and relying on mobile materials such as books, magazines, flash cards, everyday items that fit into a backpack, and a small foldup white board.

Materials

New and different materials need to be developed that reflect the multilingual practices described above and suit domestic migrant workers' local and workplace contexts. This means that materials need to consider and reflect migrants' social, cultural, sociolinguistic, and ethnic contexts (cf. McKay 2003b for a discussion of materials devised within a Chilean context). Textbook writing could be used as part of the multilingual practices approach, addressing themes salient to domestic migrant workers rather than 'imaginary content' Cook (2001: 219). Themes could include, for example, looking for housing, job hunting, family, going shopping, taking public transportation, meeting new people from different cultures, and addressing the homeland and missing it, while simultaneously including components of the dominant culture in order to promote mutual understanding and respect. The themes addressed and the language presented in such books must be relevant to domestic workers' everyday lives and workplace environments. Specifically, they need to attend to small talk, household items, furniture, and cleaning products to name but a few. By doing so, domestic workers would be able to better relate to the various themes and contexts presented in books. In his discussion of bilingual pedagogy and strategies, Cummins (2005: 588) even lists the 'creation of student-authored dual language books by means of translation from the initial language of writing to the L2'. Such an activity could be part of a larger project within a course. Flashcards could be created to resemble everyday household items and teachers can even use real life articles. Audio CDs could be designed that reflect authentic conversational exchanges (Kirkpatrick 2007) between clients and domestic workers as well as domestic workers in their everyday lives, that is, at the supermarket, bank, restaurant, or on the bus.

The language used for these materials should be multilingual (McKay 2003b; Cummins 2005) rather than monolingual and reinforce language use within the learning environment. Examples of code-switching should be included in the written and oral materials developed, and oral materials should stress different ELF speakers with a range of foreign accents in order for learners to be comfortable speaking English with an accent, rather than measuring themselves against NS, which is an 'impossible target' anyway (Cook 2002: 331). Although materials should focus on fostering oral communicative competence, not all areas need to be stressed equally. In the case of the domestic workers I interviewed, priority should be given to speaking and listening skills, followed by reading and writing skills since this is what they both desired and required.

Regarding content, primary emphasis should be placed on the areas which domestics claim to have greatest difficulty with – grammatical competence in terms of vocabulary, word and sentence formation as well as strategic competence, that is, asking for clarification, slower speech, and repetition (Canale and Swain 1980).

Employing a communication-skills-based curriculum means that learners are aware and exposed to NNS–NNS communication and are encouraged to become engaged in similar interactions themselves. By doing so, NNSs would get used to hearing different languages being produced by other NNSs and possibly become more comfortable and confident in their own English language production.

This suggests that, in terms of course content, a traditional English for specific purposes course ('English for domestic labour') based on linguistic features presumed to be typical of the discourse community would not be appropriate. Content needs to be defined in terms of local needs analysis since the circumstances of domestic labour vary worldwide.[5]

Conclusions

The suggestions made here concerning ELF pedagogy within the context of domestic migrant workers have taken previous ELF and EIL pedagogical research as a starting point. In this chapter I have outlined the pedagogical implications for teaching domestic migrant workers and developed concrete recommendations concerning ELF teaching within a very specific group of ELF learners and users. The recommendations made here should inform educators and teachers about the lives and challenges faced by domestic migrant workers and assist them in developing different teaching methods, approaches, and materials while creating more comfortable and flexible learning environments that promote multilingualism among teachers and learners alike. This requires a different approach, one that views English as a language that should be taught and learned for communicative purposes rather than identification (House 2003). A teaching curriculum needs to be developed that is based on communicative skills (Sifakis 2004). The methods used should focus on mutual intelligibility (McKay 2002; Seidlhofer and Jenkins 2003; Seidlhofer 2004; Kuo 2006), help learners develop interactional strategies (McKay 2002: 127), and promote the use of code-switching (Martin 2005; McKay and Bokhorst-Heng 2008) and creativity among L2 learners within the learning environment. The approach taken should be sensitive concerning the choice of material and respectful of the local migrant culture of individuals' learning context. By assisting individuals with their language learning efforts and use of ELF in their workplaces, this new direction in ELF pedagogy can make a difference among domestic migrant workers who continue to lead 'un-globalized lives' in a globalized world.

Engagement priorities

This chapter attempts to fill a gap in ELF studies concerned with workplaces that until now have looked primarily at 'white collar workplace' contexts. Holmes (2012) recently states that 'few researchers have ventured into blue collar worksites; they tend to be noisy and dirty and often rather uncomfortable places for academics undertaking research'. Although this chapter has taken previous EIL and ELF pedagogical research as a starting point, I have argued for a new direction in ELF pedagogy among domestic migrant workers. This entails developing different teaching methods and approaches, and creating new and relevant material aimed at migrant workers, as well as reassessing the learning environment.

1) Do you agree with Holmes' statement concerning research and blue collar worksites? What other factors besides being 'noisy, dirty and uncomfortable' do you think may contribute to the lack of research in this domain?
2) While many ELF researchers claim that English should be taught for communicative purposes rather than identification (House 2003) and that a teaching curriculum should focus on communicative skills (Sifakis 2004), what can teachers and material developers do in order to make such claims possible and realistic for migrants wanting to learn English?
3) In this chapter I argued that a teacher's knowledge base should include their learners' L1s and that multilingualism would foster and promote a positive learning environment for their students, particularly in the area of grammar explanations and students' confidence levels. I also mention that, as a result, code-switching, the 'let it pass principle', and being creative with students' L2 are approaches that should be used within such learning environments. Do you think teachers would be open to such ideas and approaches? Can you list pros and cons for employing multiple languages within a migrant learning context?

Appendix

Transcription conventions

[	= start of overlap
@@	= signals laughter (the number of @ indicates approximately the duration of laughter)
wo::rd	= perceptible vowel or consonant lengthening
,	= pause shorter than one second
(.)	= noticeable pause
(1.0)	= pause lengths in seconds
?	= rising intonation, often signals interrogative sentences
=	= latched talk
XXX	= incomprehensible speech
CAPS	= marks emphatic stress

Notes

1. The work of Lorente (forthcoming) focuses on scripted language of Filipino domestic workers in Singapore.
2. The interviews with the migrant women were conducted in July 2011 at the base of the cleaning company, to which I had access through familial ties. They were held in European Portuguese, Luso-Brazilian Portuguese, Spanish, and English, and reflected

the language preferences of each interviewee. The English-speaking interviews were carried out with clients of the company, who, since they frequented the Ironbound regularly, felt comfortable in volunteering for the study. The interviews with the English-speaking visitors were carried out in their homes, located in towns 10 to 20 kilometres from Newark. The interviews were recorded and lasted between 16 minutes to one hour and 30 minutes, producing a total of 21.5 hours of recordings. All of the recordings were transcribed and resulted in two different sub-corpora – a Portuguese and Spanish corpus (82,792 words) and an English corpus (103,607 words). All interviewees were women of 24–63 years of age. The 'English-speaking visitor' interviewees were two men and 18 women of 36–72 years of age. Due to the data-driven nature of this study, hypotheses were not addressed in an *a priori* fashion.

3. The interviews covered a number of topics ranging from migration, integration, and missing the homeland to communicative practices in their workplace. Questions were not aimed specifically at eliciting information about language learning, but several thematic categories involving language practices emerged from the interview transcripts and corpora. These included code choice in the workplace, at home, and in their local communities, language learning attempts on the part of the migrants, and perceptions of English use by domestic workers, clients, and language brokers.

4. Bianca is not only responsible for driving domestics from the Ironbound to their respective homes, but is also in charge of coordinating the schedule together with Magda. Bianca is in charge of the cleaning company whenever Magda is away on vacation, for example. Therefore, within the cleaning company network's hierarchy, Bianca's status as 'driver' and Magda's 'right-hand man' positions her differently from the rest of the cleaning staff.

5. According to the International Labour Organization (ILO), there are roughly 100 million domestic migrant workers worldwide. These consist of nannies, cleaning ladies, and caregivers.

References

Adey, P. (2010). *Mobility*. New York: Routledge.

Anderson, B. (2000). *Doing the Dirty Work? The Global Politics of Domestic Labour*. London: Zed Books.

Arthur, J. and Martin, P. (2006). Accomplishing lessons in postcolonial classrooms: Comparative perspectives from Botswana and Brunei Darussalam. *Comparative Education* 42: 177–202.

Bauman, Z. (1998). *Globalization: The Human Consequences*. Cambridge and Oxford: Polity Press.

Block, D. (2007). *Second Language Identities*. London: Continuum.

Blommaert, J. (2010). *The Sociolinguistics of Globalization*. Cambridge: Cambridge University Press.

Breen, M. P. (1984). Process Syllabus for the language classroom. In Brumfit, C. J. (ed.), *General English Syllabus Design: ELT Documents 118*. Oxford: Pergamon Press, pp. 47–60.

Canagarajah, S. (1999). *Resisting Linguistic Imperialism in English Teaching*. Oxford: Oxford University Press.

Canagarajah, S. (2007). Lingua Franca English, multilingual communities, and language acquisition. *The Modern Language Journal* 91: 923–939.

Canagarajah, S. (2011). Translanguaging in the classroom: Emerging issues for research and pedagogy. In Wei, L. (ed.), *Applied Linguistics Review 2*. New York: Mouton de Gruyter.

Canale, M. and Swain, M. (1980). Theoretical bases of communicative approaches to second language teaching and testing. *Applied Linguist* 1 (1): 27–31.

Chang, G. (2000). *Disposable Domestics: Immigrant Women Workers in the Global Economy*. Cambridge, MA: South End Press.

Cogo, A. (2010). Strategic use and perceptions of English as a Lingua Franca. *Poznan Studies in Contemporary Linguistics* 46 (3): 295–312.

Cogo, A. (2012). ELF and super-diversity: A case study of ELF multilingual practices from a business context. *Journal of English as a Lingua Franca* 1 (2): 287–313.

Cook, V.J. (1999). Going beyond the native speaker in language teaching. *TESOL Quarterly* 33 (2): 185–209.

Cook, V. J. (2001). *Second Language Learning and Language Teaching*. London: Arnold.

Cook, V. J. (2002). *Portraits of the L2 User*. Clevedon: Multilingual Matters.

Creese, A. and Blackledge, A. (2010). Translanguaging in the bilingual classroom: A pedagogy for learning and teaching? *Modern Language Journal* 94(1): 103–115.

Cummins, J. (2005). A proposal for action: Strategies for recognizing heritage language competence as a learning resource within the mainstream classroom. *Modern Language Journal* 89: 585–592.

Del Torto, L. M. (2008). Once a broker, always a broker: Non-professional interpreting as identity accomplishment in multigenerational Italian-English bilingual family interaction. *Multilingua* 27: 77–97.

Dewey, M. (2012). Towards a post-normative approach: learning the pedagogy of ELF. *Journal of English as a Lingua Franca* 1 (1): 141–170.

Ehrenreich, S. (2009). English as a Lingua Franca in multinational corporations – exploring business communities of practice. In Mauranen, A. and Ranta, E. (eds), *English as a Lingua Franca: Studies and Findings*. Newcastle: Cambridge Scholars Press, pp. 126–151.

Firth, A. (1996). The discursive accomplishment of normality. On 'lingua franca' English and conversation analysis. *Journal of Pragmatics* 26: 237–259.

Garcia, O. (2009). *Bilingual Education in the 21st Century: A Global Perspective*. Oxford: Wiley Blackwell.

Gonçalves, K. (2012). The semiotic landscapes and the discourses of place within a Portuguese-speaking neighborhood. *Interdisciplinary Journal of Portuguese Diaspora Studies*, 71–99.

Holmes, J. (2012). Discourse in the Workplace. In Hyland, K. and Paltridge, B. (eds), *Continuum Companion to Discourse Analysis*. London: Continuum, pp. 185–198.

Holt, E. (1996). Reporting on talk: The use of direct reported speech in conversation. *Research on Language and Social Interaction* 29 (3): 219–245.

Holt, E. (2000). Reporting and Reacting: Concurrent Responses to Reported Speech. *Research on Language and Social Interaction* 33 (4): 425–454.

Hondagneu-Sotelo, P. (1990). *Gender and the Politics of Mexican Undocumented Immigrant Settlement*. PhD dissertation, University of California, Berkeley.

Hornberger, N. H. (2002). Multilingual language policies and the continua of biliteracy: An ecological approach. *Language Policy* 1: 27–51.

Hornberger, N. H. (2005). Opening and filling up implementational and ideological spaces in heritage language education. *The Modern Language Journal* 89: 605–609.

House, J. (2003). English as a Lingua Franca: A threat to multilingualism? *Journal of Sociolinguistics* 7 (4): 556–578.

International Labour Organization. (2011). *Text of the Convention Concerning Decent Work for Domestic Workers*. Geneva. Available at http://www.ilo.org/wcmsp5/groups/public/---ed_norm/---relconf/documents/meetingdocument/wcms_157836.pdf (accessed 15 July 2014).

Jenkins, J. (2000). *The Phonology of English as an International Language. New Models, New Norms, New Goals.* Oxford: Oxford University Press.

Jenkins, J. (2007). *English as a Lingua Franca: Attitude and Identity.* Oxford: Oxford University Press.

Kankaanranta, A. and Louhiala-Salminen, L. (2007). Business communication in BELF, focus on teaching column. *Business Communication Quarterly* 70: 55–59.

Kankaanranta, A. and Louhiala-Salminen, L. (2010). 'English? – Oh, it's just work!': A study of BELF users' perceptions. *English for Specific Purposes* 29: 204–209.

Kirkpatrick, A. (2007). *World Englishes: Implications for International Communication and English Language Teaching.* Cambridge: Cambridge University Press.

Kramsch, C. (1997). The privilege of the nonnative speaker. *PMLA* 112 (3): 359–369.

Kramsch, C. (2014). Teaching Foreign Languages in an Era of Globalization: Introduction. *The Modern Language Journal* 98 (1): 296–311.

Kramsch, C. and Sullivan, P. (1996). Appropriate Pedagogy. *ELT Journal* 50 (3): 199–212.

Kuo, I-Chun (Vicky). (2006). Addressing the issue of teaching English as a Lingua Franca. *ELT Journal* 60 (3): 213–221.

Lan, Pei-Chia. (2006). *Global Cinderellas: Migrant Domestics and Newly Rich Employers in Taiwan.* Durham and London: Duke University Press.

Lin, A. M. Y. (2005). Critical, transdisciplinary perspectives on language-in-education policy and practice in postcolonial contexts: The case of Hong Kong. In Lin, A. M. and Martin, P. W. (eds), *Decolonisation, Globalisation: Language-in-education Policy and Practice.* Clevedon, UK: Multilingual Matters, pp. 38–54.

Lorente, B. (forthcoming). *Scripts of servitude: language, labor migration and domestic work.* Clevedon, UK: Multilingual Matters.

Louhiala-Salminen, L., Charles, M. and Kankaanranta, A. (2005). English as a lingua franca in Nordic corporate mergers: Two case companies. *English for Specific Purposes* 24 (4): 401–421.

MacKenzie, I. (2014). *English as a Lingua Franca: Theorizing and teaching English.* New York: Routledge.

Martin, P. (2005). 'Safe' language practices in two rural schools in Malaysia: Tensions between policy and practice. In Lin, A. M. and Martin, P. W. (eds), *Decolonisation, Globalisation: Language-in-education Policy and Practice.* Clevedon, UK: Multilingual Matters, pp. 74–97.

Matras, Y. (2009). *Language Contact.* Cambridge: Cambridge University Press.

McKay, S. L. (2002). EIL curriculum development. In Rubdy, R. and Saraceni, M. (eds), *English in the World: Global Rules, Global Roles.* Bangkok: IELE Press at Assumption University.

McKay, S. L. (2003a). Toward an appropriate EIL pedagogy: Re-examining common ELT assumptions. *International Journal of Applied Linguistics* 13 (1): 1–22.

McKay, S. L. (2003b). Teaching English as an International Language: The Chilean context. *ELT Journal* 57 (2): 139–148.

McKay, S. L. and Bokhorst-Heng, W. D. (2008). *International English in Its Sociolinguistic Contexts: Towards a Socially Sensitive EIL Pedagogy.* New York: Routledge.

Medgyes, P. (1994). *The Non-Native Teacher.* London: Macmillan.

Milroy, L. (1987 [1980]). *Language and Social Networks*, 2nd ed. Oxford: Blackwell Publishing.

Newark City Data. (2014). http://www.city-data.com/city/Newark-New-Jersey.html (accessed 15 July 2014).

Norton, B. (2000). *Identity and Language Learning.* Harlow: Pearson Education Limited.

Papastergiadis, N. (2000). *The Turbulence of Migration: Globalization, Deterritorialization and Hybridity*. Cambridge and Oxford: Polity Press.

Parkinson, S. (1988). Portuguese. In Harris, M. and Vincent, N. (eds), *The Romance Languages*. Oxford: Oxford University Press, pp. 131–169.

Parreñas, R. S. (2001). *Servants of Globalization. Women, Migration, and Domestic Work*. Stanford, CA: Stanford University Press.

Planken, B. (2005). Managing rapport in Lingua Franca sales negotiations: A comparison of professional and aspiring negotiators. *English for Specific Purposes* 24(4): 381–400.

Planken, B. and C. Nickerson. (2009). English for specific business purposes: intercultural issues and the use of business English as a lingua franca. In Belcher, D. (ed.), *English for Specific Purposes in Theory and Practice*. Ann Arbor: University of Michigan Press, pp. 107–126.

Poncini, G. (2004). *Discursive Strategies in Multicultural Business Meetings*. Bern: Peter Lang.

Pullin Stark, P. (2009). No joke – this is serious! Power, solidarity and humour in business English as a Lingua Franca (BELF) meetings. In Mauranen, A. and Ranta, E. (eds), *English as a Lingua Franca: Studies and Findings*. Newcastle: Cambridge Scholars Press, pp. 153–177.

Rogerson-Revell, P. (2007). Using English for international business: A European case study. *English for Specific Purposes* 26: 103–120.

Rogerson-Revell, P. (2008). Participation and Performance in International Business Meetings. *English for Specific Purposes* 27(3): 338–360.

Rollins, J. (1985). *Between Women: Domestics and Their Employers*. Philadelphia: Temple University Press.

Romero, M. (2002). *Maid in the U.S.A.* London: Routledge.

Ruiz, L. V. (1987). By the day or the week: Mexicana domestic workers in El Paso. In Ruiz, V. L. and Tiano, S. (eds), *Women on the U.S. – Mexico Border: Responses to Change*. Boston: Allen and Unwin, pp. 61–76.

Seidlhofer, B. (2001). Closing a conceptual gap: the case for a description of English as a Lingua Franca. *International Journal of Applied Linguistics* 11(2): 133–158.

Seidlhofer, B. (2004). Research perspectives on teaching English as a Lingua Franca. *Annual Review of Applied Linguistics* 24: 209–239.

Seidlhofer, B., Breiteneder, A. and Pitzl, M. (2006). English as a lingua franca in Europe: Challenges for applied linguistics. *Annual Review of Applied Linguistics* 26: 3–34.

Seidlhofer, B. and Jenkins, J. (2003). English as a Lingua Franca and the politics of property. In Mair, C. (ed.), *The Politics of English as a World Language*. Amsterdam: Rodopi, pp. 139–154.

Sifakis, N. C. (2004). Teaching EIL – teaching international or intercultural English: What teachers should know. *System* 32(2): 237–250.

Sifakis, N. (2009). Challenges in teaching ELF in the periphery: The Greek context. *ELT Journal* 63(3): 230–237.

Shin, S. J. (2005). *Developing in Two Languages: Korean children in America*. Clevedon, UK: Multilingual Matters.

Tannen, D. (1989). *Talking Voices: Repetition, Dialogue, and Imagery in Conversational Discourse*. Cambridge: Cambridge University Press.

Urry, J. (2000). *Sociology Beyond Societies. Mobilities for the Twenty-first Century*. London: Routledge.

9

Teaching through ELF at International Post-Secondary Institutions: A Case Study at United World Colleges

Veronika Quinn Novotná and Jiřina Dunková

Introduction

This chapter explores the use of English, especially in its Lingua Franca (LF) function, at United World Colleges (UWCs). UWCs are international, globally based, multilingual post-secondary schools with a standardised curriculum geared towards the International Baccalaureate (IB) diploma. Our chief focus is to describe how English is viewed and used as the main means of instruction and the main tool of social and academic interaction among students and staff at UWCs, using questionnaire survey data. We use this data to identify several key teaching and learning practices that facilitate the integration of Content and Language Integrated Learning (CLIL) through ELF in multilingual settings. This is an important area of investigation since the relationship between multilingual environments and CLIL (Juan-Garau and Salazar-Noguera 2015) and between ELF and CLIL (Smit 2010 a, b; Knapp 2011) have only recently started to be explored in depth.

The chapter is divided into two parts. The first part provides a general framework of international schools, a brief history of the International Baccalaureate® (IB) programme and the UWCs background. The second part of the study explores the pedagogical implications of these policies, drawing on empirical data collected at UWCs to describe the key tendencies of ELF usage in the schools and make recommendations for ELF-aware teacher training programmes.

International schools and ELF usage

In this section we describe the make-up and language background of international schools. We then focus on UWCs, describing ELF usage in the schools using data from a research study carried out in 2012 and 2013 (Quinn Novotná, Grosser and Dunková 2013).

International schools – qualifications, language policies

International schools are not easily defined (see Wilkinson 1998). They are generally characterised in terms of 'multinational composition' (Hayden and Thompson 2004: 28) and described as 'market actors' whose 'stage is becoming increasingly global' (Hayden and Thompson 2004: 9). The history of international schools is connected with post-WWII developments and the globalisation trends that have characterised the last three to four decades. The International Schools Association (ISA), created in 1951 and based in Geneva, was 'one of the earliest attempts to incorporate supranationality' (Hayden and Thompson 2004: 9).

International schools can only function as international schools thanks to a shared linguistic code. This has been facilitated by the rise of English as a global language (Crystal 1997) and/or a global lingua franca. In the 1950s, however, the perception and spread of English was far different from what it is now or even what it was 20 years ago. Nowadays, even though regional LFs may be utilised at certain institutions, the role of English as a dominant institutional language at international schools is unshakable and is indeed one of the vehicles of globalisation (see also Wallace 2002; Dewey 2007; Gnutzmann and Intemann 2008; Coupland 2010; Saxena and Omoniyi 2010). With the growing number of international schools operating in English there is now an urgent need to research the role of English at these institutions (see, e.g., Hayden and Thompson 2013; Mahboob and Barratt 2014).

The International Baccalaureate Diploma

The IB organisation was founded in 1968 in Geneva and is run both privately and by the state. According to the IB website, the first IB schools were 'predominantly private' and its current guiding principles include the 'development of intercultural awareness and understanding among young people', the promotion of 'holistic education' and 'higher-order cognitive skills such as critical thinking, analysis, problem-solving and creative thinking.'

The International Baccalaureate® (IB) offers four recognised international education programmes to more than one million students aged 3–19 in 146 countries. The International Baccalaureate Diploma Programme (IB DP) is a two-year pre-university course for students from 16–19 years of age. The organisation is a non-profit educational foundation and evolves around its mission 'to create a better and more peaceful world through intercultural understanding and respect'.

IB DP and English – official policy

The relationship of IB DP and English is quite straightforward. The IB Language Policy (cf. IB Language Policy) clearly states that English is the 'organization's internal working language, in which most operational and development activities take place. It is also the language of its governance, management and academic committees'. Hence, English is not only a key language of instruction in the IB and IB DP but it is also one of the administrative languages of the organisation, that is, it is used in formal situations, official documents and correspondence, and serves as a means of communication with the public. The language policy of the UWC is described below (see 'Language policy and proficiency').

UWC – educational policy, CLIL and LA

United World Colleges were selected as a case study for several reasons. First, they are represented on a truly global scale, that is, on four continents. They are also closely connected with the beginnings of the IB programme – UWC Atlantic College was the first school to abandon the national curriculum in favour of the International Baccalaureate Diploma Programme (IB DP). More importantly, however, our previous research (Quinn Novotná, Grosser and Dunková 2013) shows that UWCs represent an 'ideal' environment for a multitude of forms, varieties and functions of English to take shape and flourish. There are 12 UWCs worldwide providing education for students from over 140 countries. Thus, they represent a wide range of nationalities, mother tongues, cultures and social backgrounds. UWCs support such values as 'international and intercultural understanding' and 'celebration of difference,' which we believe 'resonate with the intellectual background of English as a Lingua Franca (ELF) as discussed by ELF researchers' (Quinn Novotná, Grosser and Dunková 2013: 51–52). The admission process to the colleges is designed to provide equal chances to students from all socio-economic backgrounds and is mostly carried out through national committees, which evaluate candidates against core selection criteria reflecting the local context of each candidate. UWC students live a residential life at their colleges and UWCs charge tuition fees for which needs-based scholarships are available. All UWC colleges offer accommodation and the students live at the schools for the whole time of their studies. The educational programmes include organised extracurricular activities, exchanges and community and volunteer programmes. In line with general IB principles, UWC policy stresses the importance of socialisation and the building up of social relationships within a multinational and multilingual community. The importance of this social policy for language learning will be discussed in the section on *Extensive language exposure*.

Our previous research (Quinn Novotná, Grosser and Dunková 2013) showed that UWCs provide a typical Content and Language Integrated Learning (CLIL) educational approach, which is characterised by an equal focus on content and language and an emphasis on multilingual and multicultural education including elements of language immersion programmes (see Coyle, Hood and Marsh 2010; Dalton-Puffer, Nikula and Smit 2010; Georgiou 2012). In relation to Coyle et al.'s typologies of CLIL, UWCs belong to a 'Model B2' (2010: 21) because of its link to international certification (in our case the IB diploma). Our previous research also highlighted the role of language awareness (LA) at the UWCs, understood as increased sensitivity towards language and the ability to reflect upon language use, culture, creativity and meaning (see James and Garret 1991; Carter 2003; Andrews 2007; Edmondson 2009). We concluded that both these areas (CLIL and LA) were specific to UWCs but were potentially transferable to similar institutions.

ELF usage at UWC – qualitative analysis

Our survey-based research[1] was designed to focus on student and teacher attitudes to ELF usage in relation to CLIL and LA at UWCs. The mix of languages and nationalities of UWCs highlighted by the survey is shown in Tables 9.1 and 9.2 below, which illustrate the background data from 9 UWCs. The numbers of teachers and students who responded to the survey is set out in Table 9.1 and their demographic data in Table 9.2.

The tables suggest that the English spoken in the UWC context is a prime example of ELF in a multilingual environment – the 315 students who participated in the survey had 87 different nationalities and spoke 71 declared mother tongues.

Key tendencies

Teaching and learning in the UWC ELF environment was explored through on-site classroom observation at one UWC[2] combined with qualitative analysis of questionnaire responses, using a set of variables that had been identified in previous research.[3] This section sets out seven main tendencies emerging from the analysis in relation to teaching and learning via the medium of English in a multilingual environment. These tendencies, which are based on perceptions of teaching and learning through ELF 'in action', can also be understood as

Table 9.1 UWCs – countries and respondents

UWC school	Students	Teachers
UWC Atlantic College Llantwit Major, UK	73	10
UWC South East Asia Singapore	46	15
Li Po Chun UWC Hong Kong SAR, China	46	6
UWC Mahindra College Pune, India	41	10
UWC Adriatic Duino, Italy	43	2
UWC in Mostar, Bosnia and Herzegovina	32	7
UWC Red Cross Nordic Flekke, Norway	32	5
UWC-USA Montezuma, New Mexico	–	5
Pearson College UWC Victoria, Canada	–	1
Total	315	64

Table 9.2 Demographic data – UWC teachers and students

UWC – Teachers

Nationality		Mother tongue		Sex	
UK	19	English	33	Male	35
USA	8	Croatian	5	Female	26
India	7	Spanish	4	**UWC based in**	
Canada	4	Polish	2	Hong Kong	6
Croatia	3	Hindi	2	India	10
Bosnia and Herzegovina	3	German	2	Singapore	15
Australia	2	Czech	2	Italy	2
Spain	2	Other	11	UK	9
Czech Republic	2	**Total**	61	Bosnia and Herzegovina	7
Other	11			Norway	5
Total	61			USA/ Canada	4/1

UWC – Students

Nationality	N.	Mother tongue		Age		Common interlocutors*	
India	39	English	81	15	2	NSs	104
UK	20	Chinese	19	16	75	NNSs	183
Hong Kong	20	Hindi	18	17	117		
USA	15	German	15	18	98	**UWC based in**	
Netherlands	14	Spanish	15	19	16	Hong Kong	46
Norway	14	Dutch	14	20	2	India	41
Germany	10	Norwegian	14	**Sex**		Singapore	46
China	10	Italian	9	Male	107	Italy	43
Italy	9	French	7	Female	202	UK	71
Canada	8	Portugal/ Danish	6	**Year of study**		Bosnia and Herz.	32
Other	151	Other	112	First	139	Norway	32
Total	310	**Total**	310	Final	171	**Total**	311

a set of teaching recommendations applicable at, and possibly beyond, other multilingual institutions.

Language policy and proficiency in English

Our previous research (Quinn Novotná, Grosser and Dunková 2013) suggested that UWCs adopted language policies that contribute significantly to the success of the UWC environment. In order to investigate further how the policies were applied and perceived, students and teachers were asked if they had been introduced to an official language policy (LP) at UWCs. Their answers provided a somewhat mixed picture, summarised in Table 9.3.

The majority of both UWC students (75.9%) and teachers (75%) had not been introduced to any official institutional language policy; most starting teachers (68.8%) had not been instructed either formally or informally to use

Table 9.3 Questionnaire answers – 'were you introduced to an official language policy?'

UWC students		UWC teachers	
Yes	76 (24.13%)	Yes	14 (21.88%)
No	239 (75.87%)	No	48 (75%)
Total	315	*	2 (3.13)
		Total	64

*'Do not wish to answer.'

English only. Table 9.3 shows that a marked portion of both respondent groups had not received any formal instruction about the language rules at the school. Only three teachers mentioned that they had been 'formally'[4] informed that all instruction was in English. One teacher reported that s/he 'know[s] there is one – though [...] haven't seen it'. The rule that English was the main medium of communication and instruction seems to be of a rather implicit nature at all participating institutions, that is, teachers speak of a(n) 'understanding', 'assumption', 'default', of being 'aware of a policy', or report that it 'seemed obvious', or mention it was 'done unofficially.' These and several other examples of unwritten language management instances, such as an unofficial ban of offensive language or a recommendation to speak clearly and slowly, seem to be implemented and enforced relatively systematically across different UWCs.

Interaction in the students' mother tongues (MTs) is not explicitly prohibited in official documents and this is mirrored by students' and teachers' comments. However, a rule preventing MT interaction is perhaps unnecessary since the number of students that speak the same language at any given institution is usually rather low anyway and English is often the only option in interactions when there are speakers of other languages (SOLs) present. What we observed is that when no SOLs were present, the common L1 and/or other linguistic resources were considered acceptable and indeed utilised. Three students reported that local languages could sometimes be a problem for those who do not speak them since this may lead to reverse discrimination of monolingual (mostly English) NSs.

As already mentioned, selecting students from enormously diverse backgrounds is a deliberate strategy of UWCs. Fluency in English is not stated as a necessary requirement for enrolment in their programmes. This means that the students' command of English varies significantly – their intake includes native speakers, bilingual speakers, proficient English users (PEUs), and speakers with fairly low knowledge of English (see also Quinn Novotná, Grosser and Dunková 2013: 56).

When it comes to language assessment, the majority of teachers (68.8%, 44) reported that students' level of English language proficiency (in terms of fluency, accuracy, grammaticality, phonological and lexical correctness) plays a role when they assess their subject knowledge. Based on the respondents' comments, we observed that the level of English proficiency mostly plays a role in English as a subject (English A, English B), when teaching and assessing 'the essay writing process' and in the 'use of accurate subject-specific terminology'; in other subjects, e.g. biology, chemistry, history, language proficiency does not play a key role in the assessment of students' subject knowledge.

In sum, English is understood and used as the language of communication and instruction at UWCs. Official language policy may be in place but it is not explicitly enforced. It is presented and demonstrated in more implied and suggestive ways, or 'made clear' through doing, that is, teachers and students' efficient language usage and verbal and non-verbal behaviour is used as a guideline, which is emulated and followed by all parties involved.

Focus on content not language form

During classroom observation we noticed an overall focus on content, on communicating ideas and conveying message. The focus on content is expressed by the teachers' fairly strict attitudes towards knowledge of the subject matter on the one hand, and quite relaxed or liberal attitudes to language form on the other. We also noticed that most of the creative uses of grammar and pronunciation were passed over in silence by both teachers and peers. The typical features of teachers' and students' LF English included the following: omission and insertion of definite and indefinite articles, heavy reliance on certain verbs of high semantic generality, omission of third-person '-s' and use of universal question tags (Seidlhofer 2005: R 92).

Teachers' attitudes to language use, expressed in questionnaire answers, were a mixture of demanding in terms of what is taught, that is, content, definitions and vocabulary, and relaxed in terms of how students express themselves. Examples of comments describing these mixed attitudes are the following: '[I] give emphasis to science as opposed to English', '[...] I try to separate "language issues" from subject matters', and '[a]s long as they can communicate what they want to say (in maths) it doesn't matter how proficient they are.' Generally, there seems to be less focus on grammatical accuracy (e.g., 'We want their ideas, not proper grammar.'), although this varies according to different subjects and tasks. Both teachers and students distinguish the subjects and tasks that may require more accuracy and focus on form than others; in other words their approach is marked by a distinct level of flexibility.

Focus on vocabulary

We detected a strong focus on subject-specific vocabulary in almost all questionnaire answers and class observations (see also Quinn Novotná, Grosser and Dunková 2013: 68–70), as exemplified by a student's comment that '[e]veryone is very relaxed about the use of english, however the teacher is demanding more of a specialised vocabulary'. A teacher also made the following comment:

> I teach subjects where the level of English influences the understanding and answering the questions. Also, there are key words which are different in English than in other languages. The subjects require precision in vocabulary. I am liberal in terms of grammar, demanding in terms of vocabulary and sentence structure.

This comment suggests that, in relation to CLIL at UWC, the importance of precise and extensive knowledge of terminology goes hand in hand with a focus on subject matter. This orientation towards lexis and the importance of how it is presented and taught (see also Eldridge, Neufeld and Hancioğlu 2010), as well as its close link to proficiency, in other words, the fact that more extensive vocabulary knowledge is perceived to be directly linked to higher language and subject-specific proficiencies, are illustrated in the following comment from a teacher, exemplifying CLIL practice at UWC:

> As part of developing their proficiency in the subject I teach, I insist that my students learn to correctly use the relevant vocabulary. I assign flashcards, give vocabulary quizzes, and instruct my students in how to write well-composed paragraphs and essays. As this level, I see my job not just as teaching 'content' but also developing fluency in the subject and its ways of expression. I hope my approach allows them to access higher-level research papers in the subject as well as critique popular depictions/usages of the subject's concepts.

A solid grasp of vocabulary also plays a key role in increasing students' linguistic self-esteem, that is, their confidence in how they utilise the language to their advantage: 'English language skills among the non-native students are being consistently enhanced, by expanding vocabulary and developing routine in use of key phrasing. They gain more confidence and gradually reach higher levels of proficiency.' Similar findings are also presented in Quinn Novotná, Grosser and Dunková (2013: 65). For more about the role of vocabulary see the section *Challenges of studying through the medium of English* below.

Teacher and peer behavioural response to English usage

The questionnaires also examined how the students perceived their teachers' behaviour towards their English usage. To prevent possible bias questions did not include labels such as 'native', 'native-like' and 'non-native' English or 'variety of English', and used the phrase 'kind of English' instead. The questionnaires also allowed students freedom to refer to teachers' linguistic or overall teaching behaviour. In their answers 53.3% of students (168) did not claim that the teachers' behaviour towards them depended on the kind of English they use, whereas 46.7% (147) observed some change, suggesting that students' perception of UWC teacher's behaviour was as varied as the body of students themselves. A minor group of respondents (3) observed 'some form of discrimination towards students with stronger english skills.' Ten respondents, which is also a relatively small group, reported some form of discrimination of NNSs by teachers; in several instances they used rather strong expressive language, with comments including words such as 'more childish', 'ignore', 'bullied', 'demeaning', 'mentally retarded', 'opinion is discarded' or 'aggressive teachers' when describing how some teachers approach students 'when their level of English is poor'; some students made the same point but in less expressive terms: 'there is obviously no bias, but students are better able to articulate themselves because of having an advantage in English get appraised by teachers', or 'some teachers tend to listen to students with good grammar than those who don't.' Since the body of responses to this question was very diversified, it was hard to detect major tendencies; the highest number of respondents (17%) agreed that UWC teachers behave so as to create a very linguistically fair and supportive environment. UWC students mention a 'patient', 'equal', 'helpful' approach. For example, '75% of the teachers have tutorials and they are VERY patient' or '[teachers offer] extra classes after the school'. 'Fair' treatment especially towards NNS students is also stressed, as shown by comments such as 'students [remarked that they] aren't favoured if they know English and the teachers do their best to be fair,' or 'Teachers treat all their students equally.'

Moreover, we inferred a high level of accommodative skills shown by UWC teachers from students' written descriptions, such as '[they/some teachers] avoid difficult vocabulary', 'simplify', 'try to be more clear', 'alter their language by using less complicated words and adjusting their speed to make sure everybody follows the lesson' and 'adapt to their levels' when interacting with their students. This seems to be characteristic of both native and non-native teachers working at UWCs. All the above strategies correspond with the implied language policy at UWCs discussed above and reflect the linguistically sensitive attitudes of UWC students and teachers (see below).

On-site classroom observation showed that the teachers' overall linguistic approach, such as talking slowly and focussing on clear and careful pronunciation towards the class rather than individual students, was stable throughout the lessons. This teaching style can be described as consistent accommodation.

During the observed lessons the attitudes of the classmates were friendly and helpful – a finding which correlates with students' written responses. For example, during one observed class (biology) students were divided into smaller groups to carry out experiments; this forced the students to cooperate and even the less-skilled non-native speakers of English were motivated to communicate with others. During this activity some of the ELF-specific features and strategies could be observed, namely the use of politeness phenomena, backchanneling supported with laughter, task-orientedness and focus on message, the let-it-pass principle, and the presence of long pauses within and between turns.

In sum, a linguistically friendly and stimulating environment is enhanced by the help and support provided by teachers and peers: 'People here understand that not everyone is a fluent English speaker and are extremely open and helpful to one another. Of course, sometimes a teacher may be demanding in the use, but that would be only to help the student in question learn faster'; or '[...] I encourage communication even using non-verbal methods is necessary (visual help). I think it is helpful in learning process to all, to those with stronger English too.' The aspect of help can also be seen in a marked ability of UWC teachers to accommodate to students with different language proficiencies.

Extensive language exposure

The amount of language exposure to English plays a vital role in the usage of English at UWCs. Almost all teachers (89.1%, 57) agreed that they observe 'massive', 'noticeable', 'marked', 'dramatic difference' in the students' English over the course of the two years of study. Indeed with respect to English, the IB programme run at UWCs and the 'immersion' in the use of English it offers seems to have, as one teacher commented, a 'transformational effect' on the students. Further, a key observation based on teachers' comments is that it is not the curriculum itself that contributes to the overall improvement of students' proficiency but also the amount of extracurricular activities and social involvement (see also *UWC – educational policy, CLIL and LA*). These were described by teachers as leading to increased 'motivation' and an intensification of language 'acquisition'. As one teacher highlighted, how much students improve 'may have something to do with how socially involved they become here at school.' The same teacher clarified that not all students' level of English improves equally: 'the progress is much more marked in those who are socially more active'; '[l]anguage immersion and the ability to express their ideas ensures they have more confidence when they leave.' We can tentatively conclude from this that it is not just extensive academic exposure but also the level of social engagement that make a big difference to students' linguistic progress and hence that 'social' ELF, that is, outside the classroom, rather than academic ELF, plays a key role in successful language learning at UWCs.

Linguistic sensitivity and management of multilingualism

In our previous study (Quinn Novotná, Grosser and Dunková 2013) our attention was drawn to the linguistically sensitive attitudes among the students. These were confirmed by several highly sensitive answers reflecting upon questionnaire respondents' own multilingualism, multiculturalism and identity.

Questionnaire results showed an awareness of the importance of accommodation strategies and supportive communicative behaviour in international settings. The high level of self-reflective and linguistically sensitive skills was also strikingly evident from students' elicited reflections and definitions of ELF and IE, such as the following: '[J]ust reading off the name, I would assume it is the notion of English as a lingua franca, or its function as a "global language" for people of all different parts of the world to communicate';

> I wasn't aware of it before now but I think it refers to a functional and communicative form of English that does not stress on the correctness of the speech. The main goal is to get the message across and now that I come to think of it, it's more or less the kind of English we use here at UWC – English as a Lingua Franca!

Other similar responses from students from across different UWCs suggest that linguistically sensitive attitudes are a systematic phenomenon characterising students and teachers at these institutions.

Such heightened students' and teachers' linguistic sensitivity, which is marked by a wide array of communicative strategies (e.g. code-mixing and code-switching, discussed in detail in Cogo and Dewey 2006; Pitzl et al. 2008; Pitzl 2009; Cogo and Dewey 2012), varied linguistic behaviour, linguistically open attitudes and acceptance of variation, as well as an ability to draw on multilingual resources, has two observable outcomes. First, it produces better communication in English as a LF; second, linguistically liberal attitudes and supportive attitudes by students and teachers promote learning: 'It is important to let students use other languages to assist in their learning'; 'The teachers don't mind if you speak languages other than English during times when you are working on problems, if it helps you to learn, and classmates will more often than not attempt to join in whatever language you are speaking'. This last comment, one of many similar ones, illustrates for us the very essence of a liberal and at the same time efficient approach to multilingualism at UWCs. It highlights how in a multilingual community which shares a common purpose other languages are embraced and cherished as a common commodity.

Challenges of studying through the medium of English

Studies of the impact of CLIL on language proficiency, motivation and cognitive progresses have shown it to be both beneficial (e.g., Coyle, Hood, and Marsh 2010: 11; Várkuti 2010) and challenging for students and teachers (e.g., Banegas 2012).

Regarding the challenges, we investigated whether non-native speakers ever felt disadvantaged in their studies because of their non-native status when studying different subjects through English. Our survey results showed that

131 (41.6%) students felt disadvantaged, whereas 81 (26%) did not; 102 students (32.38%) selected the option 'Not applicable'. The following comment provides a good summary of the disadvantages felt by students: '[I felt disadvantaged] [b]oth academically as well as socially sometimes, if I don't manage to convey a message.' Most of the challenges described by students who claimed to be 'disadvantaged' were of a linguistic nature, connected to a lack of subject-specific vocabulary and the (in-)ability to express ideas and to join in conversations. Students also made several culturally sensitive comments which touch upon the fact that, for example, a different language is closely linked with different thinking and different reasoning and that coming from a different cultural background can make learning content more difficult since, as one student explained, it is hard to '[adapt] education in a language in which you do not have any cultural bargain.'

Students who are comparatively weak in English struggle with 'basic English', difficult subject matter and 'complicated terms in English'. On the other side of the spectrum, however, three NSs and PEUs report being slowed down by these students: for example, 'It is challenging to study subjects alongside others with a significantly lower level of English than me. I feel as though their presence often holds my own progress and speed and efficiency of work back', while others show sympathy and understanding of the extra challenges faced by their fellow students.

Overall, studying through the medium of English poses a variety of challenges to NNS students. Based on the numerical response count, several subjects, such as biology and history, seem to be more difficult than others in this respect, suggesting that more pedagogical focus should be given to these more challenging areas.

Conclusions and recommendations

This chapter has explored the pedagogical implications of ELF by looking at its role and functionality at an international teaching institution. Based on our research data, we observe that teaching through ELF need not be a 'struggle' (Holliday 2005) but can be done successfully if the right teaching priorities and attitudes are adopted. Our particular research context at UWCs revealed that these institutions provide a unique multilingual setting which enables English in all its forms, varieties and functions to flourish as a mutually shared code of understanding and an efficient vehicle for learning, regardless of the individual particularities and idiosyncrasies of its many users. This has a number of implications for teaching and teacher training.

First, our results suggest that the following teaching practices should be pursued: application of liberal language policies, focus on content, focus on (subject specific) vocabulary, help and support from teachers and peers, high level of language exposure to English, and development of linguistically sensi-tive attitudes and the ability to draw on multilingual resources and focus on extra challenges that NNS students may experience when studying through the medium of a FL (CLIL). In our view these recommendations are essential for best practice in international multilingual post-secondary institutions that teach CLIL through ELF.

Second, if we want to learn from efficient teaching practices observed at the UWC institutions and apply them at other multilingual institutions that inte-grate ELF and CLIL, we envisage the need for a broader understanding and/or re-definition of language proficiency, accuracy, standards and teaching goals. Applying an ELF perspective in these areas can bring about a shift in attitudes[5] which may have positive teaching and learning outcomes. Our results show that proficiency is not necessarily seen as native-like or near-native competence, rather it is defined by international intelligibility and comprehensibility (see also Jenkins 2000 and Sifakis 2006), wide range of vocabulary and ability to accommodate to different speakers from different linguistic and cultural back-grounds. Hence, we can no longer insist on trying to replicate NS-like English speakers, rather we want to educate individuals (PEUs) who are not afraid to use English[6,7] and other languages actively and who focus on communicating ideas rather than fear linguistic 'imprecision'. Moreover, achieving higher profi-ciency seems to be intrinsically connected with students' increased self-esteem and generally better learning results. This is enhanced by encouraging students' social involvement through ELF.

Third, our results have illustrated the compatibility between liberal multilin-gual policies and teaching practices, and an ELF-speaking environment. For this reason we recommend that ELF-informed theory is incorporated into training programmes for CLIL teachers working in similar ELF-speaking environments. Increasing awareness and theoretical knowledge about ELF, however, will not suffice if new ideas and attitudes are not translated into the actual practices applied in the classroom (see Dewey 2012: 153, 158; Giorgis 2013; Dunková 2014). We argue that the gap between theory and practice can be filled dur-ing teacher training by implementing seminars on WEs and ELF which would include reflective activities (see also the 'transformative perspective' in Sifakis 2014) that can then be related to hands-on application during teaching prac-tice.[8] Given the importance of language awareness at UWCs, that is, the ability to reflect upon the language used and to act accordingly, on the part of students and teachers in the creation of a successful learning environment, we also recommend that training programmes seek to develop future teachers' meta-linguistic skills, showing them how they can increase their students' linguistic sensitivity (see also Carter 2003: 64–65; Tulasiewicz 2000: 8–9). As Howard (2013: 78) puts it '[i]ncreased conscious reflection on language by the students and the teachers leads to improved language use and better overall education.'

Engagement priorities

To translate our findings into practice we pose the following questions and problems for further reflection by teachers and teacher educators.

1. How much training concerning multilingual awareness have you received throughout your studies and teaching practice? What is your idea of a multilingual teacher? What do you think would help teachers and students to become more open to multilingualism and how could they benefit from it?
2. Based on our findings regarding language policy (LP) at UWCs, do you think similar LP could be applied at other multilingual institutions? What implications could adopting such LP have?
3. Are the recommendations which we formulated for multilingual contexts (e.g. focus on content; focus on subject-specific vocabulary; help and support provided from teachers and peers; high level of language exposure to English; developing linguistically sensitive attitudes and the ability to draw on multilingual resources) feasible in your particular local (monolingual) context? What other ways of replicating and/or simulating multilingual environment can you think of?
4. At UWCs teachers place great importance on the students' knowledge of subject-specific vocabulary and content, and less emphasis on other language elements such as pronunciation or grammatical correctness. If you teach or are thinking of implementing CLIL in your local context, would this CLIL-based focus on vocabulary work with your students?

Notes

We would like to thank Julie Harris from UWC Atlantic in Wales for her kind assistance with organizing our visit. We would also like to thank David Grosser for helping to collect some of the data and Tamah Sherman, Ph.D. for providing her invaluable sociolinguistic expertise.

1. This consisted of an 11-question survey for students and a ten-question survey for teachers. The on-line questionnaire, which was voluntary and anonymous, was designed in Survey Monkey. Upon approval of UWC representatives, a link was sent to all 12 UWC institutions attending the particular institution this academic year. Nine institutions agreed to participate.
2. The observation took place at the UWC in Wales and consisted of five lessons and four semi-structured interviews. All information was recorded in a form of field notes in specifically devised Observation Sheets.
3. These variable were as follows: linguistic proficiency, knowledge of language forms, language models, efficient (LF) communicative strategies; language confidence; linguistic identity; personal and professional attitudes to language use; metalinguistic skills – general linguistic sensitivity, ability to reflect upon language; general study skills – studying through the medium of a FL; school language policy.
4. Single quotation marks are used to indicate the students' verbatim quotes. These quotes were not corrected for grammar and spelling with respect to Standard varieties.

The motivation for keeping their original spelling and grammar was twofold; first, we wanted to maintain the authenticity of the comments; and secondly, we wanted to illustrate the actual usage which we believe represents authentic written ELF.

5. The changes in attitudes and teaching priorities seem to be in line with major paradigmatic changes happening globally on many levels (see Quinn Novotná 2012: 110).
6. In a pedagogically 'ideal scenario', primary education would provide a solid foundation of this 'basic skill' (Graddol 2006: 72), in the 'traditional' EFL sense, i.e. with a strong phonological and grammatical focus in line with ICE standards. Beyond this stage the focus should shift to confident LF and FL language use underscored by a vast knowledge of vocabulary as a necessary toolkit for such active use.
7. A decade ago, Howatt (2004: 353–4) predicted in a chapter on 'recent trends' a future shift away from the strictly formal instruction to more emphasis placed on the 'ability to actually use the language'. In the light of our and other current WEs and ELF research, such ability has a much wider scope than might have ever been anticipated. Hence there arises the necessity to redefine certain EFL paradigm concepts.
8. Jenkins, Cogo and Dewey (2011: 306) recommend opening up 'the possibility of incorporating a multi-norm, multi-method approach.'

References

Andrews, S. (2007). *Teacher Language Awareness*. Cambridge: Cambridge University Press.

Banegas, D. L. (2012). CLIL teacher development: Challenges and experiences. *Latin American. Journal of Content & Language Integrated Learning* 5(1): 46–56.

Carter, R. (2003). Language awareness. *ELT Journal* 57(1): 64–65.

Cogo, A. and Dewey, M. (2006). Efficiency in ELF communication: From pragmatic motives to Lexico-grammatical innovation. *Nordic Journal of English Studies* 5: 59–93.

Cogo, A. and Dewey, M. (2012). *Analysing English as a Lingua Franca: A Corpus-driven Investigation*. London: Continuum.

Coupland, N. (ed.) (2010). *The Handbook of Language and Globalization*. Oxford: Wiley-Blackwell.

Coyle, D., Hood, P. and Marsh, D. (2010). *CLIL: Content Language Integrated Learning*. Cambridge: Cambridge University Press.

Crystal, D. (1997). *English as a Global Language*. Cambridge: Cambridge University Press.

Dalton-Puffer, Ch., Nikula, T. and Smit, U. (eds) (2010). *Language Use and Language Learning in CLIL Classrooms*. Amsterdam: John Benjamins Publishing Company.

Dewey, M. (2007). English as a Lingua Franca and globalization: An interconnected perspective. *International Journal of Applied Linguistics* 17: 332–354.

Dewey, M. (2012). Towards a post-normative approach: Learning the pedagogy of ELF. *Journal of English as a Lingua Franca* 1(1): 141–170.

Dunková, J. (2014). *Learner Goals and Attitudes to Mistakes from an ELT and ELF Perspective*. Unpublished Masters thesis. Faculty of Arts, Charles University, Prague.

Edmondson, W. (2009). Language awareness. In: Knapp, K., Seidlhofer, B. and Widdowson, H. (eds), *Handbook of Foreign Language Communication and Learning*. Berlin: Mouton de Gruyter, pp. 163–190.

Eldridge, J. Neufeld, S. and Hancioğlu, N. (2010). Towards a lexical framework for CLIL. *International CLIL Research Journal* 1(3): 88–103.

Georgiou, S. I. (2012). Reviewing the puzzle of CLIL. *ELT Journal* 66(4): 495–504.

Giorgis, P. (2013). Mind the gap EFL/ELF: What lies in between what teachers teach and what students use, and its pedagogical implications. *Boğaziçi University Journal of Education* 33(1): 87–98.

Gnutzmann, C. and Intemann F. (eds) (2008). *The Globalization of English and the English Language Classroom*. Tübingen: Gunther Narr.

Graddol, D. (2006). *English Next. Why Global English May Mean the End of 'English as a Foreign Language'*. London: British Council.

Hayden, M. and Thompson, J. (2004). *International Education: Principles and Practice*. Abingdon: Routledge Falmer.

Hayden, M. and Thompson, J. (2013). *International Schools and International Education: Improving Teaching, Management and Quality*. London: Routledge.

Holliday, A. (2005). *The Struggle to Teach English as an International Language*. Oxford: Oxford University Press.

Howard, N. (2013). Language awareness and second language development. In: C. James and P. Garret (eds), *Language Awareness in the Classroom*. New York: Routledge, pp. 78–96.

Howatt, A. P. R. (2004). *A History of ELT, Second Edition*. Oxford: Oxford University Press.

IB DP General Information. Available at: http://www.ibo.org/diploma/ (accessed 1 November 2014).

IB DP History. Available at: http://www.ibo.org/history/ (accessed 1 November 2014).

IB Language Policy. Available at: http://www.ibo.org/mission/languagepolicy/ (accessed 30 December 2013).

James, C. and Garret, P. (1991). *Language Awareness in the Classroom*. London/New York: Routledge.

Jenkins, J. (2000). *The Phonology of English as an International Language*. Oxford: Oxford University Press.

Jenkins, J., Cogo, A. and Dewey, D. (2011). Review of developments in research into English as a Lingua Franca. *Language Teaching*, 44(3): 281–315.

Juan-Garau, M. and Salazar-Noguera, J. (eds) (2015). *Content-based Language Learning in Multilingual Educational Environments*. Heidelberg: Springer.

Knapp, A. (2011). Using English as a Lingua Franca for (mis-)managing conflict in an international university context: An example from a course in engineering. *Journal of Pragmatics* 43(4): 978–990.

Mahboob, A. and Barratt, L. (eds) (2014). *Englishes in Multilingual Contexts: Language Variation and Education*. Heidelberg: Springer.

Pitzl, M. L. (2009). 'We should not wake up any dogs': Idiom and Metaphor in ELF. In Mauranen, A. and Ranta, E. (eds), *English as a Lingua Franca. Studies and Findings*, Newcastle: Cambridge Scholars Publishing, pp. 298–322.

Pitzl, M. L., Breiteneder, A. and Klimpfinger, T. (2008). A world of words: Processes of lexical innovation in Voice. *Vienna English Working Papers* 17: 21–46.

Quinn Novotná, V. (2012). *World Englishes and English as a Lingua Franca: A Reflection of Global Paradigmatic Changes in the Czech Republic*. Unpublished doctoral thesis, Faculty of Arts, Charles University, Prague.

Quinn Novotná, V., Grosser, D. and Dunková, J. (2013). UWC schools: An ideal ELF environment? *Boğaziçi University Journal of Education* 33(1): 51–76.

Saxena, M. and Omoniyi, T. (eds) (2010). *Contending with Globalization in World Englishes*. Bristol, Buffalo and Toronto: Multilingual Matters.

Seidlhofer, B. (2005). English as a Lingua Franca. In Wehmeier, S. (ed.), *Oxford Advanced Learner's Dictionary of Current English*. 7th ed. Oxford: Oxford University Press, p. R 92.

Sifakis, N. (2006). Teaching EIL: Teaching *international* or *intercultural* English? What teachers should know. In Rubdy, R. and Saraceni, M. (eds), *English in the World: Global Rules, Global Roles*. London: Continuum, pp. 150–168.

Sifakis, N. C. (2014). ELF awareness as an opportunity for change: A transformative perspective for ESOL teacher education. *Journal of English as a Lingua Franca*, 3/2: 317–335.

Smit, U. (2010a). *English as a Lingua Franca in Higher Education: A Longitudinal Study of Classroom Discourse*, Berlin: Mouton De Gruyter.

Smit, U. (2010b). CLIL in an English as a lingua franca (ELF) classroom. On explaining terms and expressions interactively. In Dalton-Puffer, Ch., Nikula, T. and Smit, U. (eds), *Language Use and Language Learning in CLIL Classrooms*. Amsterdam: John Benjamins Publishing Company, pp. 259–278.

Tulasiewicz, W. (2000). Whither language awareness? Enhancing the literacy of the language users. In White, L. J., Maylath, B., Adams, A. and Couzijn, M. (eds), *Language Awareness – A History and Implementations*. Amsterdam: Amsterdam University Press, pp. 5–21.

UWC – Core selection principles. *UWC Documents*. Available at: http://www.uwc.org/includes/documents/cm_docs/2013/c/core_selection_criteria_selection_policy.pdf (accessed 1 January 2014).

UWC guiding principles. *UWC Documents*. Available at: http://www.uwc.org/includes/documents/cm_docs/2013/g/guiding_principles_new.pdf (accessed 1 January 2014).

UWC – Mission and values. *UWC Homepage*. Available at: http://www.uwc.org/about_uwc/mission_and_vision.aspx (accessed 12 December 2013).

Várkuti, A. (2010). Linguistic benefits of the CLIL approach: Measuring linguistic competences. *International CLIL Research Journal* 1(3): 67–79.

Wallace, C. (2002). Local literacies and global literacy. In Block, D. and Cameron, D. (eds), *Globalization and Language Teaching*. London/New York: Routledge, pp. 101–114.

Wilkinson, D. (1998). International education: A question of access. In: M. Hayden and J. Thompson (eds), *International Education: Principles and Practice*. London: Kogan Page, pp. 227–234.

10

ELF, Teacher Knowledge and Professional Development

Martin Dewey

Introduction

ELF research has consistently generated substantial debate regarding the perceived relevance (or for some commentators, irrelevance) of lingua franca interaction for language learning and teaching. Researchers are not only commenting at greater length on the implications of their work for language pedagogy; it is a significant development that we are also now beginning to do so in domains that are more directly connected to ELT (e.g., Jenkins, Cogo and Dewey 2011). As each of the chapters in this volume attests, there are many ways in which empirical data and theoretical discussions represent some quite major implications for language teaching. However, what is equally clear, is that the practical implementation of an ELF perspective in pedagogy is far from straightforward.

Developing any kind of new practice can be a complex matter. This is especially true in the context of ELF, since responding to research and debate in practical ways requires us to adopt a profoundly different perspective on language than probably most teachers have been accustomed to. Adopting an ELF perspective will in many contexts require a radical departure from widely accepted beliefs about good practice (see Dewey 2012 for further discussion). It is therefore necessary for research to become much more thoroughly engaged with teachers' existing beliefs, and for researchers to pay closer attention to teachers' levels of awareness of ELF and their understanding of what ELF means for learners and teachers in specific pedagogic contexts. This is essential if we want to properly focus on how the many implications of ELF may be developed into classroom applications, and how these might thus become an integral part of teachers' professional knowledge base.

In this chapter, I address the need for this engagement in light of recent curriculum developments for the main accredited language teaching awards in the UK. Reference to ELF is now explicitly stated in the current syllabus guidelines for the most widely accepted language teaching qualifications in the UK, the CELTA and Delta schemes, awarded by Cambridge English Language Assessment, part of the University of Cambridge. These are respectively: the Certificate and the Diploma in Teaching English to Speakers of Other Languages.[1]

My purpose in focusing specifically on these teaching awards is several-fold. Firstly, these are the teacher education contexts with which I am most familiar – from both a practitioner and a research perspective, having previously been a course tutor for both, and more recently having collected empirical data through observation, questionnaires and interviews with course participants. Secondly, while my discussion focuses on practice and experience in these teacher training courses, many of the issues that emerge relate to broadly universal aspects of teacher knowledge and teacher preparation, and are therefore likely to be equally relevant in a wide range of teacher education contexts. Finally, the teaching awards in question are very popular and very widely recognized internationally – according to Cambridge English, there are over 300 centres worldwide offering courses that lead to these qualifications, with more than 12,000 successful candidates taking CELTA each year (http://www. cambridgeenglish.org/exams-and-qualifications).

Combined with the prestige that unfortunately (often erroneously) continues to be assigned to native-speaker teachers (regardless of level of experience and qualification), the popularity of these courses means the Cambridge awards exert considerable and widespread influence in the profession. This influence has manifested itself over the years in several ways, but can predominantly be evidenced in a relatively global move towards what can broadly be described as a communicative methodology. This has steadily gathered pace since the 1980s, when CLT (Communicative Language Teaching) began to take hold as the dominant methodology. In short, the type of practices promoted on CELTA and Delta courses become the practices and approaches that are valued elsewhere, even in contexts that might be very far removed from those in which these were originally devised, and even where they might not be locally appropriate.

In a number of contexts, it has in fact been shown that implementing a communicative approach may well be directly in conflict with existing beliefs and practices (see e.g. Choi 2013 on the impact on Korean teachers of an educational policy aimed at promoting communicative methodology). This debate, however, goes beyond a consideration of pedagogic methods. One vital consequence of the promotion of CLT is the subsequent effect this can have on the relative levels of prestige attached to native and non-native speaker teachers. In contexts where CLT is actively promoted, teachers are put under greater pressure to use English (and sometimes *only* English) as the medium of instruction, which creates additional expectations regarding teachers' perceived levels of proficiency. This pressure is exerted from all directions and involves all stakeholders: education policy makers, educational management and school hierarchies, students, parents and of course teachers themselves. Choi's (2013) doctoral study of educational policy in Korea demonstrates very clearly how the promotion of CLT methodologies is intricately tied up with notions of English language proficiency and perceptions of Korean teachers' levels of expertise.

This may be a very specific case, peculiar to the Korean context. It is, however, also quite indicative of a much broader trend to replace existing methods and practices with less localized ones. Globalization has brought about increased demand for high levels of English language proficiency in growing numbers of contexts across the world. The effects this is having on educational policy include: a move towards earlier introduction of English into the curriculum; an increase in the length and/or number of English language classes in the timetable; and in many settings a move towards adopting more communicative approaches. CLT has thus continued fairly inexorably to become the single most dominant theoretical model of English language teaching worldwide, with recent attempts to promote communicative methodologies having taken place in a wide variety of contexts. As has been quite widely discussed (see e.g. Littlewood 2007), the promotion of CLT is regularly a requirement rather than an option, and it is often promoted with little consideration of local context and practices. In relation to Bangladesh, for example, Chowdhury and Phan (2008: 305) argue that a communicative approach is not always well suited to the contexts in which it is being implemented:

> Even though CLT claims to create a democratic classroom that is responsive to students' needs, it is often inappropriate and incompatible, neither sophisticated nor responsive enough for the complex educational needs and cultures of students in certain settings.

Chowdhury and Phan comment how policy-led reforms in practice may in fact create considerable friction for practitioners who continue to value and uphold more traditional approaches.

English language competence (leaving aside for now the complex matter of determining how this ought to be conceptualized) is widely seen as a precondition for gaining access to economic, social and educational opportunities. The curriculum changes this has brought about have led to an escalation of teacher training activity that focuses on communicative methodologies. This has involved groups of teachers being sent to the UK (and to a lesser extent Australia and the US) for intensive training courses, and/or to teacher training courses being arranged locally, usually through partnership with organizations such as the British Council and Cambridge English. These courses are predominantly taught and assessed by teacher trainers from the UK. They are broadly modelled on CELTA and Delta type schemes in so much as they tend to prioritize the mastery of classroom procedures and techniques, where the focus is almost exclusively on practical skills, generally with little to no discussion of theoretical principles.

In the context of these intensive training programmes, with their strong emphasis on classroom procedures and a reliance on outsider 'experts' to 'deliver' course content, there is typically little scope for a discussion of the local educational setting. In many of these courses, teachers are quite literally 'flown in' from the UK. The trainers therefore have no experience of the local context, nor much time available to gain an understanding of teachers' beliefs and expectations. This will also mean of course that there is little opportunity to discuss the language itself, with typically little to no consideration given to the type of communicative settings that students are most likely to encounter or what kind of English they would benefit from. As has been commented on at some length in relation to ELF, in the absence of explicit discussion of language models, the default practice in education is to adhere to dominant NS norms, in other words British or American English (see e.g. Jenkins 2013). In addition, it is unclear what level of awareness of ELF the teacher trainers are likely to have. In previous research with CELTA and Delta course tutors, it has generally been the case that there is still relatively little discussion of ELF on teacher education courses (see e.g. Dewey 2011).

Given the disproportionate and widespread influence of UK-based teacher education, it is thus paramount that we look closely at existing practices on both pre-service and in-service teaching awards. This is essential for several reasons: first to determine current levels of awareness of ELF among teacher educators; second to establish whether and to what extent this awareness is beginning to shape syllabus content; and finally to explore ways in which ELF might be further incorporated in the curriculum for language teacher education. The following discussion will thus address the relevance of ELF for practitioners involved in the Cambridge English schemes, from the perspective of course tutors as well as candidates.

Researching ELF in teacher education

In-depth investigation into the role and status of ELF in language teacher training is becoming a matter of some prescience, especially given the recent changes to the CELTA and Delta syllabus guidelines mentioned above. In the case of the Delta scheme, the current syllabus documentation explicitly states that candidates should not only be aware of the global status of English, but also '[r]elate the role of English as a global language to developments in learning and teaching in a range of international contexts' (University of Cambridge

ESOL Examinations 2011: 5). The relevance of this is made even more explicit with regard to ELF in the syllabus descriptions of learning outcomes. According to these specifications, relating this global status to teaching and learning will require candidates to demonstrate an understanding of '[d]ifferences in English in different world contexts (e.g. English as a global language; World Englishes; English as a *lingua franca*)' (University of Cambridge ESOL Examinations 2011: 4).

The syllabus guidelines for CELTA and Delta are deliberately broad in their focus, however, dealing with fairly generic issues regarding teacher knowledge. This is essentially because the awards are overseen and administered by Cambridge English but delivered locally in individual centres. There is thus considerable scope for flexibility in how syllabus specifications are interpreted and then translated into actual course content. There are very broad guidelines on topic areas, but no detailed specification of precisely what topics should be included or how much attention should be devoted to each syllabus item. In practice, there are essentially as many different CELTA and Delta awards as there are providers. The findings presented in this chapter must be viewed in light of this diversity of practice. Whilst broad claims may be made about the syllabus guidelines, any research carried out on the training programmes themselves will concern the particular centre in question. We have to be cautious therefore in whatever claims we make about current levels of provision regarding ELF in teacher education programmes in the UK.

Nevertheless, there are at this stage some fairly strong indications that uptake of ELF in the curriculum is still relatively limited. Research into teacher awareness of ELF concepts has thus far tended to show that there is a growing awareness among some teachers of terms such as 'World Englishes', but there is generally limited meaningful integration of these terms and the concepts they represent in existing practices (see Dewey 2012 for a fuller discussion of teacher awareness of ELF).

Furthermore, existing preparation materials for CELTA and Delta, and past exam papers for Delta, so far suggest that there is relatively little provision made for bringing ELF into the curriculum (for a thorough discussion of preparation materials and a more detailed account of the syllabus guidelines for both awards see Dewey, forthcoming). Language focused tasks in the Delta exam, for example, typically concern teachers' knowledge of metalanguage and some analysis of short language samples (for sample papers see http://www.cambridgeenglish.org/exams-and-qualifications/delta/how-to-prepare-for-delta/). In the case of the former candidates might be asked to match a term, say *cohesion* or *coherence*, to an appropriate definition. In the latter, candidates might be asked to comment on the form and meaning of highlighted words. In both cases, the task is entirely decontextualized: there is no mention of a teaching context in either and the language samples nearly always consist of lists of single, isolated sentences. In other words, it is impossible to see how a test of this nature could be used to assess a candidate's awareness of sociocultural and sociolinguistic factors regarding the role of English as a global lingua franca.

Perceptions of English in initial teacher training

In this section I discuss a recent small-scale study of an intensive four-week, pre-service course leading to the CertTESOL qualification. This is very similar in scope and purpose to the Cambridge CELTA award, and is widely recognized as an alternative qualification. As with CELTA, the qualification is administered centrally, in this case by Trinity College London, and then delivered locally by individual accredited centres. There is a similar set of syllabus guidelines, which specify quite broadly the objectives of the scheme and the syllabus topic areas, with descriptors provided for the desired learning outcomes for candidate teachers (for details see http://www.trinitycollege. co.uk). In terms of objectives and approach the two awards are direct equivalents, with language schools accepting either as valid initial ELT qualifications. In previous studies, I have focused on tutors and trainees participating in CELTA courses (see e.g. Dewey 2011). In this study I opted to collect data from a CertTESOL programme with a view to increasing the variety of specific teacher training contexts being investigated, and to thus broaden the scope of my research in this area and get a fuller picture of current practice in ELT teacher education.

The particular course in question took place at a private sector language school in London. Fifteen candidates were enrolled on the course (12 native English speakers and three non-native English speakers), some with minimal prior experience of English language teaching, but most with no teaching experience, and none with any prior formal training. All of the participants in the study can thus be described as novice teachers. The course operates on a full-time, face-to-face basis, with a very intensive daily timetable consisting approximately of three hours of input (comprising methodology and language awareness, and totaling approx. 60 hours of content training), one hour of supervised lesson preparation, then finishing with a two-hour teaching practice session, with follow-up group feedback seminars (constituting 60 hours in which the focus of training is on the practicum). In addition, course requirements stipulate that candidates must observe four hours of experienced ESOL language teaching, for which they need to write a reflective journal, as well as work independently on lesson preparation and written assignments. All in all, this is a highly concentrated and demanding programme.

For the penultimate input session, I arranged with the lead tutor of the course to provide a one-hour guest seminar focusing on Global Englishes and ELF.[2] The purpose of this was to provide appropriate input relating to the following learning outcome, as stipulated in the CertTESOL syllabus, that candidates should demonstrate 'awareness of geographical varieties of English, including the emergence of English as a lingua franca, and associated implications for teaching' (Trinity College London 2013: 11). The guest input session was designed both for research purposes and with pedagogic objectives. It was intended to serve as a means of exploring how ELF can be introduced into the curriculum on an intensive pre-service course. As well as presenting the input session, this entailed investigating novice teachers' existing levels of awareness regarding ELF – obtained either as a result of having come into contact with the concept prior to the course or during the course input received thus far. To this end, a questionnaire was given out to candidates prior to the input session. The questionnaire responses are discussed here as a first phase of what will be a much larger, long-term project involving further questionnaire studies and follow-up interviews with trainers and trainees (for a full discussion of this work see Dewey, forthcoming).

The initial questionnaire (see Appendix) was aimed primarily at eliciting trainee teachers' awareness of language diversity. This involved participants indicating whether or not they had come across a number of terms to describe different varieties or types of English, including: *World Englishes, Global Englishes, English as a lingua franca*, and several named varieties, *Indian English* and *Singlish*. Participants were asked to indicate on scales from 0 to 5 how familiar they were with each term, and then how confident they were about the concept they thought each represented (with zero signalling 'not at all familiar'/'confident' and five signalling 'very familiar'/'confident'). Participants were then asked in open questions to comment on what they understood by the terms *English as a lingua franca* and *Standard English*.

The questionnaire concludes with two more open questions, aimed at investigating participants' perceptions of knowledge about language and whether their views on this had changed as a result of taking part in the CertTESOL course. The questions were as follows: *Based on what you knew already, and what you have learned on this course, what do you think language teachers need to know about English in order to be effective teachers?*; and then finally *Have your views changed on this matter as a result of taking this course. If so, please could you briefly state how?* My purpose was first to try to determine how the participants are beginning to conceptualize subject knowledge as novice language teachers, anticipating that this was likely to conflict with an ELF perspective on language. Second, I was interested in knowing how and to what extent their thinking had been influenced by the training they had received on the course in an attempt to gain further insight into current practices in initial teacher education.

In the following sections, I will first comment on the rating task provided in the initial questionnaire before then moving on to consider some of the participants' responses to the open questions.

Questionnaire responses: rating scales

Although the first questionnaire task involves the collection of numerical data, at this stage the number of respondents is still very low (13 completed questionnaires were returned following the input session). For this reason the responses have not yet been treated to any statistical analysis. It will, however, be important to carry out statistical tests to verify the significance of the findings as more data becomes available. At the time of writing the questionnaire is due to be administered on an additional four CertTESOL programmes, each of these with a seminar session on ELF timetabled to take place towards the end of the course. In addition, a parallel study is planned for participants enrolled on a Delta course, the in-service teaching award discussed above (see Dewey, forthcoming, for a more extensive examination of both research projects). My purpose here is to present some preliminary findings, drawing on descriptive accounts of the available quantitative data combined with a discussion of the more qualitative data provided by participants' responses to the open questions. My interpretation of what this means with regard to the current status and relevance of ELF in the teacher education curriculum is at this stage still more exploratory than conclusive.

To return to the questionnaire data, given the relative lack of experience of the teachers involved in this study, it is unsurprising that the rating scores for all items in both the familiarity and confidence tasks were generally quite low. As should be expected from novice teachers pursuing an initial qualification, participants tended to report relatively little familiarity with most of the terms, and in turn they broadly tended to assign still slightly lower ratings when reporting levels of confidence. Table 10.1 lists all 13 scores assigned by the participants for each of the items in this question (ranged across the top row, moving from World Englishes in the first column to ELF in the final one). At the end of each column there are two additional cells, one with the total score for each language variety or type (a tally of the 13 individual ratings), and one with a mean score for each type/variety.

What the table clearly reveals is that some fairly strong patterns are emerging (even with this limited volume of data) with regard to which language types participants feel relatively familiar or unfamiliar with. As should inevitably be expected, the highest rating (49 overall, 3.7 average) is by some margin for Standard English (SE). This is the only language variety receiving an average rating above 3, and the only variety to have been given the highest rating by more than one respondent. *International English* was the only other item to receive a familiarity score of 5 – this was given by only one teacher and appears to be something of an outlier response as it is substantially above the average rating for this variety (2.3). The ratings for SE are also very consistent, with nine out of 13 participants assigning a value of either 4 or 5 in terms of familiarity. Broadly speaking, the scores regarding how confident the participants felt

Table 10.1   Familiarity with language varieties and types

Familiarity ratings (0–5)

World Englishes	Singlish	Standard Eng.	Global Englishes	International Eng.	Indian Eng.	ELF
2	1	2	1	2	3	3
3	0	2	3	2	0	0
2	3	4	2	1	2	0
2	0	4	1	2	2	0
2	0	5	4	5	0	0
2	0	4	0	2	2	1
3	0	3	1	3	4	4
1	0	3	0	0	2	2
3	0	4	3	3	0	0
1	0	4	3	3	2	0
1	0	4	1	0	1	0
4	0	5	4	4	2	0
4	5	5	3	4	0	0
Total 30	9	49	26	31	20	10
Avg rating 2.307	0.692	3.769	2	2.384	1.538	0.769

in terms of knowing what concepts these terms represent are very similar to those given for familiarity.

As Table 10.2 shows, the rank order of the seven items is almost identical for the confidence dimension as it is for familiarity. In other words, there is a very close correspondence between levels of familiarity and of confidence, with all but one of the participants recording either the same score for both dimensions in every item, or a score one or two points lower. As expected, the two dimensions correlate closely: where there is a difference, this is (a) relatively minor and (b) in the direction we would anticipate since it is wholly counterintuitive to feel confident about defining a term that is relatively unfamiliar. Furthermore, even with a high level of familiarity, most people would probably exercise slightly more caution when reporting how confident they are about a term's concept. What remains most immediately striking, though, in the findings displayed in both tables is the consistently high scores assigned to SE.

There are several conceivable explanations for the comparatively high rating values for SE. They can in part be explained by the educational setting of the study, a relatively formal, institutional context where the participants are students enrolled on a course leading to a recognized qualification, the assessment of which places substantial emphasis on being able to speak and write in SE. In addition, each of the participants has presumably spent a significant amount of time in formal education prior to the course, and will thus have been exposed to commonplace expectations about the use of SE in pedagogic

Table 10.2 Confidence in knowing about language varieties and types

Confidence ratings (0–5)

World Englishes	Singlish	Standard Eng.	Global Englishes	International Eng.	Indian Eng.	ELF
2	0	2	1	2	2	3
2	0	2	3	2	0	0
2	2	3	1	0	1	0
1	0	4	1	1	2	0
2	0	5	3	3	0	0
2	0	4	0	2	1	0
2	0	2	1	2	2	3
0	0	2	0	0	1	1
3	0	4	4	4	0	0
4	1	4	4	4	4	1
1	0	4	1	0	1	0
4	0	5	4	4	2	0
4	4	4	3	4	0	0
Total 29	7	45	26	28	16	8
Avg rating 2.230	0.538	3.461	2	2.153	1.230	0.615

contexts (although there are no formal entry requirements with regard to qualifications, Trinity College specify that course participants should have sufficient educational background to allow them to enter university). This will also mean that they have been exposed to the influences of standard language ideology (see e.g. Milroy and Milroy 2012). Finally, it is entirely feasible that the course itself has reinforced this ideology of SE due to the existing practice of orienting towards language in a predominantly normative way in ELT (see Dewey 2012 for further discussion). The responses provided in the subsequent section of the questionnaire, where participants are asked to comment on what they understand by the term *Standard English*, reveal some evidence of the influence of standard language ideology.

The overall familiarity scores for the following items, *World Englishes*, *Global Englishes* and *International English*, are all fairly close (respectively 30, 26 and 31), with participants displaying a slight tendency to rate *Global Englishes* as a marginally less familiar term. There was a broad level of consistency regarding how familiar and confident participants were with these three items, with individual teachers generally providing similar scores for each. One tenable interpretation of this is that there is a tendency for teachers to see the terms as broadly synonymous with each other, which would also suggest there is little awareness of the important conceptual distinctions made between the three terms (see Cogo and Dewey 2012, Chapter 1, for a detailed discussion of terminology). This is borne out by the lack of reference to any of the terms in the more open questions. It would appear that for these novice teachers there is a general understanding that English is international in scope, but possibly little awareness of what this means precisely with regard to linguistic diversity.

In contrast to the rating of SE, there was however considerably more variability across individual participants' reported levels of familiarity and confidence with these terms. Across the 13 participants there were typically four or five different rating scores for each of these three items in terms of both familiarity and confidence, and in the case of *International English* all possible scores (i.e. 0, 1, 2, 3, 4 and 5) were recorded for the familiarity dimension. In other words, there are substantial differences among these CertTESOL course participants regarding their apparent awareness of the role of English as a global language. This provides convincing evidence that these topics should be given much more attention than they are currently receiving on pre-service teaching awards.

It also appears that the novice teachers in this study have relatively limited awareness of the extent or nature of linguistic diversity. The three items receiving the lowest overall scores for familiarity and confidence were, in descending order, *Indian English, ELF* and *Singlish*. In other words, when it comes to thinking about specific named varieties of English, participants were unaware of the terms used to describe anything other than SE, and not at all confident that they knew what these terms mean. Most strikingly, especially given the inclusion of the term in both the CELTA and CerTESOL syllabus guidelines, the rating for ELF is the second lowest of all (with overall scores of 10 for familiarity and 9 for confidence, and average ratings of 0.769 and 0.615 respectively). Nine out of the thirteen participants assigned a value of 0 for both dimensions, familiarity and confidence. The only teacher assigning a high value to ELF (4 for familiarity and 3 for confidence) was one of only two who had previous teaching experience: in this case, two years working at a primary school in China, and some experience of one-to-one tuition in Spain. On the whole, participants seem almost completely unaware of the term ELF or what it denotes, even though the study was undertaken on the penultimate day of an intensive and relatively comprehensive pre-service training course.

Questionnaire: open responses

There were four open-ended questions. In the first two, participants were asked to comment on what they understood by *English as a lingua franca* and *Standard English*. As a reflection of the low familiarity ratings assigned to ELF, eight of the participants either left this section blank or wrote an entry such as 'nothing' or 'no idea'. Despite reporting a familiarity and confidence rating of 0 for ELF, two of these participants were also prepared to hazard guesses at what the term might mean, both of which were in fact quite idiosyncratic answers: 'English as a language in France perhaps?'; and 'is it to do with family of languages?' (an interesting reflection of participants' general willingness to take part in this kind of study – i.e., even where respondents have no idea about a concept some will be prepared to make wild guesses, no matter how outlandish).

What was surprising though, given the low ratings for ELF, is that the remaining five participants – including one who gave a 0 rating on both dimensions – were able to provide quite accurate (in one or two cases very accurate) descriptions of the role of English as a global lingua franca. The five answers are as follows, with the rating values from that participant given in brackets (the first figure signals the familiarity rating and the second represents the confidence rating):

The one language that many people from all over the world commonly use to communicate with each other (2, 1).

English used as the language communicated between people of other nationalities, i.e., Italian person speaking English to a French person (??) (1, 0).

English used for administrative purpose in a country where there are various national languages. English acts as a language to communicate between various languages (4, 3).

English as being a language that everyone can 'fall back on' for communication in EU. (3, 3).

English as a world language spoken by non-native speakers where the basics of communication is transmitted/communicated to the detriment of grammar, tenses, etc. (0, 0).

Apart from the last of these referring to the concept of ELF from a deficit perspective, 'to the *detriment* of grammar, tenses, etc.', these are fairly workable accounts of ELF use or ELF settings. What is also notable is that there is not always much correspondence between a participant's reported levels of familiarity with a term and willingness and ability to provide a definition. So although the novice teachers were as a group reporting a general unawareness regarding ELF and quite a lot of uncertainty about the meaning of the term, several of the participants have at some point either encountered the term before and/or developed some appreciation of the role of English as a contact language. What is clear, however, is at this relatively late stage in their training course there has been no mention of ELF or Global Englishes of any note.

The subsequent open question asked participants to comment on what they understood the term SE to mean. All 13 participants included some entry for this question, but responses varied quite considerably in terms of length and style. These ranged from single word answers and short phrases, including 'RP', 'Queens' English' and 'Oxford dictionary English', up to much longer descriptions that attempted to specify the term in more detail. Each of these longer entries is presented below:

- the English that is used by everyone in normal speech;
- general English spoken every day – the 'proper' form of English;
- official English in a given region – RP in the UK;
- English taught in school – British English;
- English in its most basic form without the use of colloquial words or different accents;
- English that is spoken by people who live in an English speaking country;
- received pronunciation (RP) – or the Queen's English – the recognized standard for (UK) English;
- standardised English as it is spoken by native speakers – the Queen's English;
- Standard English is what native speakers use, not the Queen or BBC.

There are several important matters arising here. Strikingly, there is first quite a strong tendency for participants to mistakenly associate SE with accent, with seven of the teachers mentioning either 'RP' and/or 'Queen's English', and with one of the responses describing SE as English 'without an accent' (see Lippi-Green 2012 on this).

As anticipated, participants also made a clear link between SE and native-speaker English, but exclusively mentioned only the UK or British English, with no reference to American English or any other standard varieties. One response alludes to SE being broader than British English, describing this as English 'spoken by people who live in an English speaking country'. However, there is no specific example given, nor any indication of what would count as an English-speaking country. Again, this suggests that for these novice teachers the notion of linguistic diversity does not really figure at all in their conceptualizations of language. These responses provide further suggestion that there has up to this point been little to no discussion of language variability or related sociolinguistic concepts, including for instance processes of standardization.

In short, the participants have a strong sense of the importance of SE, but not a particularly well-informed understanding of the linguistic or sociolinguistic/sociopolitical nature of standard languages. If we look at the responses to the final two questions, we can see what impact this has on the teachers' developing sense of subject knowledge. To recap, the penultimate question asked participants to comment on what they felt language teachers needed to know in order to be effective teachers. Two participants left this section of the questionnaire blank. In the remaining 11 questionnaires, responses tended to focus on aspects of content knowledge, with a clear preponderance for grammar, lexis and phonology (seven respondents mentioned grammar and/or lexis and phonology in one combination or another). Longer entries tended to specify discrete aspects of grammar and lexis, as can be seen in the following example:

> Differences between use and meaning. How to form tenses (and other grammatical things). Collocation and knowledge of vocabulary. They need to have a good knowledge of everyday conversational English.

In addition, several participants made reference to aspects of pedagogic content knowledge (principles relating to how teachers convey subject knowledge to learners; see Tsui 2003 on categories of teacher knowledge). These included comments such as 'grading language', 'staging language' and 'ability to think on your feet', while two other respondents made reference to aspects of language acquisition, but simply stated very broadly that teachers need to become aware of 'how language is acquired and how it can develop'.

In relation to the syllabus guidelines discussed above, there were only two responses that included comments on the learning context as a relevant aspect of teacher knowledge. In both cases, however, this related to learning strategies and styles, and was more an expression of awareness of micro-contextual issues regarding classroom procedures and task type than a concern for the social dimension of language. In other words, none of the participants mentioned wider social contexts of language learning and use, nor any aspects of learning or teaching that related to the role of English as a global lingua franca. Again we can conclude that this area of syllabus content of the qualification is largely not being dealt with.

In terms of the perceived impact of CertTESOL training on participants' thinking – the final question in the study – there was again a focus on content knowledge and pedagogic content knowledge, but no reference to language varieties or aspects of sociolinguistics. This is a complex area though, and being able to articulate ways in which a course (still ongoing at the time of this study) has impacted on existing ideas about teaching is not a straightforward matter. Unsurprisingly, when asked if their views on teacher knowledge had changed as a result of taking the course, eight of the participants left this section blank or wrote 'no', 'none' or 'not at all'. There was only one longer response to this question, with the participant giving details on how the course had influenced his thinking in terms of language teaching methods: 'I have learnt many new techniques of teaching a language. There are too many to list here but in brief you need to follow a logical process to teach new words'. I end my discussion of the questionnaire study here, as this comment is a very apt reflection of the way Cambridge English and Trinity College teaching awards have for many years now shown a strong tendency to focus on classroom procedures and practical skills, often at the expense of other areas of the syllabus.

Concluding remarks

This study represents a small but important step towards further exploring the role of ELF in the development of expertise among English language teachers. The questionnaire findings (although as yet rather preliminary) reveal that to date professional qualifications in ELT are still somewhat lacking with respect to incorporating an ELF perspective in practice, despite the inclusion of ELF in the current syllabus guidelines. In terms of initial teacher preparation in the UK, attention is still predominantly on how 'best' to teach English and very little on the nature of the subject itself. The input session was designed to make at least some contribution to the introduction of ELF in the curriculum. The restricted availability of time, as well as the late timetabling for this session (the penultimate class of the course), mean that the potential impact on these teachers' approaches to language will be relatively limited. However, it is hoped that by raising awareness of ELF and linguistic diversity so early on in the trajectory of a teacher's professional development, the practical relevance of ELF in teachers' perceptions of expertise will be quite prominent.

Introducing change in educational practice is no easy task, however. As Suzuki (2011) reports with regard to her attempts to introduce greater awareness of the diversity of English among a group of English language teachers in Japan, although teachers developed a better understanding of linguistic diversity, there was still a reluctance to include different varieties of English in their future practice. Suzuki concludes that 'single-shot instruction' (2011: 151), that is, a one-off module that focuses on diversity, is unlikely to be sufficient to bring about lasting change in terms of teachers' thinking about English. Suzuki ascribes this to 'the student teachers' deeply ingrained beliefs that there is a single useful form of English for international communication [...] i.e. American and British English (in their eyes)' (2011: 151).

The focus on ELF in the teacher education curriculum must therefore begin early on in teachers' professional learning. Elsewhere, I have reported that ELF has begun to feature prominently in teachers' perceptions of English (Dewey 2012). However, for the most part to date, teachers have tended only to become exposed to ELF in a sustained and systematic way on high-level in-service teacher education programmes, typically on MA TESOL or MA ELT modules. These tend to focus on theory and debate surrounding ELF, with little attention then given to the practicalities of incorporating ELF in classroom practices. So far, there has been relatively little attention given to the development of practical tasks for use with novice teachers. It is essential therefore that in ELF research we do not stop at the discussion of the 'implications' of ELF for pedagogy. We cannot simply say that it is up to teachers to develop their practice in response to ELF; we need much further engagement with practitioners in order to make ELF more prominent in teachers' professional development (see Dewey, forthcoming, on what practical measures can be taken to further integrate an ELF perspective in the teacher education curriculum). Educating the educators must be an essential aspect of this, since not all teacher trainers in the UK take an MA course with a focus on ELF and Global Englishes.

Finally, given the complex nature of implementing change in pedagogy, it will be particularly valuable to carry out empirical research from a longitudinal perspective. The impact on teachers of the study reported here is likely to be greater if this kind of intervention can be followed up by further involvement between researchers and practitioners. It would be especially interesting to carry out interviews and/or classroom observations with teachers who have taken modules in ELF, say six or 12 months afterwards, to further determine to what extent and in what ways teachers are able to incorporate an ELF perspective in practice.

Engagement priorities

In the case of ELF, 'engagement' is an exceptionally important concept. Up to this point, discussion of ELF theory and research has predominantly been concerned with identifying the key areas of language pedagogy for which ELF raises *implications* for current practice. If practitioners are to move beyond these implications towards incorporating an ELF perspective in *application*, initial teacher education programmes are key. As we have seen in this chapter, there is significant scope in existing programme documentation on certificate level teaching awards for ELF to be better incorporated in the teacher training curriculum. However, the challenge is to reconceive the way English is oriented to in the classroom and during assessment of teaching practice, and to reconsider existing practices to determine where there are opportunities to insert ELF perspectives in the timetable. In order to achieve this, the following priorities need to be addressed:

- Beyond simply incorporating an introductory session on ELF, teacher educators could consider which aspects of training are most relevant to approach from an ELF perspective, thus integrating ELF further by relating ELF to activity type, language models, materials selection and so on.
- More time needs to be devoted to discussing the nature of language itself, with a focus on the extent of linguistic diversity in English and the importance of language variation.
- Discussions of learning and teaching contexts must consider macro as well as micro-level aspects of context. This will need to involve teacher educators developing greater awareness of the role of English globally and the impact this has on how the language is used.

- Teachers can be encouraged to reflect on current and future teaching contexts, with further consideration given to the type of communicative settings that their future students are most likely to encounter and what kind of English they would benefit from.

To what extent do these priorities apply to your own situation? Are some more important than others? What other priorities, if any, would you add to the list?

Notes

1. Somewhat confusingly perhaps, the acronyms by which the awards are usually known (i.e., CELTA and Delta) do not exactly match the full title of each qualification. This is largely an indication of the popularity and widespread recognition of these awards, which have been in existence for many years and have gone through various name changes along the way. They were previously referred to as CTEFLA (Certificate in Teaching English as a Foreign Language to Adults) and DTELFA (Diploma in Teaching English as a Foreign Language to Adults). The title of the award was changed to CELTA (Certificate in English Language Teaching to Adults) and DELTA (where 'D' again signals 'Diploma') in an attempt to better reflect the scope of the awards (i.e., that the qualifications were not limited solely to EFL contexts). This was then subsequently changed to the current full title. The most recent name change has simply not been carried over in the acronym, as this has now gained quite considerable and widespread currency in the profession, and changing it would likely have substantial commercial implications.
2. Prior to this, the particular course in question had not included an input session on ELF. After a meeting with the course leader it was agreed that I would give an introductory session towards the end of the programme, both for the purpose of my own research and as a means of experimenting with ways in which the existing timetable might be updated to include a session on ELF. Since conducting this 'guest' session the school management decided to reconfigure the four-week schedule, with the result that there is now a regular slot in which ELF is introduced. This session is taught by course tutors at the centre, using materials designed by the course leader. Patsko (2014) provides a detailed account of this course.

References

Choi, T. (2013). Curriculum innovation through teacher certification: Evaluation of a government intervention and its effects on teacher development and English language pedagogy in South Korea. Unpublished PhD Thesis, King's College London.

Chowdhury, R. and Phan, L. H. (2008). Reflecting on Western TESOL training and communicative language teaching: Bangladeshi teachers' voices. *Asia Pacific Journal of Education* 28(3): 305–316.

Cogo, A. and Dewey, M. (2012). *Analysing English as a Lingua Franca: A Corpus-driven Investigation*. London: Continuum.

Dewey, M. (2011). Accommodative ELF talk and teacher knowledge. In Archibald, A, Cogo, A. and Jenkins, J. (eds) *Latest Trends in ELF Research*. Newcastle: Cambridge Scholars Press, pp. 205–208.

Dewey, M. (2012). Towards a *Post-normative* approach: Learning the pedagogy of ELF. *Journal of English as a Lingua Franca* 1(1): 141–170.

Dewey, M. (forthcoming) *The Pedagogy of English as a Lingua Franca*. Berlin: De Gruyter.

Jenkins, J. (2013). *English as a Lingua Franca in the International University: The Politics of Academic English Language Policy*. Abingdon: Routledge.

Jenkins, J., Cogo, A. and Dewey, M. (2011). Review of developments in research into English as a lingua franca. *Language Teaching* 44(3): 281–315.

Lippi-Green (2012). *English with an Accent: Language, Ideology and Discrimination in the United States*. 2nd ed. New York: Routledge.

Littlewood, W. (2007). Communicative and task-based language teaching in East Asian classrooms. *Language Teaching* 40: 243–249.

Milroy, J and Milroy, L. (2012). *Authority in Language: Investigating Standard English*. 3rd ed. Abingdon: Routledge.

Patsko, L. (2014) Talking to novice teachers about ELF: Dealing with ELF in pre-service TESOL course. Paper presented at ELF 7, the 7th International Conference of English as a Lingua Franca, Athens, 4–6 September 2014.

Suzuki, A. (2011). Introducing diversity of English into ELT: Student teachers' responses. *ELT Journal* 65(2): 145–153.

Trinity College London (2013) *Certificate in Teaching English to Speakers of Other Languages (CertTESOL). Syllabus – from June 2013*. London.

Tsui, A. (2003). *Understanding Expertise in Teaching: Case Studies of Second Language Teachers*. Cambridge: Cambridge University Press.

University of Cambridge ESOL Examinations (2011). *Cambridge English for Teaching. Delta Syllabus Specifications*. Cambridge.

11
ELF-Oriented Pedagogy: Conclusions

Hugo Bowles

The concern of this collection has been to address the many challenges facing language teachers who work with ELF, a global language, at a local level. This concluding chapter will review the main issues raised and solutions proposed in the collection in relation to pedagogy and ELF; the final section will look ahead to possible future developments in these areas.

Interest in the relationship between teaching and ELF is a relatively recent phenomenon, since early ELF research was reluctant to stray into pedagogical areas, claiming that it was up to ELT practitioners rather than researchers to decide the relevance of ELF to their own teaching context (Jenkins 2012: 492). However, ELF's status as 'a globalised phenomenon that is continuously being localised during its countless interactions' (Jenkins, Cogo and Dewey 2011: 304) provides both a description and a perspective on English that is now widely recognised and debated in relation to pedagogy. Since the first overview on the teaching of English as an international language by McKay (2002), book-length additions to the pedagogical ELF literature have been added, including edited collections by Sharifian (2009), Alsagoff et al. (2012), Matsuda (2012), Kirkpatrick and Sussex (2012), Marlina and Giri (2014) and Bayyurt and Akcan (2014). On top of this, the proceedings of recent ELF conferences (Bayyurt and Akcan 2013a, 2013b; Lopriore and Grazzi, forthcoming) include a number of papers dedicated to pedagogy. This increase is not only an indicator of a burgeoning interest in the teaching of ELF but also highlights the pedagogical areas that recent ELF research has led applied linguists to address.

Pragmatics, intelligibility and culture: pedagogical issues

ELF-oriented pedagogy has moved away from the traditional ELT focus on language components and skills and incorporates typical ELF concerns in the area of pragmatics, culture and intelligibility. This section will briefly explore the main questions that the recent applied linguistics literature has raised in relation to these three areas before moving on to pedagogical applications.

Pragmatics and pedagogy

With regard to pragmatics, the hybridity and fluidity of ELF interaction highlighted by ELF research (Cogo, Chapter 1) makes it difficult to be too prescriptive in the areas of pragmatics teaching. McKay (2009) has argued for a context-sensitive approach to the teaching of ELF pragmatics in the classroom, pointing to three areas in which the teaching of pragmatics could concentrate: introducing and practising repair strategies, the use of conversational gambits and the development of negotiation strategies. Murray (2012) takes a similar line, calling for 'a bespoke social grammar for each interaction according to the particular characteristics of their interlocutor and of the broader context in which that interaction takes place' (p. 325). This would involve an explicit focus on those features of ELF pragmatics that have been shown to facilitate communication in ELF interaction. House (2013: 198–199) provides a list of speech act sequences and discourse features which in her view need to be introduced in class from a cross-cultural pragmatic perspective, while Murray provides a similar list, including the let-it-pass principle, code-switching, repetition, paraphrase, clarification, the use of certain discourse markers and self-repair. The question of how such complex packages of pragmatic input can be presented in the classroom in order to produce the accommodation skills on which ELF research sets a high premium is discussed below (see *Awareness-raising in the classroom*).

Intelligibility and pedagogy

Intelligibility is not only concerned with the decoding of sounds but is affected by listeners' attitudes to accents and by what Seidlhofer (2011) calls the 'willingness to understand' (p. 36). It is also closely associated with the process of accommodation and the adjusting of speech in order to become intelligible. In this respect, as noted by Pickering (2006), ELF blurs the distinction between intelligibility and comprehensibility and this in turn affects the way the teaching of areas such as pronunciation, listening and speaking is viewed.

In terms of individual sounds, as Walker (2010) has stressed, an ELF orientation to pronunciation in the classroom means that teachers need to differentiate sound reception and production. According to traditional ELT models pronunciation teaching involves approximation to NS phonemes – students are required to listen to and produce the same English sounds. From an ELF perspective, the sounds that students hear are not necessarily the sounds they will produce. Teachers therefore need to be aware that a focus on intelligibility means being able to manage different sound features for reception and production.

To improve intelligibility it is recommended that teachers provide students with greater exposure to the different accents of proficient NSs from different speaking cultures (see, e.g., Bayyurt and Altinmakas 2012). However, this kind of exposure requires different approaches in monolingual and multilingual groups. On the production side, teachers of monolingual groups can be made aware of the kind of intelligibility problems that are caused by the different phonological realisations of English, such as Japanese English vowel length (Oda and Tajima 2010). On the reception side, teachers can focus on which accents of English are less easily understood by the L1 group. With multilingual groups, this kind of approach to the management of intelligibility is made more complex by the fact that the range of possible intelligibility problems increases in proportion to the number of different L1s in the class. A suggestion for surmounting the problem of differentiated intelligibility in a multilingual class is to focus on features of spoken production, known as the lingua franca core (LFC), which are argued to produce maximum intelligibility in spoken interaction. The implementation of LFC features to assist mutual intelligibility in multilingual classrooms aims to provide a pragmatic target rather than a specific model for the exact replication of individual English phonemes (Jenkins 1998).

The role of students' and teachers' own attitudes to accents of English is also emerging as an important feature in the teacher's assessment of which approach to intelligibility to adopt in the classroom. Li (2012), for example, warns of a conflict between a student's desire to express their own identity through L1 accented English and a fear that this may cause intelligibility problems, and recommends that 'the pedagogic option of the teaching of the local(ised) accent should be considered with care, for such an important decision might turn out to be unpopular and possibly meet with learner resistance in class' (p. 109). Overall, the management of intelligibility in the classroom requires an expert mix of sensitivity, phonetic knowledge and pedagogical skill. Practical teaching suggestions in the area of intelligibility are illustrated below (see *Awareness-raising in the classroom*).

Culture and pedagogy

What is the culture of ELF interaction, what is its role in the language classroom and how can teachers address it? Baker (2011) has pointed out that for ELF speakers, whose communicative strategies are those of multicultural language users rather than native English speakers, no 'target culture' actually exists. The existence of online communities, for example, where ELF discourse flourishes, calls into question the very notion of 'cultural authenticity' (Kern 2014). Very often English cannot be confined within a single community of practice but is connected to a range of communities where there is no explicit link between nation, language and culture. As a result, Baker argues that ELF users need a flexible model of culture that enables them to adapt their English as it moves between communities and that this kind of 'intercultural communicative competence' can only be achieved by developing intercultural awareness (ICA).

The concept of ICA has considerable pedagogical significance. A high level of ICA is needed by a wide range of communities of practice, particularly business communities and academia, where intercultural expertise needs to be acquired in order to achieve professional goals through the medium of English, and immigrant communities and displaced ethnic groups, where English is used as a lingua franca. ICA, it is argued, enables such communities to deal with communicative situations with which they may not be familiar. As with the teaching of pragmatics and intelligibility, the aim of an ELF-orientation to the teaching of culture is to enhance the flexibility of the ELF user so that they adapt to interactions as they are taking place and are not hindered by cultural stereotyping or expectations as to how interaction should proceed. The practical task of developing this kind of intercultural awareness has now begun to be addressed (see, e.g., Feng, Byram and Fleming 2009). The classroom is now seen as both a source of knowledge of diverse communicative practices and a forum for critical discussion and reflection, and practical suggestions for the teaching of intercultural awareness are illustrated in the *Intercultural Awareness* section below.

An ELF-orientation to teaching: some pedagogical suggestions

Having explored some of the issues raised in the applied linguistics literature relating to ELF and teaching, we now turn to practical pedagogical answers provided in this collection and elsewhere. It needs to be said first that although many of the chapters in the collection describe pedagogical aspects of ELF in a specific part of the world (Taiwan, Italy, Switzerland, China, Turkey, Greece, the United States and the Czech Republic), their analysis is framed in relation to particular communities of practice rather than geographical areas. These communities may be monolingual schools and university classrooms, or involve language learners with a multilingual repertoire from a variety of linguacultural backgrounds, such as international schools and migrant communities. Secondly, as stated in Chapter 1, ELF is not a variety of English that needs to be taught, nor is the relationship between ELF and pedagogy a methodology that needs to be prescribed (see Alsagoff 2012: 6 for a similar non-prescriptivism within EIL pedagogy). As a consequence, although the aspects of language teaching covered by individual authors are familiar ones – materials analysis (Lopriore and Vettorel, Chapter 2), writing skills (Grazzi, Chapter 4), and student/teacher perceptions of language usage (Wang, Chapter 6), textbook usage (Yu, Chapter 3), teaching practices (Bayyurt and Sifakis, Chapter 7) and oral presentations (Schaller-Schwaner, Chapter 5) – teaching recommendations are not necessarily based on the analysis of linguistic content. Instead they explore the issues arising in an ELF-related approach to a language practice, skill or community and describe possible implications for language teaching.

The relationship between ELF and pedagogy is described below in terms of ELF-aware teaching, which is the foundation of an ELF-orientation to teaching. It then looks at how this orientation is expressed in terms of language policies, materials development and classroom practice.

ELF-aware teaching and learning

All of the chapters in the collection deal to a greater or lesser extent with ELF awareness-raising, which emerges as the bedrock on which an ELF-orientation to pedagogy is founded. From a pedagogical perspective, the awareness-raising process describes a movement from *ELF-informed* teaching, which involves the supply of appropriate ELF information to teacher educators, trainees, teachers and learners, to *ELF-aware* teaching, which involves appropriate use of this information in the classroom. The kind of ELF-awareness training provided to students or trainee teachers by the ELF-informed educator is the main focus of Wang's study (Chapter 6).

Regarding *ELF-informed teaching*, the kind of ELF data that informs pedagogy can come from primary or secondary sources: primary ELF data, that is, data from actual ELF interaction, can be used analytically by comparing it with NS data, or it can stand alone as material in the language class as an illustration of English usage; secondary sources might include articles about ELF research or global English for use with university students or teacher trainees as background reading for discussion purposes, as recommended by Wang (Chapter 6). In relation to primary data, there is general agreement that information should be both *diverse* and *authentic*. Diversity refers not only to the inclusion of the nonstandard and unpredictable forms that are characteristic of ELF but also to the switching and mixing of codes and registers (Kramsch 2014: 301). In relation to the authenticity of primary data, Wang (Chapter 6) argues that the principle of using authentic English in class applies to ELF as much as it does to NS English and that since ELF is just as real as NS English, it is equally applicable in the classroom. Other authors note, however, that the use of authentic English, native or ELF, which can be highly complex, needs to be calibrated in terms of the local age group, level and motivation of the class.

Intercultural awareness

The development of intercultural awareness relates to both the teacher's own intercultural awareness as well as that of language learners. As regards teacher awareness, ELF-oriented teaching is contingent upon local learning, and intercultural awareness is needed by teachers if they are to be able to engage with their local teaching world and match local practices with classroom activities so that they 'resonate with the local linguistic landscape' (McKay 2012: 37). For Yu (Chapter 3) teachers also require intercultural awareness for critical engagement with languacultural dominance. Increasing teachers' intercultural awareness through teacher education is therefore an important step, and Bayyurt and Sifakis (Chapter 7) provide an interesting account of successful awareness-raising during in-service teacher training. Currently, however, as Dewey (Chapter 10) notes, there is little room for engagement with local educational contexts in standard teacher training courses.

An important part of the teacher's intercultural repertoire is awareness of local needs. The ethnographic study by Goncalves (Chapter 8) highlights the importance of the teacher having an understanding of the languacultural background of an entire discourse community in which ELF is being used in order to maximise language learning at the workplace. Schaller-Schwaner (Chapter 5) shows that intercultural features also need to be analysed in the classroom itself, where they may be a significant factor in determining the intelligibility of learner interaction – for her students, the intelligibility of spoken ELF depended a great deal on the specificity of the L1 and L2 language backgrounds of speakers and listeners. This kind of teacher awareness is quite a sophisticated one, involving an ability to understand how the phonological makeup of the L1 and L2 affects the production and reception of spoken ELF, and then to devise strategies that will enable students to accommodate to it.

Regarding the development of intercultural competence in learners, Baker (forthcoming) notes 'the lack of focus on the intercultural in teacher training, teaching materials, teacher syllabi and language testing' and how culture is still very low in terms of teacher priorities. A number of recommendations have been made for developing learners' intercultural awareness along the lines suggested by Baker's ICA model (see above). Kirkpatrick (2012), for example, recommends the teaching of individual regional cultures of English, while comparative methods can also be used to raise awareness, for example by comparing cultures in terms of their different communicative practices.

Learner awareness will also be improved with better intercultural materials. Encouragingly, Lopriore and Vettorel (Chapter 2) find that there is a distinct improvement in the diversity of intercultural language activities in textbooks, noting that they are at the same time 'broader (that is, not solely related to the anglophone world) but more localised'. The emergence of culturally-nuanced teaching ideas is also confirmed elsewhere. Doludenko and Baste (2013), for example, have highlighted how communicative practice in the target (English) language could focus on comparing native and adopted cultures (Russian and Adyghe in their case), using cultural blogs and cultural wiki-projects. In these contexts language use is a form of mediation between shared or different cultures and languaging activities that articulate intercultural experience are seen to be particularly beneficial. Wang (Chapter 6) describes how discussion of intercultural encounters in the classroom is important for ELF-related knowledge construction. Lopriore and Vettorel (Chapter 2) also strongly recommend using telecollaboration of the kind exemplified by Grazzi (Chapter 4), as well as virtual spaces such as social media and blogs. These virtual spaces, by providing both resources and a forum for intercultural activities, are seen as an ideal platform for fostering intercultural competence.

Awareness and agency

A further benefit of ELF-awareness activities is the development of learner *agency*. Schaller-Schwaner (Chapter 5) illustrates the importance of learner agency in contributing to language awareness through her recommendation that learners discover their own intelligibility through recording and discussion with other learners. Discussion and debate is not a new idea in ELT since communicative language teaching methods have always strongly advocated group discussion as a form of skills practice. However, from an ELF-informed perspective, student-led discussion is also an enabler of agency because it allows students to take charge of their own language learning with considerable benefits for learner motivation and engagement with English (Ushioda 2013). In this respect, as Lopriore and Vettorel (Chapter 2) argue, reflection on sociolinguistic aspects of language use is itself motivating for learners.

The agency of the learner can also be viewed politically. Yu (Chapter 3) and Wang (Chapter 6) advocate using ELF teaching to promote a more critical approach to awareness-raising, viewing it also in terms of consciousness-raising. This stance sees learning language as a potentially empowering political activity in which students should be encouraged by teachers to question and challenge what they are doing in language classrooms – an approach aimed more at a change in student thinking rather than a change in their language use.

Awareness-raising in the classroom

Awareness-raising activities are described in some detail by authors, particularly Lopriore and Vettorel (Chapter 2), in relation to a variety of age groups and classroom contexts (schools, universities and migrant communities) and in relation to both language learning and teacher training. On the one hand, language activities in the classroom, particularly in universities, can be used to raise awareness of English within WE and an understanding of ELF. Wang (Chapter 6), for example, describes the benefits of using WE/ELF material as background for reading or listening activities. Having already processed the material through language activities, learners are better able to discuss the content of the material itself and this improved discussion leads in turn to improved awareness of ELF issues. As regards awareness-raising in teacher training, Yu (Chapter 3) claims that the ELF approach provides theoretical and practical support to a more critical stance by teachers in relation to their classroom practices because it acts a point of reference for comparison with more traditional approaches.

However, the purpose of awareness-raising through language activities is not necessarily for critical or purely metalinguistic purposes, that is, learning about language for its own sake. In fact, the emphasis placed on awareness-raising in the ELF-oriented classroom is largely because of its direct relation to second language learning. According to Swain (2006), the production of language output produces metalinguistic awareness, which in turn leads to improved learning. This is a mutually-reinforcing process in which *languaging*, the articulation of thought about language through language, is the pedagogical means employed to achieve the learning outcome. Lopriore and Vettorel (Chapter 2) describe in detail the kind of languaging activity that can be used in school classrooms for language learning purposes and a number of chapters provide other examples. Grazzi (Chapter 4) in particular, focusing on the use of ELF by secondary school students in creative writing through telecollaboration, showcases the way in which awareness-raising activities are combined with ELF language practice. Here the use of the Internet as both the source of ELF material and the means of collaboration through which student languaging takes place neatly combines ELF with innovative pedagogic practice to provide an excellent example of an ELF-informed teaching activity.

Awareness-raising activities are recommended in the area of pragmatics and intelligibility described above. Regarding pragmatics, House (2013) recommends using awareness-raising to train students to notice the existence and usage of pragmatic features and to equip students with 'a meta-language with which to describe interactional moves and strategies' (p. 198), while Murray (2012) recommends both deductive activities include analysis and discussion of speech act performance and breakdown in ELF interaction, as well as more inductive activities would include speech act translation, guided discussion and student ethnography. The case study by Wang (Chapter 6) suggests that exposure to awareness-raising activities can develop more tolerant attitudes to intelligibility in students, and there are welcome signs that awareness-raising activities and materials in the area of accents of English and intelligibility are starting to be developed (Bayyurt and Altinmakas 2012: 180; Matsuda and Sumannamai Duran 2012: 218).

Language policies, standards and models

Although ELF itself is not defined in terms of geography or culture, the work of teachers clearly is. Teachers are often bound to observe language policies, which have traditionally been set at national or institutional levels in accordance with descriptions of NS English or nativised Englishes and have then been translated into language syllabi and curricula (Modiano 2009). ELF-based descriptions, on the other hand, which stress the localised diversity of English usage within and across national boundaries, are fluid, transitory and hard to fit in with the standardisation of English as a prescriptive entity. For many language teachers this creates a conflict in the area of assessment – they may recognise the complexity and diversity of the language usage their students need to be prepared for, but lack familiarity with the concepts needed to evaluate that usage owing to the influence of Standard English ideology (Dewey, Chapter 10).

Taking an ELF approach to this teaching dilemma requires rethinking the whole issue of standards in a post-normative way (Dewey 2012). This relates to the application of standards through testing procedures (Hu 2012: 129ff.) and to language teachers' qualifications, where nativeness is no longer viewed as an advantage for English teaching (Braine 2010). In this respect, the proficient and qualified bilingual teacher is highlighted by Goncalves (Chapter 8) as being of particular value to migrant communities.

The application of standards in the classroom is a particularly controversial area. The fact that the fluidity of ELF defies linguistic standardisation has been used to claim that ELF cannot have much relevance to language teaching since ELF descriptions cannot provide a specific standard for learners to aspire to. Three types of answer are given to this objection in the collection: firstly, that ELF standards certainly exist but they prioritise certain functional areas such as intelligibility and pragmatic competence over more formal linguistic criteria such as grammatical accuracy; secondly, that it may be the responsibility of teachers and learners themselves to establish what standards they want to achieve – authors in the collection agree that decisions about language teaching standards and materials have to be ELF-informed and be taken in relation to the needs of the local context; thirdly, they stress how problematic the imposition of NS standards can be in some learning contexts – how it can act as a brake on motivation for textbook users (Yu, Chapter 3), or a cause of insecurity among migrant workers (Goncalves, Chapter 8). One chapter also provides an interesting example of how an ELF perspective can deploy standard language teaching resources in new ways; according to Schaller-Schwaner (Chapter 5), the use of standard phonemic symbols for the 'visual anchoring' of sounds may be a necessary process for improving the intelligibility of her ELF learners' oral presentations.

Finally, the main vehicle for encouraging teachers to rethink their attitudes to language policies, standards and assessment, as well as their implementation of them, is to incorporate ELF awareness-raising into the teacher training process along the lines indicated in Dewey (2012). The reasons why this is proving to be such a challenging task is explained by Dewey (Chapter 10), who illustrates in a case study how even though a knowledge of ELF may be a syllabus requirement in a training course, that course may not be able to turn the requirement into an effective change in teachers' knowledge base or behaviour.

Materials – diversity and availability

It is now well established that teachers have to equip students to communicate both globally and locally with multiple varieties of English (Matsuda 2009) and diversity of materials is essential if teachers are to be able to achieve this objective. Diversity of representation in materials implies 'a range of different ELF scenarios in which participants were from a range of different cultural and linguistic backgrounds and communicating for a variety of purposes and in various contexts' (Murray 2012: 323) and Lopriore and Vettorel (Chapter 2) and Yu (Chapter 3) both raise concerns in relation to the lack of diversity in the materials available for teachers or students to choose from. This lack of diversity may be *linguistic*, relating to a lack of contextual variety of ELF usage, and/or *cultural* – when content has an inherent NES languacultural bias and does not match the cultural background that teacher and students can relate to.

A second general concern is the *lack of local ELF material*, that is, material that is inclusive of ELF usage in a local community. The materials analysed by Lopriore and Vettorel (Chapter 2) and Wang (Chapter 6) are all produced by international or national publishers, while local materials produced by teachers on an ad hoc basis are not available for evaluation. Given the benefits that the matching of materials with familiar local contexts and practices can have on learning and motivation (Lopez Barrios and Debat 2014), it is worth reflecting on the reasons for the lack of locally prepared and produced materials. It may be due to the fact that materials writing is time-consuming and local production expensive, with the result that local materials are not being produced in sufficient quantities, or because researchers are simply not paying sufficient attention to them since they are hard to collect and evaluate. Local material production may also be hindered by lack of access to local sources of ELF usage or by the problem of lack of technology (Graves and Garton 2014: 270) providing access to ELF usage globally. Many of the pedagogical activities recommended by authors in this collection, particularly in the area of intercultural awareness and exposure to diversity, depend heavily on teachers being able to find spoken and written ELF materials online and reproduce them in the classroom. The problem of access to technology not only involves Internet availability and the use of computers, projectors and speakers in classrooms, but also forms of telecollaboration and networking both within individual classrooms and between classrooms in different locations of the kind described by Grazzi (Chapter 4).

Regarding choice of material, Yu's exploration (Chapter 3) of the way that teachers evaluate and use materials suggests that awareness-raising during teacher training can allow teachers to take greater control of the choosing of materials, while her illustrations of student perceptions of materials assessment suggest that teachers should also take notice of the kind of material that learners themselves say they would like to be exposed to. They may very well be receptive to diversity; Buckingham (2014), for example, argues that since Omani students are receptive to the accents of proficient NNESTs, commercial materials for the Gulf market should include accented English of NSs of South Asian languages, Arabic and Kiswahili.

Multilingual classroom practices

As well as the focus on awareness-raising described above, authors identify a number of specific classroom practices as being potentially beneficial and whose deployment depends on the teacher's sensitivity to a particular language learning context. Many of these practices are characteristic of the multilingual classroom described by Kramsch (2014). The ELF-informed teacher is above all one who understands the makeup of the particular language learning community – the language background of each of the students s/he is teaching as well as the language of the local community. This is particularly true in multilingual institutions such as the internationals schools surveyed by Quinn Novotna and Dunkova (Chapter 9). Understanding of languacultural background can inform and shape the kind of classroom practices teachers adopt, as exemplified by Schaller-Schwaner (Chapter 5), who shows how important it is for teachers to look carefully at the future contexts in which their students are likely to be using English as well as their perceptions of and attitudes to different accents of English before ruling in or ruling out the teaching of non-essential NS pronunciation features. Using the resources of the multilingual classroom may also mean encouraging teachers to accept communicative practices that have been traditionally regarded as not conducive to language learning; these include translanguaging techniques (Canagarajah 2011), that is, using the linguistic features of language x to maximise the communicative potential of interaction in language y, which are argued by Goncalves (Chapter 8) to act as confidence-boosters for the learning of grammar.

Translation is a good example of a multilingual classroom practice that is potentially a highly productive process that combines ELF and ICA awareness-raising with language learning. The links between translation and ELF have been set out in Cook (2012) and the pedagogical issues raised by the spread of ELF in translation training have been explored in Taviano (2013). Taviano notes that 'traditional notions of texts written in a clearly identified language and addressed to a specific culture and readership are no longer valid' (p. 160) and that translators increasingly have to deal with texts that may not originate in a specific cultural context or have a specific national target readership, or may have been written by a number of authors; these 'hybrid' texts constitute ideal material for combining classroom language work with cultural awareness raising. She also points out (Taviano 2013: 161) how ELF-based, non-professional translation practices such as fansubbing (online translation by fans) and crowdsourcing (online translation of materials by Internet communities) can be adapted to the language classroom. In the area of the teaching of translation, Stewart (2013) discusses the difficulties of translating for a heterogeneous international readership, concluding that translation teachers need 'to acknowledge the usefulness of operating within codified boundaries, and to be open to linguistic diversity, accommodating as far as possible the sundry requisites of the target readers' (pp. 228–229).

ELF-oriented pedagogy: looking ahead

It is significant that many of the authors in this collection have drawn pedagogical conclusions on the basis of their own ELF research projects or their own teaching, and their engagement priorities encourage teachers and students to carry out their own research and reflect on it together. Most of the research in the collection is ethnographic in origin and involves qualitative analytical methods. Yu's snapshots of dialogue (Chapter 3) are used to provide insight into the nature of ELF and to guide subsequent discussion and teacher reflection. Other chapters include a case study based on focus group discussion (Wang, Chapter 6), analysis of questionnaire surveys (Dewey, Chapter 10), interviews (Goncalves, Chapter 8) or combinations of these with observation (Bayyurt and Sifakis, Chapter 7; Quinn Novotna and Dunkova, Chapter 9; Schllaer-Schwaner, Chapter 5). Future developments in the area of ELF and pedagogy are likely to stem from similar kinds of qualitative research conducted in the classroom by teachers themselves. If teachers can be encouraged to carry out their own empirical research by recording and analysing spoken and written ELF interaction and localised practices inside the classroom, an increasingly detailed picture of how an ELF-orientation to language teaching is implemented and received in class will be built up, developing what Yu (Chapter 3) calls 'a two-way relationship' between ELF and classroom practice.

Given the expansion of English as a medium of education in schools and universities, the CLIL classroom, studied by Quinn Novotna and Dunkova (Chapter 9), is likely to become a particularly productive area for ELF-based research with a pedagogical slant. Ethnographic and discourse research on CLIL is still in its infancy and is generally not conducted from an ELF perspective (Nikkula, Dalton-Puffer and Llinares 2013), but as the internationalisation of secondary and higher education programmes increases, the volume of ELF research undertaken in the area of CLIL is likely to grow with it. This kind of classroom research is particularly needed since, as Dewey (Chapter 10) notes, for the many local contexts in which demand for English is increasing, traditional communicative language teaching is often an inappropriate teaching methodology.

Overall, however, the future contribution of ELF to pedagogy will ultimately depend on how far it is understood and valued by teachers themselves. This is most likely to be achieved through direct interaction with teachers of the kind outlined by Dewey (2012, forthcoming). As Dewey notes (Chapter 10), this professional engagement needs to take place at a much more practical level than has hitherto been the case. It is hoped that responses to the engagement priorities and issues raised in this collection can help teachers make that practical connection and enable them to apply their own ELF-orientation to pedagogy in the classroom.

References

Alsagoff, L. (2012). Another book on EIL? Heralding the need for new ways of thinking, doing and being. In Alsagoff, L., McKay, S. L., Hu, G. and Renadya, W. A. (eds), *Principles and Practices for Teaching English as an International Language*. London: Routledge, pp. 1–6.

Alsagoff, L., McKay, S., Hu, G. and Renandya, W. (eds) (2012). *Perspectives and Practices for Teaching English as an International Language*. New York: Routledge.

Baker, W. (2011). Intercultural awareness: Modelling an understanding of cultures in intercultural communication through English as a Lingua Franca. *Language and Intercultural Communication* 11(3): 197–214.

Baker, W. (forthcoming). Research into practice: Cultural and intercultural awareness. *Language Teaching* 48(1).

Bayyurt, Y. and Akcan, S. (eds) (2013a). *Bogazici University Journal of Education* 30(1). Special Issue on the 5th International Conference of English as a Lingua Franca.

Bayyurt, Y. and Akcan, S. (eds) (2013b). *Proceedings of the 5th International Conference of English as a Lingua Franca*. Istanbul: Bogazici University Press.

Bayyurt, Y. and Akcan, S. (eds) (2014). *Current Perspectives on Pedagogy for English as a Lingua Franca*. Berlin: De Gruyter Mouton.

Bayyurt, Y. and Altinmakas, D. (2012). A WE-based English communications skills course at a Turkish university. In A. Matsuda (ed.) *Principles and Practices of Teaching English as an International Language*. Bristol: Multilingual Matters, pp. 169–182.

Braine, G. (2010). *Nonnative Speaker English Teachers: Research, Pedagogy and Professional Growth*. New York: Routledge.

Buckingham, L. (2014). Attitudes to English teachers' accents in the Gulf. *International Journal of Applied Linguistics* 24(1): 50–73.

Canagarajah, S. (2011). Translanguaging in the classroom: Emerging issues for research and pedagogy. In Wei, L. (ed.), *Applied Linguistics Review 2*. New York: Mouton de Gruyter, pp. 1–28

Cook, G. (2012). ELF and translation and interpreting: Common ground, common interest, common cause. *Journal of English as a Lingua Franca* 1(2): 241–262.

Dewey, M. (2012). Towards a post-normative approach: Learning the pedagogy of ELF. *Journal of English as a Lingua Franca* 1(1): 141–170.

Dewey, M. (forthcoming). *The Pedagogy of English as a Lingua Franca*. Berlin: De Gruyter.

Doludenko, E. and Baste, F. (2013). English as mediator in teaching Adyghe (Circassian): cultural values to repatriate students of Circassian origin. In Bayyurt and Akcan (eds) *Proceedings of the 5th International Conference of English as a Lingua Franca*. Istanbul: Bogazici University Press, pp.14–20.

Feng, A., Byram, M. and Fleming, M. (eds) (2009). *Becoming Interculturally Competent Through Education and Training*. Bristol: Multilingual Matters.

Graves, K. and Garton, S. (2014). Materials in ELT: Looking ahead. In Garton, S. and Graves, K. (eds), *International Perspectives on Materials in ELT*. Basingstoke: Palgrave Macmillan, pp. 270–279.

House, J. (2013). Developing pragmatic competence in English as a Lingua Franca: Using discourse markers to express (inter) subjectivity and connectivity. *Journal of Pragmatics* 59: 57–67.

Hu, G. (2012). Assessing English as an International Language. In Alsagoff, L., McKay, S. L., Hu, G. and Renadya, W. A. (eds), *Principles and Practices for Teaching English as an International Language*. London: Routledge, pp. 123–144.

Jenkins, J. (1998). Which pronunciation norms and models for English as an International Language? *ELT Journal* 52: 119–126.

Jenkins, J. (2012). English as a Lingua Franca from the classroom to the classroom. *ELT Journal* 66(4): 486–494.

Jenkins, J., A. Cogo and M. Dewey (2011). Review of developments in research into English as a lingua franca. *Language Teaching* 44(3): 281–315.

Kern, R. (2014). Technology as *pharmakon*: The promise and perils of the internet for foreign language education. *The Modern Language Journal* 98(1): 340–357.

Kirkpatrick, A. (2012). English as the international language of scholarship: Implications for the dissemination of 'local' knowledge. In F. Sharifian (ed.) *English as an International Language: Perspectives and Pedagogical Issues*. Bristol: Multilingual Matters, pp. 254–270.

Kirkpatrick, A. and Sussex, R. (eds) (2012). *English as an International Language in Asia*. Dordrecht: Springer.

Kramsch, C. (2014). Teaching foreign languages in an era of globalisation: Introduction. *The Modern Language Journal* 98(1): 296–311.

Li, D. (2012). Researching non-native speakers' views toward intelligibility and identity: Bridging the gap between moral high grounds and down-to-earth concerns. In F. Sharafian (ed.) *English as an International Language: Perspectives and Pedagogical Issues*. Bristol: Multilingual Matters, pp. 81–118.

Lopez Barrios, M. and de Debat, E. V. (2014). Global vs. local: Does it matter? In Garton, S. and Graves, K. (eds), *International Perspectives on Materials in ELT*. Basingstoke: Palgrave Macmillan, pp. 37–52.

Lopriore, L. and Grazzi, E. (eds) (forthcoming). *Intercultural communication: new perspectives from ELF*. Roma: Roma Tre Press.

McKay, S. (2002). *Teaching English as an International Language*. Oxford: Oxford University Press.

McKay, S. (2009). Pragmatics and EIL pedagogy. In Sharifian, F. (ed.) *English as an International Language: Perspectives and Pedagogical Issues*. Bristol: Multilingual Matters, pp. 227–241.

McKay, S. (2012). Principles of teaching English as an International Language. In Alsagoff, L., McKay, S., Hu, G. and Renandya, W. (eds.), *Principles and Practices for Teaching English as an International Language*. London: Routledge, pp. 28–46.

Marlina, R. and Giri, R. A. (eds) (2014). *The Pedagogy of English as an International Language: Perspectives from Scholars, Teachers and Students*. Switzerland: Springer International Publishing.

Matsuda, A. (2009). Desirable but not necessary? The place of World Englishes and English as an international language in English teacher preparation programs in Japan. In F. Sharifian (ed.) *English as an International Language: Perspectives and Pedagogical Issues*. Bristol: Multilingual Matters, pp. 169–189.

Matsuda, A. (ed.) (2012). *Principles and Practices of Teaching English as an International Language*. Bristol: Multilingual Matters.

Matsuda, A. and Sumannamai Duran, C. (2012). EIL activities and tasks for traditional English classrooms. In Matsuda, A. (ed.) *Principles and Practices of Teaching English as an International Language*. Bristol: Multilingual Matters, pp. 201–237.

Modiano, M. (2009). EIL, Native-speakerism and the failure of European ELT. In Sharifian, F. (ed.) *English as an International Language: Perspectives and Pedagogical Issues*. Bristol: Multilingual Matters.

Murray, N. (2012). English as a lingua franca and the development of pragmatic competence. *ELT Journal* 66(3): 318–326.

Nikkula, T. Dalton-Puffer, C. and Llinares, A. (2013). CLIL classroom discourse: Research from Europe. *Journal of Immersion and Content-Based Language Education* 1(1), 70–100.

Oda, S. and Tajima, J. (2010). Analyzing speaker and learner factors affecting the intelligibility of Japanese English. *Asian English Studies* 12: 61–78.

Pickering, L. (2006). Current research on intelligibility in English as a lingua franca. *Annual Review of Applied Linguistics* 26: 219–233.

Seidlhofer, B. (2011). *Understanding English as a Lingua Franca*. Oxford: Oxford University Press.

Sharifian, F. (ed.) (2009). *English as an International Language: Perspectives and Pedagogical Issues*. Bristol: Multilingual Matters.

Stewart, D. (2013). From pro loco to pro globo. *The Interpreter and Translator Trainer* 7(2): 217–234.

Swain, M. (2006). Languaging, agency and collaboration in advanced language proficiency. In Byrnes, H. (ed.) *Advanced Language Learning: the Contribution of Halliday and Vygotsky*. London: Continuum, pp. 95–108.

Taviano, S. (2013). English as a Lingua Franca and Translation. *The Interpreter and Translator Trainer* 7(2): 155–167.

Ushioda, E. (2013). Motivation and ELT: Looking ahead to the future. In Ushioda, E. (ed.), *International Perspectives on Motivation: Language Learning and Professional Challenges*. Basingstoke: Palgrave Macmillan, pp. 233–240.

Walker, R. (2010). *Teaching the Pronunciation of English as a Lingua Franca*. Oxford: Oxford University Press.

Index

Printed and bound by CPI Group (UK) Ltd, Croydon, CR0 4YY